Quote Poet Unquote

QUOTE
POET
UNQUOTE

Contemporary Quotations
on Poets and Poetry

Edited by

Dennis O'Driscoll

Copper Canyon Press
Port Townsend, Washington

Cover art: Jules Remedios Faye, *Monkey Business,* 2001.
Letterpress print, 11" × 14", detail.

Copper Canyon Press is in residence at Fort Worden
State Park in Port Townsend, Washington, under the
auspices of Centrum. Centrum is a gathering place for
artists and creative thinkers from around the world,
students of all ages and backgrounds, and audiences
seeking extraordinary cultural enrichment.

LIBRARY OF CONGRESS CATALOGING-IN-PUBLICATION DATA

Quote poet unquote: contemporary quotations on
poets and poetry / edited by Dennis O'Driscoll.
p. cm.
Includes bibliographical references and index.
ISBN 978-1-55659-270-6 (pbk.: alk. paper)
1. Poetry—Quotations, maxims, etc.
2. Poets—Quotations. I. O'Driscoll, Dennis. II. Title.
PN1064.Q68 2008
809′.1—dc22
2007042705

2 4 6 8 9 7 5 3
FIRST PRINTING

COPPER CANYON PRESS
Post Office Box 271
Port Townsend, Washington 98368
www.coppercanyonpress.org

CONTENTS

A poem is
language distilled
into premium
whiskey, no mix,
no ice, no little
paper umbrella.

PENNY DYER,
The Chattanooga Pulse,
24 May 2006

⌣

v

Poetry says more about the psychic life of an age than any other art. Poetry is a place where all the fundamental questions are asked about the human condition.

CHARLES SIMIC,
The American Poetry Review, September–October 1991

ِ

Poetry is memory
become image,
and image
become voice.

Octavio Paz,
The New York Times,
8 December 1991

⌣

INTRODUCTION

BOSWELL: Sir, what is poetry?
JOHNSON: Why, Sir, it is much easier to say what it
is not.

A defining mark of poetry is that it defies definition. On this, if nothing else, poets and critics of all stripes, camps, and persuasions tend to agree. Like "Bogland," in the poem of that title by Seamus Heaney, poetry always seems to be "Missing its last definition / By millions of years." But this very elusiveness inspires the multitude of attempts to freeze-frame the art, pin it down and definitively describe how it works. As with the frantic search in science for a "theory of everything," poetry readers and practitioners continue to reach beyond "the *best* words in the best order" (Coleridge) and "emotion recollected in tranquillity" (Wordsworth) for a more perfect encapsulation of their tantalizing art. Somehow, though, every would-be watertight "last definition" proves to be as slippery, porous, and unstable as bogland.

"To circumscribe poetry by a definition will only shew the narrowness of the definer," Samuel Johnson contended rather witheringly. He is right in the sense that even the niftiest definition may quickly become redundant, outmaneuvered by the next poem that is written. Yet his barb ignores the pleasures to be derived from attempting the impossible and the fact that definitions, however provisional, enable readers—if I may rephrase one of the doctor's own most quoted remarks—better to enjoy poetry, or better to endure it. Otherwise, we are abandoned to the utilitarian option enunciated by the poet who held that poetry is what you get when you ask a bookseller for a book of poems.

Some of the best poets of the last century (T.S. Eliot, Ezra Pound, Marianne Moore, Wallace Stevens, W.H. Auden, Patrick Kavanagh, Robert Frost, and Philip Larkin, among many others) were masters of the epigrammatic utterance in both poetry and prose. The words of contemporary poets such as Seamus Heaney, Les Murray, Billy Collins, Robert Pinsky, Charles Simic, Wendy Cope, Dana Gioia, Nuala Ní Dhomhnaill, George Szirtes, Jane Hirshfield, and the redoubtable William Logan form epigrammatic clusters even on the most casual occasions. Gifted from the start with a facility for the *mot* jest, Don Paterson has published two books of epigrams. Michael Longley—a poet with a classical cast of mind—coined a number of epigrammatic remarks that have gained wide currency, especially, "If I knew where poems came from, I'd go there," a gold-standard quotation that is the most frequently borrowed of all the entries here.

This book, however, consists less often of self-contained epigrams than of remarks—excerpted from essays, reviews, interviews, broadcasts, and (on rare occasions) poems—that are capable of surviving outside of their original habitats. The quotes trapped and caged in *Quote Poet Unquote* entered my sights over the past twenty years; if "what oft was thought" is to be found here, it will ne'er have been expressed so pithily or freshly or topically (or downright foolishly, in some cases). In 1987, while I was editing *Poetry Ireland Review,* the notion occurred to me that I might at last be able to justify the reading time I was lavishing on newspapers and literary magazines by recording contemporaneous remarks that cut to the nub of some poetry-related topic or put a bright new gloss on old chestnuts. The jotting habit became an obsession, and the obsession ensured the longevity of my quarterly quotations column called Poetry Pickings and Choosings; also crucial was the generosity of my successors in the rotating editorial chair at *Poetry Ireland Review,* most of whom indulged the column with commodious accommodation.

A certain casualness characterized the columns at first; I had conceived of them as existing for the duration of the shelf-life of the magazine—no "second life" for the quotations was predicted or even aspired to, let alone an afterlife between book covers. If I am no prophet, neither am I a scholar, and the earliest columns were published without the dates of the journals from which the quotations were drawn. However, in 1992 I readily adopted the suggestion of then-editor Dr. Peter Denman that I should make full disclosure of my sources. Although I have now added dates to many of the early quotations, some eluded traceability; my academic credentials, were I possessed of any, would doubtless be called into question by my untidy inconsistency in this respect. Another moment of change clicked into place in 1999, when I came of Internet age and began exploring poetry cyber-space—especially the peerless *Poetry Daily* site of Don Selby and Diane Boller. Surfing the Internet or trawling through the countless literary periodicals to which I subscribe, I make the reading and enjoyment of the texts my priority; whether an article or interview yields a quotable catch is a secondary consideration.

The best of these quotations are "sound bites" only insofar as they sound out ideas memorably—encapsulating larger debates in bonsai form—and the adjective *sound* means "judicious." That there are some unsound and meretricious remarks here is part of the book's dialectic (and of its entertainment value, too) as we watch contentions contradicted, assumptions undermined, and paradoxes perpetrated. Everything and its opposite may no more be true in poetry than in anything else, but someone always seems ready to take a contrary view or a controversial one. I selected remarks for their vitality no less than their plausibility.

This collection was assembled without consulting any dictionaries of quotations and makes not the slightest claim to comprehensiveness. If a reader's quest is for those hallowed remarks about poetry that are already enshrined on the standard reference shelf, this book—which aims to originate, not to duplicate—cannot help. *Quote Poet Unquote* is, in effect, a commonplace book: a contemporary compilation, not a canonical work of reference. Having multitasked as indexer, research assistant, and office gofer, as well as editor, I cannot evade responsibility for any errors. Yet this is a populous and polyphonous book, too—a chorus of hundreds of voices (raised and hushed, earnest and ironic, wise and provocative) from daily newspapers and literary monthlies, radio broadcasts and weblogs, small-circulation poetry periodicals and sources as unlikely as the *Irish Farmers Journal, Vogue,* and *Harpers & Queen.* I am enormously grateful to everyone quoted: the vigor and passion with which poetry is discussed in print, on-line, and on air—albeit primarily by practitioners and academics—prove the art to be reassuringly alive and, in more senses than one, kicking.

"Poetry, like traditional music, is a product of, and a repayment to, community," Bernard O'Donoghue asserts. I'd like to think that this book—a product of the literary community—is repaying that companionable and cantankerous community in a modest way by preserving and disseminating vibrant recent remarks about poetry. And although "remarks are not literature," as Gertrude Stein snapped, some of these quotations are so eloquent in construction and so economic in language as to come close to the status of poetry itself.

After an earlier book-length selection from my Pickings and Choosings column was resourcefully edited by the Irish poet Tony Curtis (*As the Poet Said,* Poetry Ireland, 1997), quotations from the volume appeared in reviews and critical essays—even in advertisements from the leading British poetry organizations and in the published poetry of at least one major writer. I hope this broader selection will animate classroom debates, stimulate critical essays, invigorate panel discussions, enliven workshops, lectures, and broadcasts, and provide *bons mots* for harried arts administrators charged with introducing obscure peripatetic bards. Ideally, too, these quotations will equip readers of poetry with heightened enthusiasm, deepened appreciation, and sharpened skepticism.

It is, of course, poetry itself that—beyond definition and discussion—matters in the end. Having, in one of her wry poems, noted that "many a shaky answer" has been given to the question "What sort of thing is poetry?", Wislawa Szymborska concludes: "I do not know and do not know and hold on to it, / as to a saving bannister." In the same spirit of the staircase, I regard these quotations as steps in the direction of a fuller understanding of poetry, irrespective of what the word *poetry* may connote or how—if at all—it is finally defined.

Dennis O'Driscoll

EDITORIAL NOTE

Quote Poet Unquote owes its publication in America to the enthusiasm and editorial guidance of Michael Wiegers, executive editor of Copper Canyon Press. I am enormously indebted to him and to his colleagues and collaborators.

The U.K.-published version of the book, *The Bloodaxe Book of Poetry Quotations* (2006), was commissioned and encouraged by the managing director and founder of Bloodaxe Books, Neil Astley. Without the support of J. Patrick Lannan Jr. and Lannan Foundation, whose generosity enabled me to curtail my day-job commitments, the very welcome Bloodaxe initiative would have proved a commission impossible. Without the column inches allocated to my Pickings and Choosings by most of the successive editors of *Poetry Ireland Review,* from John Ennis to Peter Sirr, my appetite for hoarding and hawking quotations might well have waned rather than waxed. I would like to thank them and Poetry Ireland's staff for their immense help across the collective years. Dr. Barbara Brown provided note-perfect keyboard transcriptions of my early Pickings and Choosings columns. Tom Guckian, former Customs colleague, counseled and proofread with customary cheer and punctiliousness. Tony Curtis, editor of an earlier selection of my columns (*As the Poet Said,* Poetry Ireland, 1997), lit the way. Julie O'Callaghan aided, abetted, and lived with my quotationmania.

A few remarks on the presentation of the quotations in this book may not go amiss. For reasons explained (but not excused) in my introduction, I only began to routinely record the dates of the quotations in 1992. While giving preference to dates over volume numbers in my listings, I am unable to be entirely consistent in this regard because of variant practices by some of the journals themselves. To complicate matters, certain Internet sites provide no hint as to the date of first posting of an essay or interview.

Where the phrase *cited in* is used, the words quoted derive from a secondary source. Orthographic consistency has not been sought; whether my source is American or British, I have taken the spelling as I found it. Similarly with proper nouns: I have used whatever versions the quotations yielded and have not presumed to standardize them.

The categories into which quotations are placed are intended to be convenient, but they cannot pretend to be definitive. Some quotes could as easily have slotted into one category as another, and many could conveniently bilocate or even trilocate. When searching this book for an apt quotation, it always pays to shop around.

My parting word of thanks must be to everyone quoted here; my parting wish is for these quotations to fuel further disputatious debate about poetry, thus spawning a whole new anthologyful of quotable remarks.

Quote Poet Unquote

WHAT IS IT ANYWAY?

Poetry: three mismatched shoes at the entrance of a dark alley.

CHARLES SIMIC, *Dime-Store Alchemy,* 1992

Poetry is a sofa full of blind singers who have put aside their canes... Poetry is the sound of summer in the rain and of people laughing behind closed shutters down a narrow street.

LAWRENCE FERLINGHETTI, *San Francisco Chronicle,* 16 January 2000

Poetry is the purest of the language arts. It's the tightest cage, and if you can get it to sing in that cage it's really really wonderful.

RITA DOVE, *Poetry Flash,* January 1993

Poetry is language at its most nourishing. It's the breast milk of language.

ROBERT CRAWFORD, *The South Bank Show,* October 1994

Poetry is like a substance, the words stick together as though they were magnetized to each other.

DAVID GASCOYNE, *Stand,* Spring 1992

Poetry is energy, it is an energy-storing and an energy-releasing device.

MIROSLAV HOLUB, *Poetry Ireland Review,* Autumn–Winter 1990

Poetry is a dividend from what you know and what you are.

CZESLAW MILOSZ, *Poets & Writers,* November–December 1993

Poetry is a diagram of reality. A distillation of reality, that may make us free.

ALICIA OSTRIKER, *The American Voice,* no. 45, 1998

Poetry is language in orbit.

SEAMUS HEANEY,
Sunday Independent,
25 September 1994

ᘐ

Poetry is an act by which the relation of words to reality is renewed.

YVES BONNEFOY, *Times Literary Supplement,*
12 August 2005

Poetry is an investigation, not an expression, of what you know.

MARK DOTY, *The Cortland Review,* October 2000

Poetry is words in space, representing words in time.

GLYN MAXWELL, *Fulcrum,* no. 4, 2005

Poetry is the art of using words charged with their utmost meaning.

DANA GIOIA, *Can Poetry Matter?,* 1992

Poetry is a verdict that others give to language that is charged with music and rhythm and authority.

LEONARD COHEN, *The Sunday Times*

Poetry is like standing on the edge of a lake on a moonlit night and the light of the moon is always pointing straight at you.

BILLY COLLINS, *Portsmouth Herald,* 23 January 2005

Poetry is a thief that comes in the middle of a new day, while the critics are still studying by night light.

JAMES LIDDY, *Éire-Ireland,* Spring 1991

Poetry expresses the newness of the day.

ADAM ZAGAJEWSKI, *AGNI* online, 2004

Poetry is either language lit up by life or life lit up by language.

PETER PORTER, BBC Radio 3, May 1995

Poetry is not a matter of feelings, it is a matter of language. It is language which creates feelings.

UMBERTO ECO, *The Independent*, 6 October 1995

Poetry is language wrought by feeling and imagination to such a pitch that it enacts and embodies the thing it says.

CHRISTOPHER MIDDLETON, *PN Review*, March–April 1993

Poetry is a dialect of the language we speak, possessed of metaphorical density, coded with resonant meaning, engaging us with narrative's pleasures, enhancing and sustaining our pleasure with enlarged awareness.

DAVE SMITH, *Local Assays*, 1985

Poetry is a fire, well banked-down that it may warm survivors in the even-colder nights to come.

HUGH MAXTON, *Dedalus Irish Poets*, 1992

Poetry is deep gossip.

LIAM RECTOR, *The American Poetry Review*, September–October 2005

Poetry is a dame with a huge pedigree, and every word comes practically barnacled with allusions and associations.

JOSEPH BRODSKY, *The New Yorker*, 26 September 1994

Poetry is philosophy's sister, the one that wears makeup.

JENNIFER GROTZ, Here Comes Everybody blog, April 2005

Poetry is the eroticization of thought—psychic vitality.

CAL BEDIENT, *Denver Quarterly* 39, no. 2, 2004

Poetry is that / which arrives at the intellect / by way of the heart.

R.S. THOMAS, *Residues*, 2002

⌣

Poetry's a zoo
in which you
keep demons
and angels.

LES MURRAY,
The Australian,
10 May 1997

Poetry is... a kind of leaving of notes for another
to find, and a willingness to have them fall
into the wrong hands.

MATTHEW HOLLIS, Poetry Book Society
Bulletin, Spring 2004

Poetry is language that sounds better and
means more.

CHARLES WRIGHT, *Quarter Notes,* 1995

Poetry is about the intensity at the centre of life, and about intricacy of
expression. Without any appreciation of those, people are condemned
to simplistic emotions and crude expressions.

ANNE ROUSE, *The Sunday Times,* 28 January 2001

Poetry is a way of communicating a vast array of thoughts and feelings
by concentrating them into minimal, or even single, points which
describe the whole.

FRIEDA HUGHES, *The Guardian,* 3 October 2001

Poetry is the meeting point of parallel lines—in infinity, but also in the
here and now. It is where the patent and incontrovertible intersects with
the ineffable and incommensurable.

JOHN SIMON, *Dreamers of Dreams,* 2001

Poetry is language pointing beyond its own capacities.

DON McKAY, *The Toronto Star,* 4 June 2007

Poetry essentially is figurative language, concentrated so that its form is
both expressive and evocative.

HAROLD BLOOM, *The Art of Reading Poetry,* 2006

Poetry is like fingerprints / on a window, behind which a child who can't sleep / stands waiting for dawn.

HERMAN DE CONINCK, *The Plural of Happiness*, 2006

Poetry is the rapture of rhythmical language.

GREGORY ORR, *The Washington Post*, 16 May 2006

Poetry is what makes the invisible appear.

NATHALIE SARRAUTE, cited in *Staying Alive*, 2002

Poetry is a perpetual redefinition of beauty and truth in patterned language. An assault on yesterday's beauty which no longer shines. An assault on yesterday's truth which has become a lie.

ROSANNA WARREN, *Fulcrum*, no. 4, 2005

A poem is words at work, on us and for us.

PETER FALLON, *The Poetry Paper*, no. 3, 2006

A poem is a machine for remembering itself.

DON PATERSON, *Strong Words*, 2000

A poem is a box, a *thing*, to put other things in. For safe keeping.

MARIANNE BORUCH, *The American Poetry Review*, September–October 2006

A poem is a cup of words open to the sky and wind in a bucket.

NAOMI SHIHAB NYE, *The Poetry Paper*, no. 3, 2006

A poem is partly grace, partly discovery, and partly a struggle to squeeze out a little bit more, to conquer another foot of territory from the unconscious.

ÁGNES NEMES NAGY, *A Hungarian Perspective*, 1998

A poem is an attempt to find the music in the words describing an intuition.

P.J. KAVANAGH,
BBC Radio 3,
December 1990

A poem is a smuggling of something back from the otherworld, a prime bit of shoplifting where you get something out the door before the buzzer goes off.

NUALA NÍ DHOMHNAILL, RTÉ 1 television, July 1995

A poem is like a ghost seeking substantiality, a soul in search of a body more appealing than the bare bones mere verses rattle.

WILLIAM H. GASS, *The Georgia Review*, Spring 2004

A poem... is the attire of feeling: the literary form where words seem tailor-made for memory or desire.

CAROL ANN DUFFY, *Out of Fashion*, 2004

Every poem is an answer to the question what poetry is for.

JAMIE MCKENDRICK, *The South Bank Show*, October 1994

Defining Moments

A successful poem, in my definition, is "a machine for re-reading."

MICHAEL HOFMANN, Poetry Book Society *Bulletin,* Summer 1999

Poems are engines, painstakingly designed to manufacture experiences in their audiences simply by describing them.

JON MOOALLEM, *San Francisco Chronicle,* 17 April 2005

Poetry... creates a metaphor, which enables the reader to experience what you have experienced with a kind of specificity and depth that is not possible in casual language, partly because the form also communicates the information.

STEPHEN DOBYNS, *The Cortland Review,* Spring 2004

Where poetry excels is as a method of experience, not expression. It has a unique capacity to render an experience in a fresh, unsettling way. I don't write a poem to express an experience, but to experience it again.

EAVAN BOLAND, *New Hibernia Review,* Summer 2006

Writing is a way not just of ordering and making sense of our experience, but actually a means of opening ourselves to experience.

PETER SANSOM, *Contemporary Poems,* 2000

Poems are words that take you through three kinds of doors: closed doors, secret doors, and doors you don't know are there.

STEPHANIE STRICKLAND, Here Comes Everybody blog, 12 March 2005

In the end we go to poetry for one reason, so that we might more fully inhabit our lives and the world in which we live them, and that if we more fully inhabit these things, we might be less apt to destroy both.

CHRISTIAN WIMAN,
Poetry, April 2004

Poetry captures ideas, emotions, fixes things, explains them, erects memorials, expands ideas, delights the ear, moves the soul, fences with the tongue, pulls perception through hoops.

PETER FINCH, *Writers' Monthly,* January 1995

Poetry is born out of the superfluity of language's own resources and energy. It's a kind of overdoing it. Enough is not enough when it comes to poetry.

SEAMUS HEANEY, *Giving Their Word,* 2002

Poetry, that art of the marvellous, of a simultaneous compression of language and an endless expansion of meaning...

FRED D'AGUIAR, *Strong Words,* 2000

Poetry does not *explain* life. It gives life to *feeling* and *seeing.*

SALAH STÉTIÉ, *Reading and Writing Poetry,* 2005

In poetry there is a nostalgia for something we have forgotten and which poetry, nevertheless, remembers.

JUAN MALPARTIDA, *Agenda,* Summer 1995

Poetry desires words that one can make part of one's destiny.

YVES BONNEFOY, *The Act and the Place of Poetry,* 1989

In poetry, language is returned to its once magical state. The words are surprised to be there. Some seem relieved, others embarrassed. The poet has brought them out of the orphanage for a day at the beach.

BILLY COLLINS, *Fugue,* Summer 2001

Poetry can open up a world which lies both within and yet beyond the ordinary world—like one of those secret chambers behind the library panelling.

RACHEL CAMPBELL-JOHNSTON, *The Times*, 12 March 2003

Much of what poetry tells us we know already, but not well enough, not keenly enough, not so that it matters. Poetry helps us realise common things better.

DAVID CONSTANTINE, *Strong Words*, 2000

Fundamentally, what I want from poetry is the preciousness and foundedness of wise feeling become eternally posthumous in perfect cadence. Good poetry reminds you that writing is writing, it's not just expectoration or self-regard or a semaphore for self's sake. You want it to touch you at the melting point below the breastbone and the beginning of the solar plexus. You want something sweetening and at the same time something unexpected, something that has come through constraint into felicity.

SEAMUS HEANEY, *Salmagundi*, Fall 1988

Poetry models something which probably all humans do. Their poetries don't usually come to fruition or get embodied as words on a page. They come out as ideologies, political systems, inventions, cars, marriages, all sorts of things like that.

LES MURRAY, BBC Radio 4

Poetry connects us to what is deepest in ourselves. It gives us access to our own feelings, which are often shadowy, and engages us in the art of making meaning. It widens the space of our inner lives. It is a magical, mysterious,

The poet's job is to find a name for everything.

JANE KENYON,
A Hundred White Daffodils, 1999

⌣

Writing poetry is a single combat between the unambiguous word and the inarticulate mood.

ÁGNES NEMES NAGY, *A Hungarian Perspective*, 1998

⌣

inexplicable (though not incomprehensible) event in language.

EDWARD HIRSCH, *The Washington Post,* 13 January 2002

Poetry is written out of the need one has to write it. There is a void in oneself that echoes the Void without.

LOUIS SIMPSON, *The Hudson Review*

Certain poems allow you to feel what you mean, even though you cannot dare to say what that is yourself.

MOLLY PEACOCK, *How to Read a Poem*, 1999

Poetry is an embarrassing affair; it is born too near to the functions we call intimate.

CZESLAW MILOSZ, *Road-side Dog*, 1998

Good poets reinvent the language, taking the given of ordinary speech and pushing it beyond itself, making in effect a translation from one sense of reality to another.

JAY PARINI, *Some Necessary Angels*, 1997

If poetry is to be poetry at all, any ordinary talk that it relies on must be a virtual talk that taps into the deeper energies of the language rather than a mere imitation of the talk of daily life.

COLIN FALCK, *American and British Verse in the Twentieth Century*, 2003

A poem is like the person at the table who won't speak unless everyone else hushes to listen. A poem is like the person whose tone announces

Enough of your jabber. Now I shall speak words worth remembering. You should want to chisel these words in marble.

MARK HALLIDAY, *The Georgia Review,* Summer 2003

Lyrics can lift one's heart, prose can make one think, and speeches can move one to action. Poetry can do all three.

ROBYN HAMMER-CLAREY, *Pittsburgh Post-Gazette,* 25 May 2003

As a poet, you're always wanting to be brought to life again by whatever you write. You want the poems to tremble for you like compass needles, and you also want them to encompass what you are. You want them to be deep in your own element, loaded down to the Plimsoll line.

SEAMUS HEANEY, *W,* Autumn 1998

Poetry's greatest task is... to foster a necessary privacy in which the imagination can flourish.

DEAN YOUNG, *Poetry,* April 2005

A poet cannot refuse language, choose another medium. But the poet can re-fuse the language given to him or her, bend and torque it into an instrument for connection instead of dominance and apartheid.

ADRIENNE RICH, *The Guardian,* 26 April 2003

Writing a poem you're not even sure you know what you're looking for—just that something is out there wild and running and for some reason you're not quite sure of you have to run after it, in the hope you might just catch sight of it, catch up.

DERYN REES-JONES, *Contemporary Women's Poetry,* 2000

Poetry exists because the heart rebels against the suppression of its inner life.

CHRISTINA VITI, *Modern Poetry in Translation,* 3rd ser., no. 3, 2005

Poetry is there in a crisis, the power cut, the sudden bereavement, the dictatorship.

RUTH PADEL,
The Independent,
18 July 1997

⁓

The art of writing poetry involves the act of placing one word next to another in such a way that a particular transformation occurs between them, which subtly changes them both and creates something new, some unexpected verbal energy, out of the juxtaposition itself.

ERIC ORMSBY, *Facsimiles of Time,* 2001

Bread is necessary; poetry isn't necessary in the way cake isn't necessary. Cake marks important occasions. Can you imagine living in a city without a bakery? Without cake?

MOLLY PEACOCK, *The New York Times,*
20 April 2000

Poetry fills a human appetite: it matters the way cuisine matters beyond nutrition, or lovemaking matters beyond procreation. Like music and dance, it is at the center of human intelligence.

ROBERT PINSKY, *Newsweek,* 12 April 2004

Every authentic poem contributes to the labour of poetry... to bring together what life has separated or violence has torn apart... Poetry can repair no loss, but it defies the space which separates. And it does this by its continual labour of reassembling what has been scattered.

JOHN BERGER, cited in *The Best American Poetry 1995*

The personal lyric is omnipresent in human cultures because it serves an essential function: to assist in the survival of individuals as they undergo existential crises.

GREGORY ORR, *The American Poetry Review,* May–June 2002

As long as poems are read at weddings and funerals, and exchanged between lovers, and given to people in times of duress, poetry is doing its work. And all the rest is a kind of scaffold to support the endeavor, so it can be there at the moments it's needed.

JANE HIRSHFIELD, *Rattle,* Winter 2006

The world consigns its myths, its religions, its dreams and deepest feelings to poetry for safekeeping: and, somehow, even its critics and doubters know where to find it in their time of need.

PAT BORAN, *Wingspan,* 2006

Lyric poetry speaks out of a solitude to a solitude. It begins and ends in silence. It crystallizes our inwardness and makes space for our subjectivity, naming our inner life.

EDWARD HIRSCH, *Five Points* 2, no. 2, 2003

A lyric poem can be seen as a number of words that, taken as a whole, become a new, compound word, whose only possible definition is the poem itself.

JANE HIRSHFIELD, *Nine Gates,* 1997

The lyric poem... is the social act of a solitary maker. It situates feeling in language and seeks to restore human connection.

EDWARD HIRSCH, *The Georgia Review,* Summer 2003

What's writing really about? It's trying to take fuller possession of the reality of your life.

TED HUGHES, *The Independent on Sunday,*
5 September 1993

Poems come out of wonder, not out of knowing.

LUCILLE CLIFTON,
Poets & Writers,
March–April 1994

❧

Poetry cannot be defined, only experienced.

CHRISTOPHER LOGUE, *Oxford Poetry,* Winter–Spring 1996

⌣∵

A poem is an adventure, a runaway horse of leaps and surprises, words that toss you out of the saddle.

CHRIS BECKETT, *The Poetry Paper,* no. 3, 2006

The poem is both the winding road and the wild horse that gallops past us as we read, so that when we come around the last bend, there it is, waiting for our shock of recognition.

ANDREW JOHNSTON, *Best New Zealand Poems 2005*

The only people who have trouble with poetry are the people who link it with "Literature." It's much more akin to mountain walking and dancing by yourself at 2 A.M.

THEO DORGAN, *The Irish Times,* 11 June 1991

Perhaps one of our problems is the concept of Poetry as a single unified concept. In fact, for a very long time, there have been several different, often mutually exclusive strands of poetry around.

TONY FRAZER, *Poetry Ireland Review,* December 2004

Poetry, because nobody agrees on what makes a good poem any more (if they ever did), excites rage, derision and misrepresentation... Secretly, everyone thinks she/he could do better.

PHILIP HOWARD, *The Times,* 29 September 1995

Taken on its own, in the abstract, the word "poetry" is both radiant and resistant. It means so many things to so many people that it is more the signal of a value than a precisely determined lexical entity.

SEAMUS HEANEY, *The European English Messenger,* Autumn 2001

The word "poetry" means a made thing and doesn't define anything.

MICHAEL DONAGHY, *The Wolf,* Autumn 2002

A poem means itself. You create something, rather than define it.

NUALA NÍ DHOMHNAILL, *Fortnight,* September 2004

The relationship of all statements about poems to the poem itself, to its felt reality, is approximately the relationship of sexual instruction hand-books to sexual intercourse.

DAVE SMITH, *Local Assays,* 1985

MAKING A START

In a poem there is no past; at its inception, everything has yet to be
done, felt, imagined.

CALVIN BEDIENT, *Parnassus* 26, no. 1

It is absolutely amazing how many great poets started as seemingly
talentless half-wits.

CHARLES SIMIC, *The New York Review of Books,* 12 April 2001

Writers are readers who go karaoke. After years of hearing the voices
of masters in the poems and stories we read, we begin, at first timidly,
humming along; then singing along, mimicking the tunes and lyrics we
most admire. Soon enough the voice we hear sounds like our own.

THOMAS LYNCH, *The Independent,* 5 August 2005

For a poet, the struggle from the beginning is to really find the confidence
and authority of your own voice, not only in terms of historical style but
how to get to the point where what you're writing on the page is, metri-
cally and in terms of the tone, the exact voice in which you speak.

DEREK WALCOTT, BBC Radio Ulster

You "find your voice" when you are able to invent this one character
who resembles you, obviously, and probably is more like you than anyone else on earth, but is not the equivalent to you.

BILLY COLLINS, *Guernica,* June 2006

Poetry is a craft that one learns over a long period of time. But you only
learn it if certain gifts are there to begin with—an imagination, the ability

to make metaphor, a sense of language and rhythm and sound, intelligence, passion, curiosity, a great deal of empathy, and a fire in the belly.

STEPHEN DOBYNS, *Rattle,* Winter 2001

It takes a lot of things-in-place just to become a merely decent poet: a passion for and a suspicion of language, for starters; empathy for otherness; contempt for sham; comfort with artifice; some balance between truth's cruelty and irony's armor; a love both of exactitude and ambiguity.

STEPHEN DUNN, *The Georgia Review,* Winter 2005

What is it that makes a poet? Interest, distinctiveness, trustworthiness; the ability to make himself heard through his lines when the poet himself or herself is long dead and gone; the assiduousness and resourcefulness with which he has been able to process his life and times into poems; his qualities as a companion to us, in our lives and our times; the sense that, try as we may, we never will be finished with reading him.

MICHAEL HOFMANN, introducing *Robert Lowell,* 2001

The fear of straight speaking, the constant, painstaking efforts to metaphorize everything, the ceaseless need to prove you're a poet in every line: these are the anxieties that beset every budding bard. But they are curable, if caught in time.

WISLAWA SZYMBORSKA, cited at Poetry Foundation online, 19 April 2006

By the time you start to compose, more than half the work has been done. The crucial part of the business is what happens before you face the empty page—the moment of first connection, when an image or a memory comes

Poetry is everywhere; it just needs editing.

JAMES TATE, *The Route as Briefed,* 1999

⁓

When one remembers how many separate talents go to make a formidable poet —talents musical, imaginative, psychological, visual, intellectual, metaphysical, temperamental —one wonders that the thing is done at all.

HELEN VENDLER,
The New York Review of Books

✌

suddenly to mind and you feel the lure of the poem-life in it.

SEAMUS HEANEY, *The Times*, 25 March 2006

When I write, it's like running my hand over a length of cloth, picking out patterns, testing the give, rubbing the fabric between thumb and forefinger to feel out the texture and the flaws.

VONA GROARKE, *Modern Women Poets*, 2005

I always write a lot of drafts, and when I do this, I like to write the whole poem out each time, in order both to fix it in my head and to see where my hand catches on the paper, so to speak—which words it snags on.

JULIA COPUS, *Desperado Literature*, February 2004

I throw drafts away all the time and I wish more people did... If you have a kitten, they love playing with rolled-up balls of paper, and that may be all a failed draft is good for. Why make a reader unhappy when you can make a kitten happy?

BILLY COLLINS, *Fugue*, Summer 2001

Never throw away a draft, a stanza, a line—someday you may wake up realizing the rest of the poem it belongs to, or how to fix it, or what transformation it might be subject to.

CAMPBELL McGRATH, *Fugue*, Summer–Fall 2006

The first-line test is a good one: has the poet seized an irresistible momentum from the flux of experience and language, or is he merely looking out the window, telling you it's a nice day, and casting round for a subject?

EDNA LONGLEY, *Krino,* no. 10, 1990

Without the initial pressure or tension—without, at least, something to wonder about—the most meticulous attention to craft and form will produce no more than an empty crate.

MOYA CANNON, *My Self, My Muse,* 2001

My optimum time to write is when I don't have much to say, as opposed to when I was young and had plenty to say about everything. My poetry was liberated by that realization. I got better right away.

BILLY COLLINS, *The Exeter News,* 6 May 2005

You can have all the language in the world but it will not add up unless you have actually something to say.

GERALD DAWE, *In the Chair,* 2002

The world of contemporary poetry spilleth over with those who have nothing to say, who are nevertheless adamant that we shall hear them saying it... Many of these voices are in university writing programs, men and women who have fought no war, loved but little, gone but short distance of time and space from their homes, and read not much.

DAVE SMITH, *Local Assays,* 1985

The first great task of the aspiring poet—the task of the imagination—is to create the self that will write the poems.

STANLEY KUNITZ, *The Christian Science Monitor,* 26 October 2000

⁖

Facing that sheet of white paper can feel like a bad movie of Scott going to the South Pole.

BILL MANHIRE, *In the Same Room*, 1992

⤳

Sometimes an image just arrives, and it's like you've got the first brick in the wall and you've got to find the rest of the bricks to put it together.

ROSITA BOLAND, *The Poet's Chair,* 2004

The start of a poem announces more than it knows. The very first line or sentence will often reveal the likely ratio of intelligence to feeling in what is to come.

MARVIN BELL, *The American Poetry Review*

I never save my "big" ideas for down the road. I start with the big idea and see how much further I can go.

PAUL MULDOON, *The Paris Review,* Spring 2004

Unless you're riding some current that's bigger than just your reporting voice, you can't get started.

SEAMUS HEANEY, RTÉ Radio 1, September 1997

Words in a novel are subordinate to the broad slices of action or characterization that push the plot forward. In a poem, the words *are* the action. That is why poems establish themselves right away—in a line or two—and why experienced readers of poetry can tell immediately whether a poem possesses any authority.

MARK STRAND, *The New York Times*

Poetry builds up in your mind like a charge. If you go in too early, you'll muck it up, if you go in too late it'll be dry... At the right moment, the poem doesn't have words. It's a pressure.

LES MURRAY, *The Australian,* 10 May 1997

Even before it is ready to change into language, a poem may begin to assert its buried life in the mind with wordless surges of rhythm and counter-rhythm. Gradually the rhythms attach themselves to objects and feelings.

STANLEY KUNITZ, cited in *Poetry London,* Spring 2002

The poet has to wait longer and harder, with more exasperation, I think, than other writers, because the sense of the poem and the music have to come together in an apparently effortless whole.

C.K. WILLIAMS, *Literary Imagination,* Winter 2005

The first duty of the poem is to teach us how to read it.

BIN RAMKE, *The Writer's Chronicle,* February 2004

✌

A properly written poem should have, implicit in its writing, the best indications as to how it should be read—how it should be interpreted is another matter, but the plainest pointer to how it should be read, built into the text, is what makes a poem a poem.

JAMES FENTON, *The Guardian,* 31 March 2007

A title... is the poem's first attempt to read itself.

J.D. McCLATCHY, *Partisan Review,* Spring 1998

A poem never recovers from a bad title.

MICK IMLAH, *Oxford Poetry,* Autumn 1983

The best poets seem able both to hook a big one and then throw it back alive.

PETER ROBINSON, *Untitled Deeds,* 2004

A writer's adventure with words starts not with Shakespeare, but with doggerel and lullabies, with slide-shows of fairy tales, with the deepest, pre-language memory of a certain smell of damp leaves.

<small>Kapka Kassabova, *Modern Poetry in Translation,* 3rd ser., no. 4, 2005</small>

All writing aspires to be poetry in the same way that all milk aspires to be cheese. But before poets get too uppity, it's worth remembering all cheese aspires to be a bacon double cheeseburger.

<small>Guy Browning, *The Guardian,* 12 May 2007</small>

INSPIRED MOVES

Rivers invite bridges, tall buildings elevators, and an exciting and unexplained world invites poetry.

KENNETH KOCH, *Making Your Own Days*, 1998

A poem cannot be seen to strain after profundity; it must arrive like an astonished, unerring sleepwalker.

K.E. DUFFIN, *Harvard Review*, Spring 1994

Nothing overtly significant need be happening in a poem. The doors of perception may be no bigger than a speck of dust, but when any one of them opens it is as if the whole of life were swirling behind it.

GEORGE SZIRTES, *The Irish Times*, 16 August 2003

I'm reluctant to begin work on a poem unless I have the title, the first line and the last, or at least a clear idea of what they should contain. I suppose I've been brought up to believe in that triumvirate as the holy trinity of a poem, around which everything else must congregate.

SIMON ARMITAGE, *How Poets Work*, 1996

The first and last lines always come to me on a direct line from God. I just have to fill in the middle.

KATE CLANCHY, *Harpers & Queen*, January 1997

Once a poem has found its form it's almost found itself and then it's more like filling in.

MIMI KHALVATI, *Magma Poetry*, Autumn 2000

I don't believe in writing every day, though I'm at my desk every day.

STANLEY KUNITZ, *The New York Times*, 2 August 2000

The act of inspiration is, I think, the sudden apprehension or grasping of metaphor. When we understand a metaphor, that understanding comes all in a flash.

STEPHEN DOBYNS,
Best Words, Best Order,
1996

Inspiration is the recognition that out of one's raw material the significant object is presenting itself. You must work your way toward it.

THOMAS KINSELLA, *Poetry Ireland Review,*
Spring 1989

My best poems present a "me" that's really an individual superior to me: calm in the face of dreadful things, wise beyond my years, etc. If that's not being inspired, I don't know what it is.

PHILIP LEVINE, *The Kenyon Review,* Spring 1999

Writing poems, for me, is a bit like mining a seam of rock. One day you get some silver, and the next day you get just rock.

EAVAN BOLAND, *The Irish Times,* 15 March 2007

Inspiration is short-lived, of course—but its fleeting presence is important, it cleanses something in us, it opens us to that voice which we understand so poorly, but whose absence would leave us little wiser than any of the other mammals.

ADAM ZAGAJEWSKI, *A Defense of Ardor,* 2004

My experience of poetic ideas is that they don't stand there waiting calmly until you're ready to receive them. You have to rush out and welcome them immediately.

IAN DUHIG, *The Stinging Fly,* Winter–Spring 2004

You can work at your poetry but you can't work at your inspiration. Self-discipline exposes what the self can't be disciplined to do.

ADAM PHILLIPS, *The Observer,* 12 March 2006

Subject Matter

What one should write about is an important question for a poet, but it is separate from the question of what *moves* a poet to write.

ROBERT B. SHAW, *Poetry,* February 2001

Poetry is more a matter of cadence than content. Intonation is its deepest mystery.

SEAMUS HEANEY, *Salon*

All the elements of the poem make the poem, are the poem. You cannot extricate "subject matter" from them, unless you really believe that clothes make the man.

JAMES TATE, *The American Poetry Review,* September–October 1996

Meaning is destroyed by readers who take one's subject to be one's "subject matter," as if the subject exists only for the poem.

WENDELL BERRY, *Standing on Earth,* 1991

Poets have to realize how richly they are praised or scolded for contents and how poorly for aesthetic quality... Writers are rich young women, *poor* rich young women, who will never be loved just for their beautiful eyes.

ÁGNES NEMES NAGY, *A Hungarian Perspective,* 1998

The selection of subject matter is a primary artistic act.

THOMAS MCCARTHY, RTÉ Radio I, April 1996

Poetry gets landscape and weather for its subjects; the novel gets boxing and tattooed women and sex.

CRAIG RAINE, *The Independent,* 30 August 1994

There are no poetic subjects, only subjects to which we pay the right kind of attention.

MARGE PIERCY, cited in *The Independent on Sunday*, 12 November 1995

⌁

I've never believed that there were some topics "unfit" for poetry; if you change the form, you can make them fit.

CAMPBELL MCGRATH, *Fugue*, Summer Fall 2006

There are no simplistic rules for poets: if there were, any duffer could write poetry. There are, however, rules of thumb, and one of the best is that getting the focus off yourself gives you the best chance of tapping your personal experience.

CLIVE JAMES, *Poetry*, February 2007

Poems have become reflexively, wearyingly, claustrophobically (or is that agoraphobically?) personal, seeking nothing but miniature epiphanies, like so many needles in the disorderly haystack of life. Poets retail the meager incidents of their lives, even if they've suffered nothing worse than an IRS audit, a bicycle accident, and a headache.

WILLIAM LOGAN, *The Undiscovered Country*, 2005

The predicament of the modern short poem is that, in the absence of a common body of cultural reference, its basis must usually be personal.

LACHLAN MACKINNON, *The Independent*, 15 August 1992

It's only in times when poetry is feeling rather weak and insufficient to the larger tasks that it becomes entirely personal lyrics, the lyric of personal emotion... whereas the great world is there for the poeticising if poets are brave enough.

ANTHONY CRONIN, RTÉ Radio 1, December 2006

I was constantly struck by how many poems published in magazines today are personal to the point of suffocation. The columnar, anecdotal, domestic poem, often with a three-stress line, can be narrow in more than a formal sense.

ADRIENNE RICH, *The Best American Poetry 1996*

Many poets now write of domestic routines, which may take the adage *Write what you know* to the point of fallacy, or suicide. In the odd limbo of the suburbs... what's lacking is intensity.

WILLIAM LOGAN, *The New Criterion*, December 2003

If you write about what you know, you will keep on writing the same thing, and you will never know any more than you do now.

GEORGE BOWERING, cited in *The Iowa Review*, Winter 2003-04

Since most poets are teachers or academics, there are certain areas of life that poetry rarely touches. When was the last time you read an office poem or a factory poem that wasn't dull or patronising?

ADAM THORPE, *The Observer*, 1 March 1992

It is often preferable to take your subjects from life or even from news-papers... than to construct mysterious fantasies at one remove from reality. There's always enough to write about; indeed, there's too much.

GAVIN EWART, *The Guardian*

You need reality to make the imagination do interesting things, to renew itself. Take the reality out of the equation and you simply repeat yourself.

CHARLES SIMIC, *The Irish Times*, 23 July 2005

A poet is an omnivore.

HANS MAGNUS ENZENSBERGER, Prague Writers' Festival *News*, February 2004

I don't usually think in terms of subject matter when I sit down to write; I think about capturing a sound or a sonic insistence.

MEGHAN O'ROURKE, *Poetry*, January 2006

.·.

If a poem does not come from life but only from an idea, its effect is terminated with the working out of that idea.

DAVID CONSTANTINE, *Poetry London*, Autumn 2003

Many poets struggle to make connections between the lumpy thing called Real Life and the shiny thing called Poetry.

IAN MCMILLAN, *Poetry Review*, Winter 1996–97

Poems generally come more out of an engagement with language, and with poetry, than with life; life provides occasions, but what matters in the end is less the grain of sand than the pearl itself.

MICHAEL SCHMIDT, StAnza lecture, March 2006

Usually, poems come out of a word or a phrase which magnetically pulls other words and phrases round about it—rather than simply coming out of an idea.

ROBERT CRAWFORD, BBC Radio 4, March 2004

Poetry is not to do with ideas, or opinions, or emotions—all of these things are a small part of poetry. Poetry is really about taking ideas, opinions and emotions, and making them, through style, into something that is a poem.

VONA GROARKE, *Reading the Future*, 2000

Ideas in the way that philosophers usually approach them have little to do with poems whose main concern is with using feelings to find what is authentic.

CHARLES SIMIC, *The New York Review of Books*, 22 June 2006

Poetry, the art of making, pushes the Idea into becoming the Thing Itself.

STEPHEN FRY, *The Ode Less Travelled*, 2005

Most poems get ruined by having too many ideas in them.

MICHAEL ONDAATJE, *Writers' Monthly*

The most difficult thing to do in a poem is to present ideas.

ROBERT PINSKY, *TriQuarterly*, Winter 1995

Roughly speaking, the American poet begins with a fact and works toward an idea, while his French counterpart begins with an idea and works to the fact.

JOHN TAYLOR, *Poetry*, October–November 2000

Nobody is truly indifferent to the ideas in a poem, and to say that you should be indifferent is really to say that poetry is a decorative art, it's contentless, it's like making lace or a quilt.

KATHA POLLITT, *Poets & Writers*, March–April 1997

Anything that gets poets to *say* less seems like a worthy project.

PETER SIRR, *Irish Literary Supplement*, Fall 1994

Poetry is here to answer the question: how do we know we exist?

SELIMA HILL, *Contemporary Women's Poetry*, 2000

Sometimes, the more promising the subject seems, the more difficult the poem is. As soon as you say, "Ah, this will make a great poem," you're probably intimidating the imagination with exaggerated expectations or too much fore-knowledge of the direction the poem will take.

B.H. FAIRCHILD, *The Writer's Chronicle*, February 2005

Poets talk about the central questions, from a marginal point of view.

OCTAVIO PAZ, Lannan Readings & Conversations, 1988

Poems, like dreams, have a visible subject and an invisible one. The invisible one is the one you can't choose, the one that writes itself.

ALICE OSWALD, *Get Writing*, 2004

A poem may have no other subject than its form, no other message than its medium.

MICHAEL HAMBURGER, *Testimonies*, 1989

There's still a real neglect of the idea that a poem can be something, rather than just be about something.

REGINALD SHEPHERD, *Verse* 20, nos. 2 & 3, 2004

When asked what I write about, I like to reply that "about" is the wrong word, it suggests the wrong relationship. I prefer to say "from" or "toward" or occasionally "through."

KATHLEEN JAMIE, Poetry Book Society *Bulletin*, Autumn 2004

Nobody writes poems about parsnips.

ANNA PAVORD, *The Independent*, 8 February 1992

He certainly knows his onions, and his parsnips.

VALENTINE CUNNINGHAM, on Craig Raine, *The European English Messenger*, Spring 1992

Anne Yeats remembers he [W.B. Yeats] was a "mean croquet player" (and didn't like parsnips).

JOHN GREENING, *The Poetry of W.B. Yeats*, 2005

WORKSHOPS AND CLASS CONFLICTS

Babies are not brought by storks, and poets are not produced by workshops.

JAMES FENTON, Ronald Duncan Lecture, 1992

All the writing schools exist to promote competence, adequacy, and a late-20th-century version of good taste. What is promoted is a kind of consensus about what things should be.

SEAMUS HEANEY, *The Christian Science Monitor,* 9 January 1989

Workshops... perhaps subvert, really unintentionally, the radical, loud, original processes that might exist in somebody and tame them, domesticate them.

GERALD STERN, *Poet's Market,* 1997

Of course, the business end of poetry is threaded through everything: Creative Writing Programs provide a livelihood, which in turn makes becoming a poet "attractive" rather than "necessary," which means too much chuff and a certain complacency in many a poet's stance, because let's face it—the university environment is hardly a microcosm of the Real World.

RITA DOVE, *The Writer's Chronicle,* October–November 2005

We have made the writing of poetry an official subject on university campuses and have gone so far as to endow poets with legitimate careers at public expense, including salaries, health insurance, tenure, pensions, and faculty meetings. (That, dear friends, is a big change. Picture Keats or Rilke or Whitman at a faculty meeting.)

PETER DAVISON, *The Boston Globe,* 9 November 2003

At some point, workshops begin to grate, because you do have that pressure for consensus, when art is something about which you shouldn't have consensus.

MARY JO BANG,
Verse 22, no. 1, 2005

⌣

Today poetry is a modestly upwardly mobile, middle-class profession—not as lucrative as waste management or dermatology but several big steps above the squalor of bohemia... The problem is not that poets teach. The campus is not a bad place for a poet to work. It's just a bad place for all poets to work.

DANA GIOIA, *Can Poetry Matter?*, 1992

American poetry [has] been subsumed by the creative writing corporation of America. It became a business in the sixties. Universities needed money, and creative writing programs were moneymakers... It exists as this bizarre, quarter of a billion dollar pyramid scheme: Go out there and express yourself and you'll be confirmed in your self-esteem and you'll get your little prize and maybe even a publication.

AUGUST KLEINZAHLER, *Poets & Writers* online, October 2003

The M.F.A. system, whatever its faults, has created a thriving, self-sufficient economy, one that allows many, many writers to have time to write, and also provides them with an engaged, literate audience. In a way the whole world reminds me of ants in a sugar bowl... They can't get back out, and yes, they're separated from the other foods by the walls of the bowl, but why should they complain? They're in a bowl of sugar.

MEGHAN O'ROURKE, *The Kenyon Review* online

The workshops, which have a monopoly on the training of poets, encourage indolence, incompetence, smugness and—most perniciously—

that sense of victimization and special entitlement that poets have now come to share with other artists who depend on government or institutional patronage to sustain their art, pay their salaries, and provide free vacations.

THOMAS M. DISCH, *The Hudson Review*, Winter 1995

A good workshop... can bring a writer to a state of crisis in relation to his or her own work. In such a state illuminations occur and discoveries are made which effect lasting change.

EAVAN BOLAND, *Poetry Ireland Review*, Winter-Spring 1991

The poet has a peculiar duty: he has to create other poets. We cannot let talent die without waking.

JAMES LIDDY, *Studies* 85, no. 340

What I tend to say at the beginning of the term to my students in poetry workshops is this: I am going to be involved with your *capacities* as writers, but your *destinies* as writers are your own business.

SEAMUS HEANEY, *Poetry Ireland Review*, Winter-Spring 1991

The way to learn to write poetry is: to write poetry. So we pass directly from the aspiration to the activity itself.

JAMES FENTON, cited in *Oxford University Gazette*, 17 November 1994

Please don't damn writing programs. You should remember that this democratic access is partly what has enabled America to have a literature that more closely resembles its humanity—the variety of our experiences—all races, all regions, all classes.

D.W. FENZA, *The Writer's Chronicle*, May–Summer 2006

⸙

There's no prepa-
ration for poetry.
Four years of
grave digging with
a nice volume of
poetry or a book
of philosophy
in one's pocket
would serve
as well as any
university.

CHARLES SIMIC,
The Paris Review,
Spring 2005

Those who want to write good poems should be reading good poetry, not how-to books. Indeed, every fine poem *is* a how-to manual.

BILLY COLLINS, *Poets & Writers,*
March–April 1995

Poetry festivals, workshops and the rest have produced an idiom of poetry-competitionese, a facile imitation of the surface, not a search for the source.

KATHLEEN RAINE, *Agenda,* Autumn 1989

The effect [of writers' workshops] on editors is, of course, to increase their workload. It means that we have yet more quite polished, but fundamentally mediocre, material to plough through.

JOY HENDRY, *Acumen,* September 1995

In the same way that each generation is taller, reaches puberty sooner, lives longer, and is more affluent than the previous ones, so does the impulse to write and publish poetry grow stronger, the need to attend creative writing workshops become more pressing.

JOAN HOULIHAN, *Boston Comment,* 2001

It is almost eerie, the number of people who want to be poets.

LOUISE GLÜCK, *The New York Times,* 29 August 2003

[W]riting poetry is not something everybody needs to indulge in. Encouraging more and more people to express themselves and, above all, to publish poems or put them on the Internet, does tend to thin the blood—of literature I mean.

ANNE STEVENSON, *The Cortland Review,* November 2000

If everybody wants to write poetry, if everybody wants to be a poet, that says something about the prestige of the art of that moment, and the prestige and success of the practitioners.

DAVID LEHMAN, cited in *Poets & Writers,* November–December 2000

Poetry classes are a bit like sex. A bad session is worse than none at all.

PAULA INGRAMS, *Poetry London Newsletter,* Autumn 1998

Poetry doesn't really lend itself to guides, manuals and confessions, any more than sex does. It says eat me and drink me. Alice didn't need any further instructions, and nor should we.

WILLIAM SCAMMELL, *The Independent on Sunday,* 9 February 1997

Most poets who offer advice to a poet should be ignored, because they want you to be just like them, only not quite so good.

ADRIAN MITCHELL, *Poetry Review,* Summer 1997

I'm very hesitant about giving advice at workshops because every writer is so different. It's like hill climbs. You have the complication of choosing the route, crossing that stream, going up that rock face, but you're doing it all to have that marvellous view from the top.

STEWART CONN, *The Dark Horse,* Winter 2006–07

What one learns ultimately from Eliot is that the activity of poetry is solitary and if one is to rejoice in it, one has to construct something upon which to rejoice. One learns that, at the desk, every poet faces the same kind of task, that there is no secret that can be imparted,

I started a Ph.D. in English at the University of Chicago because I loved poetry— which I now realise is like saying I studied vivisection because I loved dogs.

MICHAEL DONAGHY, *Verse* 14, no. 1, 1997

only resources of one's own that are to be mustered, or not, as the case may be.

SEAMUS HEANEY, *Agenda,* Spring 1989

It took time for me to understand that everybody, in the end, generates his or her own ecosystem as a writer. And, if you don't, nobody else is going to give it to you.

EAVAN BOLAND, *The New Yorker* online, 26 October 2001

Poetry emerges where it will, to the bafflement of those who think they can control it.

BARRA Ó SEAGHDHA, *Poetry Ireland Review,* March 2005

You can't say "This is what poetry should be." Poetry comes from where it shouldn't.

JOHN KINSELLA, *The Courier-Mail,* 13 September 2006

I believe that "should" is the enemy of poetry.

DAVID LEHMAN, *The Writer's Chronicle,* February 2006

Poetry—thank goodness—is the animal that always escapes.

JOHN BARR, *Poetry,* September 2006

Too often in workshops and classrooms there is a concentration on the poem's garments instead of its life's blood.

LINDA GREGG, *American Poet,* Spring 2001

Nuts and Bolts

Poetry is the most lapidary of the forms of literature. It's the one where you really do need to be able to fit words together as jewellers fit gems together.

PETER PORTER, *Acumen,* October 1992

I have never ever written a poem that wasn't the most important thing in the world to me at that moment, that I would not have gone hungry for, or screwed over the phone company for, or worse.

THOMAS SAYERS ELLIS, *AGNI* online, 2005

The thing that nourishes poetry is not an ocean; it's a very small mountain stream.

DEREK WALCOTT, BBC Radio 3, April 1999

To submit a poem to a magazine is like putting out a tender plant in the spring.

BIDDY JENKINSON, *Poetry Ireland Review,* Summer 2000

The incalculable excess of possibilities at any moment of writing a poem should make us speak of literary composition in terms of impossibility rather than possibility.

KEVIN HART, *Heat* 14, 2000

A piece of writing [has] to use sound, resonance, syntax. Imagination has to hover over it. It has to be decorated, but not over-decorated. It has to seek memory, but it has to also prod memory. It has to create the actuality, and also create the utopia that one must try to find through the actuality.

JAMES LIDDY, *The Burning Bush,* Autumn 2002

Although a poem tries to convince, it isn't an argument; although it tries to be exact, it isn't analytical; although it tries to be consistent, it isn't logical, even though it can contain elements of argument, analysis and logic within it.

STEPHEN DOBYNS, *Best Words, Best Order*, 1996

∿

A poem is not an encoded message, nor is it an idea set to metre. It is a unique linguistic creation. It calls for a pitched, almost painful, sensitivity to the potencies of syntax, concept, association, metaphor and cadence.

PETER ABBS, *Agenda*, Autumn 2006

Just as a tapestry cannot be woven out of a single set of threads because you need another set of threads as counterweave, so too I think of a poem as consisting of these crossweavings of thought and image and feeling.

STANLEY KUNITZ, *Interviews and Encounters with Stanley Kuntiz*, 1993

Poetry is more than the shape of its verse, it's more than its line-turnings, and its pirouettings. It's a combination of some form of truth, wisdom, and a new way of seeing it, of saying it—as a refreshment of what you know.

SEAMUS HEANEY, *The Independent*, 31 October 2002

The poem has to be an organism—a self-sustaining ball of life. Not just a splurge of words, which happens to be nearest the heart or off the top of the head.

CHRISTOPHER REID, *The Sunday Times*, 30 June 1991

A poem is somehow alive. There's a more-than-enoughness of life and of language in it. It is that to which your being says Yes.

SEAMUS HEANEY, BBC 2, October 1997

The making of a poem ought to be a sprinkling of words and experiences with gunpowder and throwing a match in.

MICHAEL MILBURN, *Harvard Review,* Fall 1994

The poet takes language, condenses it, charges it with energy, gives it a bit of oomph—and there's the poem!

JULIE O'CALLAGHAN, RTÉ Radio 1, January 1987

A poem can't just be interesting. It has to have some passionate meaning somewhere in it. Or it has to create a passion.

C.K. WILLIAMS, *The New York Times,* 4 October 2000

If you make a good box, it's like making a good poem. You really have to get the corners squared if you're doing a quatrain.

DEREK WALCOTT, BBC Radio 4

Technique is important. I think that if most people who called themselves poets were tightrope-walkers they'd be dead.

MICHAEL LONGLEY, cited in *Fortnight,* June 1992

To write a good line of poetry is successfully to walk a high wire from perception to perception without falling into banality or self-indulgence, to retain a musical rhythm without breaking into conventional song, and to express meaning without lecturing or posturing.

F.D. REEVE, *Poets & Writers,* March–April 1996

Poets are like aerialists: the wire they walk stretches from history to eternity, fact to dream, language to silence. When they get

Poetry will wither on the vine if you don't regularly come back to the simplest fundamentals of the poem: rhythm, rhyme, simple subjects—love, death, war.

JAMES FENTON, *The New Yorker,* 25 July 1994

⌣

The world is full of poets with languid wrenches who don't bother to take the last six turns on their bolts.

X.J. KENNEDY,
Seneca Review 21, no. 2

across we feel rapture. They've taken us with them.

MARGO JEFFERSON, *The New York Times*,
11 May 2003

Trying to write a good poem is like running off a cliff to see if you can fly. Most of the time you can't, but every once in a while something happens.

MARVIN BELL, *The American Poetry Review*,
January–February 2003

Writing poetry is like trying to catch a black cat in a dark room.

ROBERT GREACEN, Irish Times Poetry Prize speech, 23 November 1995

A good poem can freeze experience even as it releases and enlarges it, the words utterly intact but ramifying, like a bell that troubles the air long after its sound has stopped.

CHRISTIAN WIMAN, *Chicago Tribune*, 19 December 2004

Any good poem is an act of taming the savage or savaging the tame.

TONY HOAGLAND, *Real Sofistikashun*, 2006

It has seemed important to me that poetry function sometimes to expand the language into areas not yet penetrated by language, thereby enlarging awareness and experience.

PATTIANN ROGERS, *The Dream of the Marsh Wren*, 1999

If there's something in your experience that moves you but seems without poetry, your challenge is to make it poetic. For modern Americans, the shopping mall is what the lake was for Wordsworth: a significant, familiar locale.

ROBERT PINSKY, *Fooling with Words*, 1999

Poetry says more about the psychic life of an age than any other art. Poetry is a place where all the fundamental questions are asked about the human condition.

CHARLES SIMIC, *The American Poetry Review,* September–October 1991

Poetry, whether it is a free verse howl, cyclonic pantoum, nuclear sonnet or double-barreled sporophyll disguised as a prose poem, has this one quality about it: it is alive. It spits, sputters, spins. It ambles forward angry and confused, chased by frightened villagers. It breaches in the ocean a thunderous hulk white and marvelous.

JOHN OLSON, *Verse* online, 10 April 2006

I've often argued that the only skill any writer needs is the ability to see his or her work from the other side. That is, to put him- or herself in the position of the reader.

SIMON ARMITAGE, *The Independent,* 8 November 2002

It is so easy to induce emotion in oneself or in the reader with rich language… The music or richness may dance the reader into a mood or beguile him into enlisting, but it is a conversion without substance. Like becoming Catholic because you like the vestments.

JACK GILBERT, cited in *Agenda,* Autumn–Winter 2005

Descriptive gifts are treacherous for poets, always tempting them to substitute the leisurely stuff of good writing for the concentrated, and less predictable, surprises of real poems.

PETER MCDONALD, *The Literary Review,* May 2005

I'd write with my Revlon Fire and Ice lipstick if I had to.

BETH ANN FENNELLY, *Poets on Place,* 2005

Description isn't just a way of telling us what the world looks like, of making what Pound called "accurate reports." It expresses the feeling a poet has for the look of things.

W.S. Di Piero, *Poetry,* January 2006

I suspect that a famous adolescent anxiety is never very far from a poet's mind... It is: "Am I doing it right?"

Jeffrey Wainwright, *The Poet's Voice and Craft,* 1994

FORMAL OR INFORMAL?

The problem with most free verse is that it locates wisdom in the self and not in the language.

GLYN MAXWELL, Bloodaxe Books Catalog, 1995

Good formalism... requires the poet to think with form and not just with ideas.

JUSTIN QUINN, *Graph*, Spring 1998

The preferred form for many poets is incoherence. Unassigned signifiers are let loose in a cloud of unknowing, in such a way as to seem to be a flight from voice, because voice implies both personality and responsibility.

MARK JARMAN, *The Hudson Review*, Summer 2006

Free verse has become a banal reflex. A lot of poets imagine that it reflects the fragmentation of the social world or something. In fact, it is just sloppy writing.

JUSTIN QUINN, *The Independent on Sunday*, 8 October 1995

Free verse has come to represent democracy, equal opportunity and self-expression. But in bulk and unaware of the forms from which it has been freed—the iambic pentameter, the alexandrine—it can be extremely depressing.

A.S. BYATT, *Times Literary Supplement*

It may be, though I can't prove it, that certain bromidic ideas about form are losing their power over us. The idea, for example, that metre and stanza are intrinsically repressive and right-wing, whereas free verse

> Form [is] any aspect of a poem that encourages it to stay whole and not drift off into chaos.
>
> BILLY COLLINS,
> *Fulcrum,* no. 4, 2005
>
> ↝

is liberating and democratic. The idea that free verse is forever original and venturesome, that it is somehow "experimental" to imitate Pound or Bill Williams decade after decade.

RICHARD WILBUR, *PN Review,* 1987

The iambic pentameter—the most typical metre in English verse—weaves together freedom and order, flexibility and regularity, the distinctive tones of an individual with an impersonal structure. This, among other things, is an idealised view of what is peculiar about English civilisation.

TERRY EAGLETON, *The Times,* 27 January 2007

Form was never a mode of civilization. Nor was it ever, nor will it ever be, a mode of evading disorder. On the contrary, it is a method of engaging it without yielding to its prescriptions.

EAVAN BOLAND, *PN Review*

A poet's resources and inspirations seem to remain constant, but our curiosity about form and technique renews the art for us.

PAUL VIOLI, *The North,* no. 35, 2004

Surrealism didn't realise that the truest defamiliarisation is that of poetic form, the breaking up of prose rhythm, prose syntax, prose convention, by devices such as the line, as metre and rhyme. It is a singing kind of defamiliarisation.

GEORGE SZIRTES online, 15 June 2005

Free verse is very exciting. But it is only exciting in the way it plays off the expectations developed by meter.

AUGUST KLEINZAHLER, BBC Radio 3, July 1995

Good metrical rhymed verse, if it's to grip the imagination and stay readable, has to have, as well as those external formal features, the same dynamo of hidden musical dramatic laws as the apparently free verse.

TED HUGHES, *The Paris Review,* Spring 1995

Metrical poetry is ultimately allied to song, and I like the connection. Free verse is ultimately allied to conversation, and I like that connection too. Not many people can mix the two.

THOM GUNN, *The Paris Review,* Summer 1995

To talk about formal verse is meaningless—poetry *is* form.

ROBERT PINSKY, *PN Review,* September–October 1998

You can't write a poem until you have a form. It's like... trying to play an untuned instrument.

LES MURRAY, *The Independent,* 29 April 1993

I think of the sonnet not as a uniform in which to dress up words but rather as a body of words in which to live for a measure of time.

RICHARD MURPHY, Australian Broadcasting Corporation, 1984

Poetry has to be embodied, just as we come in bodies. We're not pure spirit. The form is the poem's way of carrying itself, of being in the world, of incarnating the spirit.

EDWARD HIRSCH, *Five Points* 4, no. 2

Rhyme, like water on a potter's wheel, keeps the material malleable until it's finished.

TONY HARRISON,
BBC Radio 4,
April 2007

❧

Poetry without form is a fiction. But that there is a freedom in words is the larger fact, and in poetry, where formal restrictions can bear down heavily, it is important to remember the cage is never locked.

C.D. WRIGHT, *Cooling Time,* 2005

Form in poetry is like the wing of a bird. It does not cause flight to happen, but without it there would be no flight.

ROBERT BRINGHURST, cited in *The Independent*, 28 October 2005

ᕽ

In general... form urges all degrees of ability to optimum performance.

CAROL RUMENS, *The Creative Writing Coursebook*, 2001

Poems that do not exhibit an interest in language and form have a short life span.

MARVIN BELL, *Planet on the Table*, 2003

Think of [learning poetic forms] as acquiring the tools of your trade, which you may or may not choose to employ. A carpenter doesn't always use a drill, though it would be disastrous for him not to know that it exists for him, and might facilitate what he wants to accomplish.

STEPHEN DUNN, *Smartish Pace*, 2004

Free verse teetotalers innocently imagine that metrics is an abstract, intellectual enterprise. For most young poets, however, studying prosody proves an intoxicating experience, a debauchery of verbal dance and music.

DANA GIOIA, *The Hudson Review*, Spring 1998

To dispense with rhyme and metre on theoretical grounds is to oppose memorability... To remove metre from verse is to remove time, or the sound of breath upon time, which is to remove the essential soundscape of any lived moment.

GLYN MAXWELL, *The Guardian*, 17 February 2007

Rhyme is a principle of change, challenging the autonomy of words and their stability in contexts high or low... High and low can be freely paired across verbal registers, making matches that stir up our assumptions about what is most valuable, and what is kin to what.

GILLIAN BEER, *The Guardian*, 13 January 2007

Rhyme and metre are a magnifying glass: if the language, rhythm and metre are inappropriate, then it will stand out. If they are used with care, they will enlarge a poet's voice to a pitch where the reader will take notice.

N.S. THOMPSON, *PN Review,* May-June 2003

The trick remains to square and combine the two elements, so that meter gives rhythm memorable shape and stability while, at the same time, rhythm animates meter with spirit and variety.

TIMOTHY STEELE, Academy of American Poets online, December 2006

The greatest tool in the service of poetry is the line of five beats, the pentameter, which was no more nor less natural in the day of Shakespeare than it is today. It simply seems to hold as an approximation of the breath, and, as such, serves as a metaphor for the experience of a moment.

GLYN MAXWELL, *The Guardian,* 5 November 2005

It is often said to be free verse poets who are in danger of wittering on with nothing much to say, because it's so easy. But poets who are extremely skilled and practised in rhyme and metre... may be in a similar danger of knocking off sonnets simply because they can.

SHEENAGH PUGH, *Poetry Wales,* Spring 2003

If you have nothing to say, a sonnet will make that clear; there's no hiding in a sonnet. It's an open window.

MARK JARMAN, *The Writer's Chronicle,* February 2007

That [Charles Bukowski's] poems get an F for craft doesn't bother him; since his life gets an F too, he achieves an extraordinary correspondence between word and action.

D.H. TRACY, *The New York Times,* 8 January 2006

Form is a straitjacket in the way that a straitjacket was a straitjacket for Houdini.

PAUL MULDOON,
The Irish Times,
19 April 2003

᠅

Craft, in the broadest sense, is a kind of pressure that the poet puts on his material in order to see what it can bear. Its primary aim is paradoxical—to exclude and accommodate.

STEPHEN DUNN,
The American Poetry Review, July–August 2007

While it is true that we are initially *drawn* to poems by their passions, their questions, and their tonal urgencies, we are *convinced* by them, finally, insofar as they can invent formal means for their impelling motives.

HELEN VENDLER, *The Breaking of Style,* 1995

Without an awareness of structure and form, personal experience remains hermetically personal, and political comment comes over as crass polemic.

SARAH MAGUIRE, *Poetry Review,* Spring 1994

The reason I work with craft and form is because when I open up a lot of literary journals, I often can't distinguish one poem from another, and form certainly helps in that respect.

KENNETH SHERMAN, *Poetry Canada* 14, no. 1

Form cannot be first if you want to reach high artistic levels, since you are then bound by form, and that form is very often a betrayal of reality. It cannot grasp reality.

CZESLAW MILOSZ, *Partisan Review,* Summer 1996

A poet who wants all rhyme and rhythm to be flawless is working on patterns instead of poetry.

TOBIAS HILL, Poetry Book Society *Bulletin,* Autumn 1996

What free verse poets deprive us of is a metrical grid that can be placed over their poems so we can see how well they are doing their metrical job. This is what critics miss.

STEPHEN DOBYNS, *Best Words, Best Order,* 1996

It was that Dutch painter who cut off his ear, but it might well have been a contemporary English poet: it frequently seems as if we have lost all sense of the importance of music in our poetry.

JOHN GREENING, *Poetry Review*, Winter 1997–98

A poet is revealed less in his subject matter, however personal, than in his rhythms—just as a painter is most truly revealed in his brushstroke.

ADAM KIRSCH, *The Wounded Surgeon*, 2005

Poetry's only crucial attribute is rhythm. This is its heart-beat. This makes it memorable. If the rhythm falters, then the poem dies of heart-failure.

MICHAEL LONGLEY, *Poetry Ireland Review*, Summer 1999

A new rhythm is a new life given to the world, a resuscitation not just of the ear but of the springs of being.

SEAMUS HEANEY, *The Government of the Tongue*, 1988

I profoundly distrust rhythms that drown the pressure of what has been felt.

ELAINE FEINSTEIN, Poetry Book Society *Bulletin*, Spring 1997

Look at rap—that's the best poetry being written in America at the moment; at least it rhymes.

DEREK MAHON, *The Sunday Times*, 11 February 1996

Rhyme is but an echo of a pre-determinant word-sound; the refrain takes us back to the beginning; the euphony of the lines implies the monotony of the eternally recurrent. It is this that enables a poem to restrain time, or indeed to bring it to a standstill, making it the only form to give lasting quality to a subjective

Good poets don't replicate forms; they adapt them.

CARMINE STARNINO, *The New Canon*, 2005

Those who proclaim the resurrection of rhyme and meter have displaced religious yearnings.

DAVE SMITH,
Local Assays, 1985

ᴗ᛬

factor that neither celluloid nor digital plastic can render.

RAOUL SCHROTT, Rotterdam Poetry Festival, 2003

When you rhyme, you're somehow engaging with something that's older than you are, that's older than your history, that's older than anything you really understand or experience. You engage with a source of power; you're plugging into Dante, plugging into Coleridge.

GLYN MAXWELL, *Atlantic Unbound*, 14 June 2001

Rhyme can make us feel, for the space of a poem, that the world is less contingent, less random, more connected, link by link.

STEPHEN FRY, *The Ode Less Travelled*, 2005

Rhyme... is a form of relationship and connection, of encounter and metamorphosis... There is something charged and magnetic about a good rhyme, something unsuspected and inevitable, utterly surprising and unforeseen and yet also binding and necessary. It is as if the poet called up the inner yearning for words to find each other.

EDWARD HIRSCH, *The Washington Post*, 17 October 2004

I see rhyme as the tracer bullets in the battle to capture a passable poem—it shows me where I should be shooting, where I'm wide of the mark and how to be accurate in the gloom of the battlefield.

GWYNETH LEWIS, *Modern Poetry in Translation*, Spring 1995

Rhyme in poems can be like the glue that has been used to put a broken pot back together. It's structurally important but you're not aware of it.

ROBERT SAXTON, *PN Review,* September–October 2005

I sometimes think there's no more reliable way of initially entering a poet's private domain than by examining what he or she rhymes with what.

BRAD LEITHAUSER, *The New York Times,* 16 July 2006

You get bad poems that rhyme and bad poems that do not. Rhyme is not what sorts them out, and neither is it an infallible way of producing good writing.

MICHAEL HOFMANN, *The Times,* 22 August 1992

What would be rare would be to have a great poet who never wrote in form... Weaker poets are the ones who only write free verse.

DAVID YEZZI, *The Cortland Review,* June 2006

Formalism, in itself, is a fetish: specific forms only become interesting when the pressure inside them is on the point of breaking them up.

GEORGE SZIRTES, Poetry Book Society *Bulletin,* Winter 2004

When we got rid of rhyme and meter it made the business of poetry harder, not easier. I consider poetry to be a long forgotten branch of science.

ED DORN, cited in *Times Literary Supplement,* 24 January 1992

In poetry, as in meteorology, two atmospheric fronts are always colliding: the warm air of our introspection meets up with the cold front of form, the chill breeze of reflection.

ADAM ZAGAJEWSKI, *A Defense of Ardor,* 2004

The Begetters

There are, I would say, three types of poet: those who write without thinking, those who think while writing and those who have figured out everything before they sit down to write.

CHARLES SIMIC, *London Review of Books,* 18 March 1999

All people talk to themselves. Some are overheard, and they are the poets.

R.S. THOMAS, *The South Bank Show*

The poet is set against the world because he cannot accept that what there seems to be is all that there is.

BEN OKRI, *The Times,* 21 December 1991

The poet is essentially a medium. You take poetry from the people and then give it back to them.

MICHEAL O'SIADHAIL, *The Irish Times,* 21 October 1992

Ever since Stephen Dedalus, poets have tended to look at themselves as if they were angels on loan from heaven, instead of scruffy old bolloxes going around the place looking for a bit of inspiration.

BRENDAN KENNELLY, *The Big Issues,* no. 32, 1995

If you are a poet, it is a gift... And if you ask where the gift comes from, then I will have to get even more corny and say, maybe it's divine. I think all art is a manifestation of that belief that a gift is a benediction.

DEREK WALCOTT, *Wasifiri,* Summer 2004

A special gift isn't bestowed on us by God Almighty, but by another God called Hard Work. I was my own creator.

RADMILA LAZIC, *PN Review,* January–February 2005

Nearly all poets continue to be drawn to the romantic allure of being thought of as "outsider" or at least "anti-establishment" (even if the only one who buys the pose is the mug staring back in the mirror). Even those sucking lavish salaries from large educational bureaucracies enjoy imagining themselves as crusaders with mask and cape come to make trouble for the empire.

ERNEST HILBERT, *Contemporary Poetry Review*, April 2006

I don't want to don the armour of ego or the costume of the stage poet, with my special set of pencils and handmade paper. I want a hand-to-hand engagement with myself—self-forgetfulness rather than self-consciousness.

SEAMUS HEANEY, *The Times*, 25 March 2006

As a poet, you mustn't have a very hard outside wall to protect you, and so you receive a great deal of damage.

ELAINE FEINSTEIN, *PN Review*, January–February 1995

Being a poet is like having an invisible partner. It isn't easy. But you can't live without it either. Talent is only 10 percent. The rest is obsession.

SELIMA HILL, *Contemporary Women's Poetry*, 2000

For the poet, poetry is a pure obsession, a sequence of questions which have no answers, of demands that have no satisfaction other than the satisfaction of obsession itself.

T.R. HUMMER, Poetry Book Society *Bulletin*, Winter 2005

To be a published poet is not a sane person's aspiration.

BERNARD O'DONOGHUE, *Oxford Poetry*, Summer 1994

Most writers of verse have several different personalities. The ideal is to find a style or a method that includes them all.

TED HUGHES, BBC Radio 4, March 1992

⌣

Any fool can write poetry, but it takes a genius to get it published.

Horace Charles Jones, cited in *The Guardian,* 17 September 1998

If you are writing poetry only to get published, you belong in some other kind of writing.

William Bronk, *Poet's Market,* 1997

If a so-called artistic work is done without the artist committing his whole personality, I am dubious about the effect. It must fully engage our liver, heart and respiration.

Zbigniew Herbert, *PN Review,* no. 26, 1982

Lyric poets / Usually have... cold hearts. / It is like a medical condition. Perfection in art / Is given in exchange for such an affliction.

Czeslaw Milosz, *The New Yorker,* 17 May 2004

A lyric poet is... the most exemplary incarnation of man dazzled by his own soul and by the desire to make it heard.

Milan Kundera, *The New Yorker,* 9 October 2006

Poetry is old, as old as time; it is poverty, little books that fall apart, pub basements. Poets used to be mad or bad; now they're mostly just sad.

Alan Jenkins, *The Independent on Sunday,* 12 September 1993

There are *jealousies* rolling about like loose cannon in the Groves of Poesie—not much chinking of money, but plenty of *grinding of teeth.*

John Whitworth, *The Spectator,* 14 March 1992

The one thing that can get a poet irritated and upset is the thought of another poet's poems.

Charles Baxter, *Michigan Quarterly Review,* Fall 1996

Mad, Bad, and Dangerous to Know

A wallop of a fist which would give you a black eye is a relatively harmless piece of machinery in comparison to a cut from a drunken poet who, with two lines, will leave you a mark for the rest of your life that will go on even into future generations.

JOHN B. KEANE, BBC Radio Ulster

Sylvia Plath's "Daddy" set a standard for modern unfairness, and gave birth to a genre of American poetry in which the author insults her nearest and dearest.

JAMES FENTON, *The Independent on Sunday*

Not giving offense, never hurting anyone's feelings is perhaps a laudable motive and hope at the dinner table, but it is a dubious goal in education and a deplorable reality in literature, our *real* conversation.

LIAM RECTOR, *The American Poetry Review,* September–October 2005

A real poet has to be somebody that you're never quite sure that he mightn't bite you. He should not be too tamed—even by old age.

JOHN MONTAGUE, RTÉ Radio I, August 2004

If you're a poet, you've earned the right to blow off whoever you want. There used to be dozens of cranks and scolds, but there aren't any anymore.

AUGUST KLEINZAHLER, *The New York Times,* 3 August 2005

Heavyweight boxing is a tame, almost gentle, spectacle compared with the contests of literary men.

RICHARD BOSTON, *The Guardian*

There's nothing like a punch in the mouth to remind you that that poem about your next-door neighbour was not as clever as you thought.

SIMON ARMITAGE,
BBC Radio 4,
January 1993

⌣⃛

It is surprising how much grousing and grieving, and beady looking at very little, goes on in the name of poetry.

KARL MILLER, *PN Review*

It is safe to assert that the culture of poetry—i.e. backbiting—is ubiquitous. If I were Noam Chomsky I might even say that it is part of the deep structure of the brain.

PETER FORBES, *Poetry Review*, Spring 1993

The struggle for existence is fierce in the endangered species of poets, and fitness to survive may depend on skills quite different from those of poetic or critical talent.

EDWARD LOWBURY, *Acumen*, April 1993

To the outsider, poetry is a peripheral activity, useful if you're in love or on the Underground; to poets and their satellites it is a battleground, bristling with factions and militant tendencies.

DAISY GOODWIN, *The Guardian*, 11 August 1993

How many attempts to get poetry on the road have foundered because the poetry entrepreneurs have rolled all over the tarmac trying to gouge out each other's eyes?

P.J. KAVANAGH, *The Daily Telegraph*, 30 April 1994

The sense of ferrets fighting for mastery of a septic tank is depressing—poetry is the national art, after all.

SEAN O'BRIEN, *The Guardian*, 10 October 1996

Poetry, ostensibly a liberal art, is actually one of the strongest remaining bastions of pre-literate tribalism. Gangs form as readily as in any deprived ghetto and the patterns of bonding rituals, territorial marking, hysterical crowd behaviour, collective log-rolling and hatchet-work, are worth the attention of the anthropologists.

PETER FORBES, *Poetry Review,* Winter 2000–01

Such as it exists, the Anxiety of Influence is mostly a business between contemporaries. The tensions are all sibling, not Oedipal.

DON PATERSON, *The Book of Shadows,* 2004

Writing comes to be associated with the outlaw parts of the self, but one really needs an orderly, bourgeois life to get work done.

ROBERT HASS, *Smartish Pace,* 2004

Character References

He could out-talk R. Buckminster Fuller and the Wicked Witch of the West put together. Even Samuel Taylor Coleridge might have found himself gasping for air and being swept away by this river of sacred conversation.

JONATHAN WILLIAMS, on Robert Duncan, *The Independent*

Talking with Philip Lamantia was like staring up into the moss-draped limbs of a three-hundred-year-old Louisiana live oak tree, dripping with talismans, voodoo grisgris, and tribal fetishes.

JAMES NOLAN, *Poetry Flash,* Summer–Fall 2005

A lover certainly, and of both women and the land of his birth. A full list of his loves would... include many other affections that composed his life: for friends, London, rugby, drink, classical languages, fast cars, idle talk, clichés, pubs, and not most of all, perhaps, but most of the time—poetry.

SAMUEL HYNES, on Louis MacNeice, *London Review of Books*

The image persists of Shakespeare as a bald, provincial, English family man, a slightly dull bank-manager type blessed with a magic quill and a character of unalloyed sweetness.

ROBERT GORE-LANGTON, *The Sunday Telegraph,* 29 June 2003

Edmund Spenser... that poet whom sculptor Seamus Murphy called a "malignant dwarf," and who referred to the province [of Munster] as "Monster," advocating the eradication of the natives: an Elizabethan Eichmann.

JOHN MONTAGUE, *The Irish Times,* 28 January 2006

Going into a room of Auden's was like going into the nest of a very untidy animal.

STEPHEN SPENDER, BBC Radio 4

He was short-sighted, absent-minded, frequently unwashed, and lived in hair-raising squalor, his "burrows" invariably carpeted with scribbled scraps of paper and banana-skins. Visitors would be offered tea or whisky in encrusted tooth-mugs.

SAM LEITH, on William Empson, *The Daily Telegraph,* 30 April 2005

[A] typical menu for guests in "The Burrow," his filthy basement flat: hard-boiled egg in bottled curry sauce followed by a doughnut soused in condensed milk, plus a tumbler of Japanese whisky.

FRED INGLIS, on William Empson, *The Independent,* 19 January 2007

If by some miracle one could undo the tragedy of [Marina] Tsvetaeva's suicide in 1941 and bring her back to earth to finish her allotted time, one might still, on seeing her approach, cross to the other side of the street. She was simply, in life, bad news.

CLARENCE BROWN, *London Review of Books,* 8 September 1994

Even Anna Akhmatova's close friends agree that she was a difficult woman; as Nadezhda Mandelstam records, old age and fame reinforced the strain of imperiousness in her character; she would react like an "angry cat" to the slightest attempt to contradict her, an observation that would provoke her to even greater fury.

AILEEN KELLY, *The New York Review of Books,* 3 November 2005

A poet shouldn't be viewed through any prism other than that of his poems.

JOSEPH BRODSKY, *Partisan Review,* Summer 1995

⌣⁖

Human failings may be forgivable, but if lack of compassion, meanness of spirit, envy or cowardice are present in the poet's nature they will be evident in his verse. You cannot fake anything if you are trying to write serious poetry.

ELIZABETH JENNINGS,
The Independent

Alexander Pushkin drank like a frat boy, treated and spoke of women as whores, alternately rebelled against and toadied to the tsar, reduced his family to penury by addictive gambling, and typically allowed his usually dirty fingernails to grow long and claw-like... He could be utterly thoughtless of others' feelings but was himself "morbidly sensitive to... appearing comic" and quickly roused to anger, jealousy and spite.

MICHAEL DIRDA, *The Washington Post*,
16 November 2003

Charles Baudelaire is the classic "brat," the John McEnroe of poetry. His life was a sequence of rows with the referee. His poems, like ace serves, brilliant volleys, conclusive match-points, or apparently effortless but unforgettable examples of pure tennis, punctuate a life of conflict, upset and eventual tragedy.

BRUCE ARNOLD, *The Independent*

Verlaine's brother-in-law described Rimbaud as "a vile, vicious, disgusting, smutty little schoolboy," but Verlaine found him an "exquisite creature." He didn't seem to mind that Rimbaud rarely washed, left turds under one friend's pillow, and put sulphuric acid in the drink of another; not to mention that he hacked at his wrists with a penknife and stabbed him in the thigh.

CHRISTINA PATTERSON, *The Independent*, 8 February 2006

Male figures excited her rage, in her later poems as throughout her life, chiefly when they exposed her to those she feared and hated who (the evidence is distasteful but it cannot be denied, it makes up a considerable part of her work) were almost exclusively women.

TED HUGHES, on Sylvia Plath, *The Independent,* 22 April 1989

Everyone I know who was acquainted with Plath and Hughes during their marriage has little good to say about her. She seems to have been a spoiled, petulant, phony, cold, ambitious, and very talented woman... And can Hughes himself have been a bowl of cherries?

J.D. MCCLATCHY, *Poetry,* June 1998

Depending on who you read, Sylvia Plath was variously perfectly normal, oppressed, manic, depressive, manic-depressive, schizophrenic, a borderline personality, a psychopath, a sociopath, a nymphomaniac, addicted to sleeping tablets, the victim of an Electra complex, a masochist, and very definitely a misogynist. Or was that a feminist?

JOHN BROWNLOW, *The Guardian,* 22 August 2003

If we conflate current hostilities in critical and biographical accounts... T.S. Eliot emerges as a closet-homosexual, misogynistic, Jew-baiting, reactionary snob.

STEPHEN ROMER, *Times Literary Supplement,* 14 November 2003

The literary-industrial complex that sprang up in order to explain T.S. Eliot now seems to exist largely to vivisect him, intent on exposing him as all too human.

DAVID BARBER, *The Boston Globe,* 1 January 2006

At a time when Woolf is a racist and Larkin a womaniser, it is frankly amazing that Byron of all people continues to elude politically correct

Wordsworth was utterly self-centered, inordinately ambitious (without ever quite being aware of it), unsociable yet exploitative of others and very nearly a cad.

MICHAEL DIRDA, *The Washington Post,* 11 February 2007

When we say a poet was a "bad man," we don't mean that he was a shotgun-toting, baby-kicking monster; we mean that he was unpleasant, disturbed, or a jerk.

David Orr, *Poetry*, December 2004

reassessment, especially given that his vices exceed those of any other writer I can think of, with the possible exception of the Marquis de Sade.

Duncan Wu, *The Independent*, 10 September 2003

He was viciously Stalinist, masculinist, pugilistic in a way that was good then but isn't now, and I would have died from his cigarette smoke. None of that confiscates his genius.

Robert Crawford, on Hugh MacDiarmid, *Oxford Poetry*, Summer–Autumn 1995

He was a communist and a nationalist, a propagandist and a plagiarist, a drinker and a messer, and he carried out all these roles with immense panache. He made enemies with as much flair as he made friends. He was a Stalinist and a chauvinist, he was Anglophobic and arrogant, but the very excessiveness which he constantly manifested... also charged his positive achievements and gave them real staying power.

Seamus Heaney, on Hugh MacDiarmid, *The Redress of Poetry*, 1995

The poet loved to quarrel, especially about politics. He would take on anybody on any topic... Whether he was discussing Ming vases or *The Simpsons* (later in life, his favorite TV show), he was in it to win.

Martha Brant, on Octavio Paz, *Newsweek*, 4 May 1998

A glamorous loner, he lived like a reclusive movie-star/wizard in a stone tower by the sea. A wife-stealing adulterer, he was a devoted husband, father, family man. He was a Protestant pagan, an Abrahamic soothsayer, a human-loathing God-disdainer, as theologically reckless and incisive as he was humble in the face of the natural world.

Peter O'Leary, on Robinson Jeffers, *Chicago Review,* Summer 2004

Irving Layton, the "Picasso of poetry," had a complicated private life: marrying a former student, encouraging lovers to change their names—his fifth wife, Annette, became Anna—writing a vitriolic book about an ex-wife. He had two more children, his last daughter arriving when he was 70. "Everything except writing poems and making love ends up finally boring me," he said.

Cathryn Atkinson, *The Guardian,* 23 January 2006

Rupert Brooke is remembered less for his poems than for his good looks and less for his good looks than for the way he abused his friends with them.

Perry Meisel, *The New York Times,* 17 January 1999

Foul-mouthed and potbellied, ravaged by self-neglect and alcohol abuse, with a huge mis-shapen head, matted hair and lumpy, pitted, porridge-coloured skin, he looked in his prime like something risen from the dead.

Hilary Spurling, on Charles Bukowski, *The Daily Telegraph,* 30 January 1999

Charles Olson was a philanderer with an appetite for co-eds and had a way of abandoning his common-law wives and offspring when they became inconvenient.

Thomas M. Disch, *Poetry,* April 1998

There has to be a line between my life and art. You don't want to sell the one as the other... I don't simply want to tell what is. I want to tell what is with all the radiations around it of what could be.

Anne Carson, *Poets & Writers,* March–April 2001

⌣

> You don't read poetry to find out about the poet, you read poetry to find out about yourself.
>
> BILLY COLLINS,
> *The Globe and Mail*,
> 15 September 2001
>
> ∴

> [A] poser and a show-off of the first order. A sponger too, a user of women, a nobility freak and little boy lost at the same time.
>
> H.C. TEN BERGE, on Rilke, *Modern Poetry in Translation*, Winter 1997

> The word "bounder" might have been coined for him. (John Berryman called him a jerk.) He was a snob, a wastrel and a parasite, who led the most skimmingly uncommitted life.
>
> MICHAEL HOFMANN, on Rilke, *The Times*, 26 March 1998

> Giggling charmer, proselytiser and enthusiast, he also emerges as a petulant depressive, tortured by worries on unresolved matters including his sexuality, social class and intellect. His furious pride left his disastrous relationships with his father and his son largely unhealed.
>
> GILLIAN DARLEY, on John Betjeman, *London Review of Books*, 31 March 2005

> So much in the life, and quite a bit in the work, exudes a repellent, smelly, inadequate masculinity.
>
> BRYAN APPLEYARD, on Philip Larkin, *The Independent*, 18 March 1993

> A death-obsessed, emotionally-retarded misanthropist who had the impudence to generalise his own fears and failings to the way things are.
>
> TERRY EAGLETON, on Philip Larkin, Channel 4, March 1993

> If we are going to judge Philip Larkin, we should do so by the written work which he chose to publish, the library he built and the fidelity he aroused in his friends and lovers.
>
> JEAN HARTLEY, *About Larkin*, April 2002

There was much ugliness in Philip Larkin's character, but what mattered most to him was beauty, and the making of beautiful objects. In this lay his greatness.

JOHN BANVILLE, *The New York Review of Books*, 23 February 2006

Great poetry has been written by adulterers galore, as well as thieves, cowards, spies, anti-Semites, and even a murderer or two.

WILLIAM LOGAN, *The Undiscovered Country*, 2005

For a poet to be great we must find ourselves repelled by some part of the poet's work. Not just mildly disquieted but actively repelled... There must be a crack in the poet of some sort. It has to be deep, privately potent, and unmendable—and the poet must forever try to mend it.

KAY RYAN, *The Yale Review*, April 2004

The thing about [great] writers is that they provoke in us a horrible sense of envy. There's nothing you can do about it—they *are* just better. In moral terms, they are equal. You can defeat them 6-nil on moral grounds, so you think.

CRAIG RAINE, BBC Radio 4, January 2007

Much of our mainstream poetry is confined by an ethic of sincerity and the unstated wish to be admired (if not admired, liked; if not liked, sympathized with). American poetry still largely believes... that a poem is straightforward autobiographical testimony to, among other things, the decency of the speaker.

TONY HOAGLAND, *The American Poetry Review*, March–April 2003

Poems still get written, naturally, but the flames, one suspects, don't burn quite so hot these days. Poets behave better, live longer and probably settle for less.

CHARLES MCGRATH, *The New York Times*, 15 June 2003

࿇

A poem is something a poet makes; it's not the life he lives.

DAVID BIESPIEL,
The Oregonian,
1 January 2006

Having surveyed the sins of the leading poets in the language, I have come to the unlikely conclusion that the only one who can be honored with impunity is George Herbert. If you refuse to read anyone you disapprove of, I should warn you that you'll end up spending an awful lot of time with "The Temple."

ANTHONY LANE, *The New Yorker,* 10 March 1997

To learn that the poet was a practicing Christian—or doctor, or stamp collector, or child molester, etc.—may help us to see why a poem fails, but not why it succeeds.

COLIN FALCK, *American and British Verse in the Twentieth Century,* 2003

Poetry has its own life, with only an ambiguous connection to the life of the person who writes it.

ADAM KIRSCH, *The Wounded Surgeon,* 2005

It's finally impossible to consider fully any poet's body of work without considering his or her character, with how it determined the work, and then with how the work may in turn have affected the poet.

C.K. WILLIAMS, *The Yale Review,* October 2000

The extent to which we are all (except a very few saints among us?) influenced in our appreciation of contemporary writing by knowledge of the personal history and personal manner and personal affinities and even personal appearance of a given author is a subject more complicated and interesting (and embarrassing) than most of us admit.

MARK HALLIDAY, *Poetry Review,* Autumn 2001

The reader under the sway of the life will always be part psychologist, part social columnist. Whatever the question was, the circumstantial life is only ever a small part of the answer.

PETER SIRR, *Poetry Ireland Review,* December 2004

One reason readers prefer biographies of poets to their poetry is that the lives are more poetic, and more unlikely, than the poems.

WILLIAM LOGAN, *Parnassus* 25, nos. 1 & 2

The confessional and the autobiographical modes are paradoxical. Two things seem to be true: the more completely personal you are, the more universal your meaning becomes. And the more honest you are, the more mysterious you appear.

FINUALA DOWLING, *The Poetry Paper,* no. 3, 2006

Becoming a poet involves the end of a kind of innocence. It is about being critical, separate. Experience is no longer just experience. It becomes material.

VICKI FEAVER, *How Poets Work,* 1996

Poets who confuse art and life often make a mess of both.

CHRISTIAN WIMAN, *Poetry,* January 1999

Ours is a fiercely autobiographical era, and we continually refuse or fail to differentiate between the person one is and the person one becomes in the act of making art.

CLÍODHNA CARNEY, *Poetry Ireland Review,* Spring-Summer 2003

Poets seem to have less trouble writing than living. Their poems tend to be their happiness.

STANLEY PLUMLY, *The American Poetry Review,* January-February 2005

POETIC RECOGNITION

Physically, the male poet falls into two types... Feral Man with his wild stare, unruly hair and booze-wrecked complexion [and] the rival brand: *l'homme sensible,* pale and pretty...

ANDREW BILLEN, *The Observer*

There are two kinds of poets: the ones who tell the stories, and the ones about whom the stories get told.

DAN CHIASSON, *The New York Times,* 9 July 2006

We do not, on the whole, want our poets to be cuddly and approachable. We don't want to think of them buying toilet rolls at Tesco or filling out their tax returns. We want our poets to be brooding, Byronic, beautiful and preferably dead.

CHRISTINA PATTERSON, *The Independent,* 6 February 2004

A lot of people have peculiar ideas about what a poet is. They imagine someone very emotional, perhaps sentimental, nostalgic—someone whose writing reflects their own personal experience, someone who is subject to bouts of melancholia.

TIMOTHY DONNELLY, *The Salt Lake Tribune,* 4 January 2004

There is still a romantic cloak attached to being a poet; dark, swirling, smelling either of magic or of death, maybe also of sexuality.

CHRIS WALLACE-CRABBE, *Heat,* no. 8, 1998

One is encouraged to think that poets are lonely, dysfunctional people; that they phrase things in a way that cannot be understood, possibly because they don't know what they are trying to say; that they are miserable sods; that they are pretentious; that they are tweedy and old-fashioned, or else impossibly, annoyingly glamorous.

WILLIAM LEITH, *Tatler,* July 1997

When it comes to gender stereotypes, I've noticed female poets are perceived as romantic airheads who flit through life tossing about scarves and rhymed couplets, as suicidal princesses of the dark literary arts or as breezy nonconformists with free spirits and loose morals. In other words, if she's a poet, she must be ditzy, wanton or damaged goods.

NANCY BREEN, *Writer's Digest,* April 2007

Male poets? They have their own image problems: Which cardboard caricature will it be? The eccentric outsider (think Boo Radley from *To Kill a Mockingbird*), the exhibitionist reprobate who can't be trusted alone in a room with young women or the consumptive milquetoast who's a little too in touch with his own feelings?

NANCY BREEN, *Writer's Digest,* April 2007

Poets are not like the rest of us. To start with, they are untidy, often failing to tuck their shirts into their trousers; they are shockingly unpunctual, and much given to talking to themselves. Some, even more reprehensible than the rest, drink more than is good for them and others beat their wives (assuming they married them in the first place, which is by no means certain).

BERNARD LEVIN, *The Times,* 2 November 1991

Two kinds of people become poets. Extroverts who go out and entertain the family friends, and introverts who hide in the bedroom and put what they write under the mattress.

JANE HIRSHFIELD, *Rattle,* Winter 2006

ᴗ

Writing satire about the poetry world is like shooting similes in a barrel. Line for line, there's no more fertile subject than the black-turtleneck crowd clutching their foundation-funded chapbooks in the student lounge.

RON CHARLES, *The Christian Science Monitor,* 20 April 2004

ـ.

Most of us would go a long way to avoid the company of poets. They're at best disagreeable, and at worst repulsive. Selfish, testy, irresponsible, humourless, swollen-headed, and infinite liars, they're like crazy aunts or men with stains on their trousers who think it's funny to swear. Most of them seem to have spent too much time in the sun or locked up in high rooms, disappointed not to have been born Milton, stewing in their own considerable juices.

IAN SANSOM, *The Guardian,* 2 March 2002

I do my best to appear as unlike anybody's idea of a poet as I possibly can. When I appear in public, I try to dress like an executive secretary and if I were a male poet I'd certainly go for the suit and tie.

WENDY COPE, BBC 2, October 1993

A poet should not strive to look like a poet except by the subtlest means. Most younger male poets strive for a touch cool and smart-informal-tough, implying they have just walked off the set of *Lock, Stock and Two Smoking Barrels.* I am too old for that. It will be flowing locks, cravat and a buttonhole for me next.

GEORGE SZIRTES online, 7 October 2005

Watching large poets work with miniaturist forms can be a bit disorienting—like meeting a heavyweight fighter out walking a chihuahua.

BLAKE MORRISON, *The Irish Times,* 27 May 1995

Poets are almost human.

EILÉAN NÍ CHUILLEANÁIN, *Ropes,* no. 5, 1997

Respondents used the word "stigma" to describe how some people regarded anyone who revealed an interest in contemporary poetry. They were seen as strange, boring, bookish... "some guy with a ponytail, a ban the bomb freak, or a tree hugger..."

ARTS COUNCIL OF ENGLAND, *Rhyme and Reason,* 2000

POETIC LICENSE

It has been my experience that when a pauperised poet finds a charitable house and an equally expansive host, the poet will dig in like a tick.

TOM WIDGER, *The Sunday Tribune*

One should not look to poets for handy hints. W.B. Yeats had trouble walking properly, let alone boiling an egg without cracking it.

CRAIG BROWN, *The Times*

It has long been a demonstrable fact that the poet as personality is a cranky, off-putting pain in the butt. Bumptious, bilious, and babbling; irresponsible, irreal, and well irrigated; lewd, loud-mouthed, and lunatic, he does not present an edifying spectacle to the society that he must portray for the delectation of succeeding generations.

FRED CHAPPELL, *The Formalist*

There is something wonderfully amenable about dead poets. The live ones are riddled with egotism and acidity, a skinless sensitivity to slights and an immoderate estimation of their own talent, not to mention an insatiable need for money and appreciation.

ANDRO LINKLATER, *The Sunday Times*, 31 January 1993

I have noticed on arts programmes that poets and so forth are often described purringly as possessing a "childlike" vision or dealing with the big wide world in a "childlike" way. Presumably this means that they are always knocking things over, tearing things up and screaming blue murder if they don't get their own way.

CRAIG BROWN, *The Sunday Times*, 28 March 1993

A poet is allowed to walk into a pub with a bandaged thumb and explain that he did it banging in a fence-post, to fall off a horse with no whit of social opprobrium ensuing, to cast a fly-rod and remove his neighbour's earlobe with no more consequence than an indulgent smile from his hooked victim, to empty his 12-bore at a standing pheasant, miss it by yards, and shatter the village church's one decent medieval window without anyone shouting anything more critical than "Oh, bad luck!"

ALAN COREN, *The Times*, 26 June 1993

Anybody who describes his vocation as poet, purveying the modern style of formless verse, is invariably among the meanest and most despicable in the land: vain, empty, conceited, dishonest, dirty, often flea-ridden and infected by venereal disease, greedy, parasitical, drunken, untruthful, arrogant... all these repulsive qualities, and also irresistibly attractive to the women.

AUBERON WAUGH, *The Literary Review*, January 1994

In the twentieth century, I think, in the English-speaking culture, a poet is somebody who is in some way effeminate or strange, incomprehensible, and not quite right.

EILÉAN NÍ CHUILLEANÁIN, *The Canadian Journal of Irish Studies* 20, no. 2

The assumption that the writer has a right to destroy others for the sake of his art seems all the more shaky when the writer in question is self-deluded, inadequately gifted, or talentless.

X.J. KENNEDY, *The Gettysburg Review*, Spring 1994

If you want to make someone pretentious and silly in a film, making them a poet is your best bet.

MICHAEL DONAGHY, BBC Radio 4, April 1995

Poetry is rarely a victimless crime.

ROBERT CRAWFORD, *London Review of Books,* 22 February 2007

Poetry tends to like blind spots; it so often burrows where it really oughtn't to, or delves past decency and approbation.

VONA GROARKE, *The Dublin Review,* Winter 2001–02

It is not reasonable in a poet to expect the applause of society. She is a troublemaker by profession, one who looks under carpets, one who notices that the emperor is wearing designer clothes. She must be independent to the point of eccentricity and is often, though not necessarily, as curst as a crow-trodden hen and as odd as one of the triple-faced holy monsters with which the Celts depicted Ogma the omniscient, gazing in all directions at once.

BIDDY JENKINSON, *Irish University Review,* Spring–Summer 1991

CALL YOURSELF A POET?

It's a life's work to write poetry. So, for anybody to say "Oh yes, I'm a poet" suggests you should be dead by now, you're finished!

JOHN F. DEANE, RTÉ Radio 1, January 2004

Anyone who begins a sentence "as a poet I" is probably not a poet. It's like calling yourself a saint.

MICHAEL LONGLEY, *Colby Quarterly,* September 2003

Poetry makes some kind of claim of honesty. If, at a party, I say I'm a poet, people have a hard time responding, almost as if I'd said I'm a priest.

TOBIAS HILL, *The Independent,* 9 August 2003

It still makes me uncomfortable to call myself a poet. I think of myself as someone in the service of poetry.

FRANZ WRIGHT, *Image,* Fall 2006

When asked what I do, I try just to say I'm a writer, because telling people you're a poet compels them to go into nervous detail about why they neither read nor understand it.

LAVINIA GREENLAW, *The Guardian,* 20 December 2003

I *loathed* the idea of the poet. The posture, the pose of the poet, the understanding of it. I *hate:* Oh, you're a poet? I'm a poet too. Or: Oh, you're a *poet.*

KAY RYAN, *Poetry Flash,* Summer–Fall 2005

I'm embarrassed
to tell people,
still, that I'm a
poet… because I
don't like poets.
They're creeps.
Some of my best
friends are poets,
but they're adult
children, almost
without excep-
tion. And the level
of self-involve-
ment is such that
it's really a won-
der, when they're
stationary, the
floorboards don't
give way.

AUGUST
KLEINZAHLER,
Poets & Writers
online, October 2003

⌣∵

If someone on a train asked me what I did for a living, I'd say I was a tax inspector, rather than a poet. I'm shy about it.

DOUGLAS DUNN, *The Irish Times*, 20 May 2000

Parents still prefer their children to be taxidermists and tax collectors rather than poets.

CHARLES SIMIC, *Michigan Quarterly Review*, Winter 1997

I'm still embarrassed to say I'm a poet. I say I'm a writer and sometimes I say I work for the Inland Revenue, which kills the conversation. To say you're a poet is even worse.

DON PATERSON, *The Independent*, 9 January 2004

It took me years to be able to say "I'm a poet" in public, but not because it was a big claim. Because it was an embarrassing claim, like saying "I'm a proctologist." Because it was a small claim, like saying "I'm a champion toe-wrestler."

ROS BARBER, Shallowlands blog, 9 October 2006

I'd sooner call myself a haddock than a poet. A haddock is a brilliant thing… A poet is pure vicariousness; he goes out into nature, all eyes, and then when he gets home he hunches long hours under a lamp. If he's lucky, he winds up with a good hunch (and a mild myopia).

HEATHER MCHUGH, *Seattle Post-Intelligencer*, 20 April 2000

Unlike other work, being a poet is a culturally demeaned occupation. It's not the kind of thing I'd use as a pick-up line. Saying you're a famous poet is tantamount to saying you're a famous croquet player.

CHRISTIAN BÖK, *Toronto Star,* 3 January 2004

It has taken me three published books, seven years of public readings, festival appearances and tours abroad, several forays into radio, television and the quality newspapers, more than my fair share of grants and prizes and, all in all, some 2,000 poems, to feel I can now say, in a whisper, that I am a poet.

GLYN MAXWELL, *Vogue,* April 1994

In England, if you say you're a poet, it's as if you have a personal hygiene problem.

GWYNETH LEWIS, BBC Radio 4, April 2005

BEST WORDS

The best collections are those with a roughly equal mixture of intellect, heart and guts, and they aren't plentiful.

SHEENAGH PUGH, *Poetry Review*

Whereas good poetry has easily recognizable truth and beauty, great poetry strains at the limits of both thought and expression—it doesn't stop at the usual safe terminals.

CAL BEDIENT, *Denver Quarterly* 39, no. 2, 2004

The best poetry—great poetry—happens when sound, rhythm, and image bring about a mysterious feeling of wholeness that somehow draws mind, body, and spirit together into what both Yeats and Eliot envisioned as a unified dance.

ANNE STEVENSON, *Poetry,* March 2007

When you read a good poem you admire it; when you read a great poem, you fear it, because something of the original fire of composition has been transmitted.

DAN CHIASSON, *Poetry,* November 2005

There are some living poets whose every other line or title is an attempt to toss the poem into the arena of Greatness or onto the great canonical track. Mostly such poems feel like marble, the overrated brain outworking the underpaid heart.

THOMAS SAYERS ELLIS, *Poetry,* March 2005

There is something to be said against merely good poetry: It steals attention away from the best, and, indefatigable as crabgrass, chokes out the more endangered species.

ALFRED CORN, *Poetry*

If good poetry is to be written, enormous amounts of bad poetry must be written too, if only because it is important for a serious poet to know what it is she/he is trying not to do.

GERMAINE GREER, *The Independent on Sunday,* 7 May 2000

It is a rare thing to write a poem which will matter to anybody fifty years down the line, but poets keep writing anyway, because in order for pure-strain poems or hybrid-delight poems which *matter* to emerge, there must first be thousands of common-or-garden specimens to secure a habitat for poetry in the first place.

MARY O'DONNELL, *Irish University Review,* Autumn–Winter 1995

Great poets come as single spies, not in battalions... And the single spies come in unexpected disguises, and are not immediately recognised.

PHILIP HOWARD, *The Times*

How good is their best? / and how good is their rest? / The first is a question to be asked of an artist. / Both are the questions to be asked of a culture.

LES MURRAY, *Harvard Review,* Fall 2002

There is no such thing as a perfectly adequate poem, because a poem into which some strange and surprising excellence has not

In everyday practice, poetry is divided into good poetry, which is written by ourselves, and bad poetry, written by others...

MIROSLAV HOLUB, *Times Literary Supplement,* 17 April 1998

In the case of living poets, there's a simple test: whose books do you wait for? It's never very many.

MICHAEL HOFMANN, introducing *Robert Lowell*, 2001

⌒∴

entered, a poem that is not in some inexplicable way beyond the will of the poet, is not a poem.

CHRISTIAN WIMAN, *Poetry*, December 2006

If it isn't great poetry, it isn't poetry at all.

GILBERT ADAIR, *The Sunday Times*, 2 January 1994

Great poetry is seldom "positive," in the way the media today is always telling us everything from politics to poetry ought to be. Great poetry is more often one of the voices of death.

JOHN BAYLEY, *Agenda*, Autumn 1993

A great poet leaves behind an opus and an aura. The opus instructs; the aura inhibits.

WAYNE KOESTENBAUM, *The New Yorker*, 1 May 1995

Performances of mediocre poems will not make the public like poetry any better... Only a great poem, a poem it remembers, can make it do that.

LOUIS SIMPSON, *Ships Going Into the Blue*, 1994

A major poet does something slightly beyond the possible. When you read a minor poet, you're not necessarily reminded of someone else... yet you're always reminded that someone else is better.

WILLIAM LOGAN, *Parnassus* 25, nos. 1 & 2

One hallmark of the finest poetry is that no other verse can diminish it, but a peculiar effect of reading deeply in certain enduring work is that for a while one is drawn into thinking that this is the only way poetry should be written.

GLYN MAXWELL, *The New Republic*, 20 December 2004

Poetry always appealed to me because it was a genre in which it seemed you could establish perfect order, a piece of writing with everything in its essential and appropriate place, every punctuation mark, every syllable, every sound.

TED KOOSER, *Argus Leader,* 18 September 2005

My own sense of putting together a selection of poetry is to avoid perfection, not to necessarily edit out some of the weaker or goofier stuff, because that has some interesting merit of its own.

GARY SNYDER, *Poets & Writers,* May–June 1995

One should try and curb the need to make a poem too perfect. Maybe one should just try and get some spontaneity in; get it down and forget about it. That's really what's going to live of the poem.

HUGO WILLIAMS, BBC Radio 4, September 2003

There are only so many ways of kicking a bad poem, and only so many ways of finding modest pleasure in the successful minor one. But the major poem is inexhaustible.

DAVID WHEATLEY, *The Irish Times,* 7 February 2004

What is it that makes a bad poem? Well, it flinches in the face of crisis. It seeks refuge in platitude or cliché, or even in Beauty with a capital B.

ALAN SHAPIRO, *Atlantic Unbound,* 30 May 2002

Remember that the poem is a gift. You're not writing it for yourself; you're writing it so you can give it to someone else. So what are you going to give them, a handful of wadded-up tissues from your trash can or a bright, shiny jewel box you've spent weeks making?

DAVID KIRBY, *Smartish Pace,* November 2000

Poems are great to the degree that they overcome a skeptical reader's permanent resistance to being powerfully moved.

DAN CHIASSON,
Ploughshares,
Winter 2006–07

⤳

the grades assigned / to meat will do nicely [for poetry]: / Prime / choice / good / commercial / utility / canners

ED DORN,
Yellow Lola, 1980

⌣̈

The greatest risk for any poet absorbed in the act of writing a poem is the loss of nerve. Many things can cause this, but chief among them remains convention, that ubiquitous goop that shows up in poems as the stock performance of emotion or the tidy notation of good sense.

PETER CAMPION, *Poetry,* June 2005

The best poets inhabit the world with quicker senses than most of us. In town or country, they see, smell and hear more.

MARGARET DRABBLE, *The Forward Book of Poetry 1994*

Criticism, at least as we've come to understand it in Western culture, is by definition hierarchical: to criticize is to admit some system of relative value. Perhaps women are less inclined to make judgments in this way, or more inclined to make that system of value wholly individual.

AVERILL CURDY, *Poetry,* December 2003

Words like "best" are competitive, male words, unfitting to any discussion of poetry, especially women's poetry. What we want is not hierarchy but infinite variety.

GILLIAN CLARKE, Bloodaxe Books catalog, 1987

There is a hierarchy of achievement in poetry, as in all the arts; denying it doesn't make it disappear, it only blunts and veils our aesthetic response.

ADAM KIRSCH, *Poetry,* March 2005

[T]he things that distinguish good poetry from bad [are] an invincible rhythm, a mastery of construction, a thesaurus of cultural imagery, arresting linguistic vitality.

HELEN VENDLER, *The New York Times,* 18 June 1995

Tone, the genetic marker of a literary personality, is the difference between technical accomplishment and art.

IAN BELL, *Sunday Herald,* 1 August 2004

I would distinguish the first-rate artist from the others by precisely this ability. He or she is first-rate to the extent of having realized, often with very great difficulty, the personal note amid the acoustical din that surrounds us all.

GEOFFREY HILL, *The Paris Review,* Spring 2000

Unity is the dream of every poem, large or small. Does each word carry, embryonically, the intent of the entire poem?

DAVE SMITH, *Local Assays,* 1985

The ideal poem... is one you want to pick up and read right away—the irresistibleness of the "excitement"—and can also endlessly revisit.

MICHAEL HOFMANN, *Strong Words,* 2000

It is not necessarily that "more means worse," but that arguments about better and worse seem beside the point when everyone gets into print.

EDNA LONGLEY, *The Southern Review,* Summer 1995

I can hardly stand listening to people who say there isn't any good poetry out there. The vitality of the genre stands in total opposition to its paucity of readers, among them people who call themselves poets. It's so obnoxious, that attitude of read just yourself or read just the dead.

C.D. WRIGHT, Here Comes Everybody blog, 28 August 2004

There ought to be a store of the best language somewhere, and poetry is one of the last few fortresses in which it could be kept and guarded.

ALAN BROWNJOHN, *Acumen*, April 1990

∽

There is really very little poetry written. Many people write poems but poetry is rarely achieved.

SEÁN Ó TUAMA, *The Examiner*, 29 November 1997

What we get to see these days are many poets, little poetry.

OBAKANSE LAKANSE, *Vanguard*, 29 August 2004

More poetry does not mean better poetry. It simply means a bigger pile of stuff to wade through.

JOSEPH S. SALEMI, *The Dark Horse*, Spring 2004

The age of giants is past.

SEAMUS HEANEY, *Gulf Coast*, Summer–Fall 2004

Many are called but few, very few, are chosen; it is a lesson that we are happy to learn about everybody's lifetime except our own.

DONALD DAVIE, *Agenda: An Anthology*, 1994

Most poetry written at any given time is bad, and all poetry written at any given time is new. Together, these facts can make it seem that poetry (in fact, any art) is always in decline.

ADAM KIRSCH, *The New Republic*, 14 June 1999

Only publish what you know is as good as it can ever be, allowing always for a sort of private footnote that it's still not good enough. Then you might be getting somewhere toward the correct view of how to live as a poet.

IAN HAMILTON, *London Review of Books*, 21 February 2002

Without a wink from heaven what does human approval mean?

RUSSELL EDSON, *Metre,* Spring–Summer 2000

I think him not only the worst of the English poets but one of the greatest... A genius, in fact, though an inverse genius, whose special gifts are the anti-climax, the bafflement of expectation, the poetic pratfall, and the groaner.

THOMAS M. DISCH, on William McGonagall, *The Castle of Perseverance,* 2002

The wobble and flop of McGonagall is the signature of his genius.

SEAMUS HEANEY, *The Times,* 25 March 1997

How is it that his every flung-away line gives you such a lift? But it does. Such a draught of liberation. Don't dismiss McGonagall.

TED HUGHES, *The Times,* 25 March 1997

While the majority of his Victorian contemporaries have passed into oblivion, McGonagall's verse has survived... His verse is memorable; it is enjoyable. One of the principal requirements of literary permanence is a distinct voice, and few are more distinct than McGonagall's.

JAMES CAMPBELL, *The Guardian,* 21 January 2006

William McGonagall is not even a one-trick pony; he's the jockey who can't get onto the horse.

GERARD CARRUTHERS, *The Sunday Times,* 5 November 2006

Being a minor poet is like being minor royalty—and no one, as a former lady-in-waiting to Princess Margaret once explained to me, is happy at that.

STEPHEN SPENDER, *The Times*

MARKETING THE STUFF

Poets of my generation—born in the early '60s onwards—haven't had criticism; they've had marketing.

PAUL FARLEY, *The Guardian*, 9 April 2005

As with any other product, there is no innate justice in the marketing and consumption of poetry.

CLIVE JAMES, *Times Literary Supplement*

Just as the richest people are the most prone to regard capitalism as even-handed competition, so the most successful poets are the likeliest to assume that the business is a pure meritocracy.

JON VOLKMER, *Parnassus* 27, nos. 1 & 2

Those who have achieved some kind of notoriety or success within the system as it stands are unlikely to criticise it; those who haven't are likely to be soured by the experience and adopt a pose of cynicism or indifference. Some poets, for their own reasons, will be noisier than others.

MICHAEL CULLUP, *Acumen*, May 2005

There has always been a lot of interest in reading poetry. But it has tended, particularly in bookshops, that poetry sections should be put in the back. A bit like pornography, poetry is always to be found in the dark recesses.

DESMOND CLARKE, BBC Radio 4

A poetry bestseller is any book that sells four or five copies in any given store.

MICHAEL WIEGERS, *Hungry Mind Review*, Spring 1997

People don't read poetry because poetry is not as widely available as trash, or as thrillers. If I were a publisher, a publisher concerned for poetry (which is a rare bird to find!), I would publish anthologies that would be sold in supermarkets. You never know what people buy in supermarkets!

JOSEPH BRODSKY, *Vogue,* February 1988

Poetry is the spinach in America's media diet: good for you, occasionally baked into other, tastier dishes (like the cameo that W.H. Auden's "Funeral Blues" made in *Four Weddings and a Funeral*) but rarely consumed on its own.

LEV GROSSMAN, *Time,* 7 June 2007

National Poetry Month is, I believe, a cause for celebration. But I understand why more than a few American poets see it as something of a scandal and an insult. Is there a National Music Month? A National Fiction Month? A National Sports Fan Month?

RON SMITH, *Richmond Times-Dispatch,* 3 April 2005

We hear a lot from socially self-conscious poets and very right-on, PC poets, who talk about bringing poetry to the people as if it was some sacred mission, like converting the natives to Christianity. But most of us don't give a toss.

MICHAEL DONAGHY, *The Independent,* 6 October 1994

I have never been one of the people who feel it essential to increase the audience for poetry. I feel that the people who need it find it.

LOUISE GLÜCK, Lannan Readings & Conversations, 16 February 2005

Poetry's become like Amnesty International or Greenpeace. Few people would dispute its merit. But they don't actively support it.

PETER FALLON, *Krino,* Winter 1993

⌣

My own prescription for making poetry popular in the schools would be to ban it—with possession treated as a serious misdemeanor, and dealing as a felony.

CLIVE JAMES, *The New York Times,* 27 March 2005

Neither most poets nor most poetry publishers are much cop as salesmen. A friend of mine has an e-mail sig: "When I'm Evil Overlord, I'm going to swap it round so the book publishers sell the hard drugs and the drug barons sell the books."

SHEENAGH PUGH, *Acumen,* September 2006

A poet's renown obviously depends on the excellence of their work, but it can be boosted powerfully by a range of extra-poetic factors. These include a sensational private life, celebrity (or proximity to it), attachment to a national or international literary project, convergence with the aims of a powerful or fashionable minority group, and close identification with an issue of some public urgency.

JOHN REDMOND, *Poetry Wales,* Autumn 2005

A group of poets living in the city of Panevezys, Lithuania, protested people's lack of interest in poetry in an interesting fashion. The poets rushed to the state farm and put on a poetry reading for a flock of sheep.

UNATTRIBUTED, *Turkish Daily News,* 26 February 2005

Profit Motives

Poets can do without much money and that's a good thing... Poets have much more aesthetic freedom precisely because nobody cares how or what they write. That freedom is priceless.

> James Longenbach, *The Boston Globe*, 8 January 2006

That's all we have in poetry land: the truth. We are not well paid, and we are not respected in our land or time, but we can tell the truth. We don't have to accede to the hypocrisies and half-truths that surround us. We are not driven by a market economy whose rewards bend and corrupt us. That's a great gift and worth the economic trade off.

> Campbell McGrath, *Fugue*, Summer–Fall 2006

Poetry values the unknown, the real, the potential, and the silent— everything, that is, which has no value.

> Paul Hoover, *The American Poetry Review*, March–April 2005

In my book, poetry is a necessity of life, what they used to call non-taxable matter.

> C.D. Wright, *Cooling Time*, 2005

If a thing isn't commercial it has a kind of holiness about it which exempts it from responsibility. Poems are chits that get you off work.

> Hugo Williams, *Times Literary Supplement*, 23 April 2004

To be reading your poetry as a breadwinning activity... commits some sin against the freedom of poetry. I do believe that poetry is in the realm of the gift and in the realm of the sacred.

> Seamus Heaney, *The Christian Science Monitor*, 9 January 1989

Poets and money are seen in each other's company only rarely.

MICHAEL ELLISON,
The Guardian,
13 October 1995

⌁

The poem I write has to have the value of a cheque, covered by what my life has deposited in the bank.

LEONARD NOLENS, *Modern Poetry in Translation,*
Winter 1997

The often aggrieved expectation that the creation of a body of poems entitles one to a stipend sufficient to subsist on *and* have free holidays at an artists' colony seems to me grasshopperism at its most presumptuous.

THOMAS M. DISCH, *The Hudson Review,*
Summer 1999

To devote a life to poetry looks to most people like a decision to ignore the benefits of modern life, in particular the power of money to effect any meaningful progress. It looks suspiciously like sulking.

HUGO WILLIAMS, *Times Literary Supplement,* 18 April 2003

I call the impulse to write poetry "the enemy," because it's trying to keep you poor. All the time and energy you pour into writing a poem is time and energy you won't be using writing something that's going to pay for the groceries.

CLIVE JAMES, RTÉ Radio 1, October 2003

The hope of permanent fame may be the second-silliest motive for a career in poetry; the first is, of course, the hope for riches.

JOSEPH EPSTEIN, *The Weekly Standard,* 2003

Poets are infinitely corruptible; but the trouble is there aren't people around to corrupt them—there are plenty of Fausts around but no Mephistopheles to be seen.

PETER PORTER, *The Age,* 3 September 2002

POET AT WORK

A good poet is an amateur who behaves like a professional.

PAUL HYLAND, *Getting Into Poetry*, 1992

It may well be the unprofessional aspects of poetry—good poets come from all sorts of backgrounds and do every kind of job—that keep the art strong.

BOYD TONKIN, *New Statesman*, 7 January 1994

Watch out for our coming campaign, called Get the Poets Back into Banks, Doctors' Surgeries and Insurance Offices, where modern poetry began.

JAMES CAMPBELL, *Times Literary Supplement*, 11 June 2004

How do you employ a poet, since any reasonably good poet is going to be a Cassandra given to psychic keening: that never went down well in the staff room.

PETER NICHOLSON, 3 Quarks Daily online, 26 September 2005

There is a certain kind of poet who is a clerk during the day. It seems to be necessary to have mundaneness, which must involve paperwork, the long, slow soporific afternoons at an office, the sedateness of security, a regular paycheck...

RACHEL COHEN, *The Threepenny Review*, Winter 2002

By day poets masquerade as mere mortals: insurance clerks, teachers, librarians. But by night they prowl like panthers, seizing words on the run and crunching raw emotion.

UNATTRIBUTED, *The Times*, 4 September 2006

A few people have brought off the strange alchemy of having a paying job and writing in their spare time, but not many... I wanted to devote my full time to poetry, give it every kind of resource I had because it's a long, slow-maturing thing anyway.

LES MURRAY,
Australian
Broadcasting
Corporation,
6 April 2006

∿

It does not take all day to be a poet and I have never understood the contentions of those eccentrics who think that a poet should not have to earn his living like the next man. Human nature is certainly not less noticeable in the ordinary world of work than it is to the genius who fancies solitude.

C.H. SISSON, *PN Review*,
November–December 1994

I think that the diversity of my life has been good for me; I've written in many genres; I've done a lot of translation; I've taught school for thirty-six years; I've served as a town committeeman, a general editor, an academy president, and a lay reader; I've been a Broadway lyricist; I've played a great deal of tennis and *bocce*; I've tramped, botanized, bicycled, and spaded my own gardens.

RICHARD WILBUR, *Between the Lines*, 2000

Every morning I would get up at four thirty, maybe five, and write until seven. Then I'd have to get my tie on and show up at the office. I worked eight hours a day, and then I was done. I wasn't correcting papers at night.

TED KOOSER, *UU World*, Winter 2005

Walter de la Mare took a post as a statistics clerk in the Anglo American Oil Company, the London offshoot of the US monopolistic giant, Standard Oil, thus becoming an employee of John D. Rockefeller... Here, for 18 years, the poet of gentle gothic whimsy... totted up columns of figures during all the hours of daylight ("the dream of Wake") before plodding home at night over London Bridge to "the dream of Sleep."

James Campbell, *The Guardian*, 10 June 2006

A career as a bureaucrat can contribute unexpectedly, and materially, to the necessary skills in handling the poetic matter, and in communicating it with a minimum of interference.

Thomas Kinsella, University of Turin address, May 2006

[I]nstead of writing in a garret, there was all the rough and tumble: he would rehearse in the morning, perform in the afternoon and then, while other actors went drinking, he would write alone. It was terribly taxing and all without tea or coffee which had yet to arrive in England.

James Shapiro, on William Shakespeare, *The Sunday Times*, 18 June 2006

Proper Jobs were all very well in the days before work expected to have all of you. And probably, when you could write poems at work in a quiet corner without anyone noticing you're not meeting your productivity targets. But, in my experience, a Proper Job nowadays really takes it out of you. By the end of the working day you're too burnt out to create anything.

Ros Barber, Shallowlands blog, 4 April 2006

I feel very much, more and more, what a privilege it is to have the time and the physical safety and the emotional easiness to be in a position to write poetry. I suppose the privilege demands our best efforts.

Kathleen Ossip, *The American Poetry Review*, January–February 2006

The makings of art are rooted in non-art labors —repetitive, toxic, body-breaking, minimum wage or less or none—that everywhere underlie those privileged creations.

Adrienne Rich, *The Virginia Quarterly Review*, Spring 2006

⌣

You want to be a poet? Then believe it, but you can't do it with one foot in the water. There's no halfway—give up your life or not, period.

GERALD STERN,
Poet's Market, 1997

ᵕ.

I don't think I could go back to being a probation officer even if I had to. Poetry has softened my hands.

SIMON ARMITAGE, Poetry Foundation online, 2006

People think they love poetry, but actually they hate it. The average punter feels that poetry is too self-conscious. I'm just grateful that I've been allowed to stay at home and do it. Oh my God. The idea of an office.

HUGO WILLIAMS, *The Observer*, 26 March 2006

A full-time job kills a poet's talent—eventually. You can't treat the muse as a bit on the side with impunity.

FIONA PITT-KETHLEY, *Poetry Review*

It's a pity to put a poet in a job that somebody else can do.

LES MURRAY, *The Irish Times*, 22 June 2002

It never does to let myself forget that, however hard it feels, writing poetry is usually a doddle compared with real work, or real confrontation.

DON PATERSON, *Verse*, Summer 1993

Poetry is work—but it is work in the way that making a garden or being a parent is work: it is, in other words, work, not effort, the work of setting aside the preordained, the resigned, the easy, the conditioned, and allowing the real to emerge and live. The real, not the conditioned, response. A surrender, not a submission. The graceful, as opposed to the merely easy.

JOHN BURNSIDE, *Poetry Writers' Yearbook 2007*

Every poet is his own taskmaster.

Thomas Lynch, *Magma Poetry* 25, 2003

That's the great thing about being a self-employed poet, you can give yourself lovely long holidays and... retire whenever you feel like it.

Pat Ingoldsby, *Northside People,* 13 January 1993

We are never free of the obligation to respond to the world... The poet doesn't keep office hours.

Lucien Stryk, *Poets & Writers,* July–August 1995

I keep Friday as... my poetry writing day, and I have to arrange for the Muse to attend between 10 A.M. and 4 P.M.

Alison Chisholm, *Poetry News,* Winter 1995

I have no work habits whatsoever. If I did, I would probably write less because I would resent having to stick to a schedule or be at my desk at a certain time.

Billy Collins, *Fugue,* Summer 2001

In poetry, you work towards the intense instant. You certainly cannot subordinate poetry to a routine.

Harry Clifton, *The Irish Times,* 17 December 2003

Everyone's waiting for that period in life when they have lots of free time, lots of energy, and no distractions. That's called death. You've got to find a way of working in a crowded life with other priorities and constant distraction.

Dana Gioia, *Business Week,* 13 November 2006

Even a moderately interesting job outside the poetry workshop business is more likely to yield high poetic dividends than unlimited leisure or a work life confined to cajoling guileless youths into believing they are our next Rimbauds.

Thomas M. Disch, *Parnassus* 20, no. 1

⸫

Sometimes teaching feels like an extraordinary price to pay for the freedom to write poems. I find myself increasingly unable to write—to make contact with my work—while I'm "talking out" so much, burning a hole in my silence, my not-knowing (which is, of course, one's deepest resource).

JORIE GRAHAM,
American Poet,
Fall 1996

⌣:

If you want to make a living as a poet, the last thing you'll be able to do is sit quietly and write poetry.

JOHN MORRISH, *The Daily Telegraph,*
8 February 1997

Poets today are running writing courses, editing, reviewing, judging poetry competitions, working in arts administration. All that may pay the rent, but it doesn't please the muse.

SUZI FEAY, *The Independent on Sunday,*
24 August 2003

[Teaching poetry] makes me think harder than I would on my own. It keeps me from being lazy... [T]aking up aesthetics that are alien to one, having to articulate and apply principles of craft, all those, I think, will make you a better poet. And they will help your own poems.

ELLEN BRYANT VOIGT, *Fugue,* Winter 2003-04

What a strange job I have—supplying / people with meter and metaphors! / I could be trying to write poems. / Instead, I've tried improving yours.

MARY JO SALTER, *Open Shutters,* 2003

It's hard to write really good poems while you're teaching. It seems as if the really good stuff kind of evaporates, as if you can't really get down to the depths of your own work when you're thinking about the work of others.

Toi Derricotte, *The Writer's Chronicle,* September 2006

Sad to say, the academy has not been a healthy home for writers. They end up overeducated and underexperienced. My advice to young poets? Work anywhere else. Write anything, but write from the heart.

Judith Kitchen, *The Georgia Review,* Spring 2006

The less a poet's job has to do with poetry the better... My work as a journalist doesn't get in the way of my poems. And it's the journalism which keeps bread on the table and keeps me in the street, where poems start.

Seán Dunne, RTÉ Radio 1

The prospect of one's child becoming a poet is a parent's nightmare, conjuring up, as Michael Dirda put it so well... "a life of little magazines no one reads, temporary appointments at junior colleges, servile groveling for National Endowment for the Arts grants and Guggenheims, joyless affairs with students that wreck marriages and, at the end, the long look down into the river or the last glance around the kitchen before turning on the gas." And all that botheration never, somehow, furnishes material for poetry or even acts as a wellspring of language.

Katherine A. Powers, *The Boston Globe,* 23 March 2003

For those of us from poorer or working-class backgrounds, the news that you were going to dedicate your life to writing serious verse was received by the community with the same panic as might be your departure for Baader-Meinhof or a transsexual circus.

Don Paterson, *New British Poetry,* 2004

It seems that when I'm writing poetry, I always have time to do it. Time just organizes itself around this different state of being.

RUTH FAINLIGHT,
The Centennial Review,
Fall 1999

I regard poetry... as a vocation. Any other work—freelance or bank-manager—simply supports the person writing it. There's no need for different hats.

CAROL ANN DUFFY, *Verse,* Summer 1991

I thought you looked for a dead-end job to support a poet's life... My fantasies were [that] I would be a caretaker of a Civil War cemetery, which didn't have that many visitors, or that I would run a bait shop—something that didn't require a whole lot of maintenance.

C.D. WRIGHT, News Channel 10,
29 September 2004

The wonderful thing about doing something you love, like writing poetry, is that it creates its own space—often as a holiday from other obligations, an aesthetically sophisticated way of playing hooky.

DAVID LEHMAN, *The Writer's Chronicle,* February 2006

It is in battling with life and tasks that one becomes a fit person to speak in poetry. A poet must in some way engage with the world. I don't think an ivory tower is a good place to write poetry.

KATHLEEN RAINE, BBC Radio 3

I've never wanted to live in a poetry-obsessed world. You need other things in your life and from the start I set out to make sure that poetry was never my primary activity.

JAMES FENTON, *Financial Times,* 7 November 1998

The idea that we should "broaden our experience" by doing some kind of proper job has always been extraordinarily popular, especially among non-writers, for whom our relaxed hours, alcoholism and hypochondria have always been taken as a sign of moral laziness.

Don Paterson, *The Cost of Letters,* 1998

There's nothing wrong with romanticizing the working man, except it's usually the work of a deskbound poet whose nearest brush with hard labor comes, these days, from what he sees in the movies.

William Logan, *The New Criterion,* December 2002

On both sides of our family we were workers in iron—and I suppose I like to think I'm a worker in iron also.

Geoffrey Hill, BBC Radio 3, April 2004

The poetry forged in what we might consider to be genuinely hefty experience—manual labor, for example—can also easily become its own template or formula: something just as repeatable as the oft-lamented "academic" poem.

Christina Pugh, *Poetry,* June 2005

The options for poem writing are so numerous and so various that, after a while, the word "academy" refers to the building where the poems are written rather than the style they're written in.

David Kirby, *storySouth,* 2003

Being an artist is a disposition, a way of interpreting the world which is distinct precisely because it isn't and cannot be subsumed into a notion of career. Poets don't have careers, they have lives.

Ann Lauterbach, *The American Poetry Review,* May-June 1992

The thing about writing is that, if you have the impulse, you will find the time.

Seamus Heaney, RTÉ 1 television, December 1995

In the present climate, where poetry is less a fate and more a career-choice... the level of conformity, from what is said and not said and about whom, to the invisible pecking order and the smart-casual dress code, makes a bankers' convention, by comparison, seem a riot of anarchy.

HARRY CLIFTON, *Metre,* Autumn 2002

A job is more tangible than talent. It can't vanish suddenly the way that inspiration often seems to.

DANA GIOIA, *Can Poetry Matter?,* 1992

In Memory

Memory is each man's poet-in-residence.

STANLEY KUNITZ, cited in *The Kansas City Star*, 16 February 2003

Poetry is memory become image, and image become voice.

OCTAVIO PAZ, *The New York Times*, 8 December 1991

The best poetry opens a window in the reader's heart and mind. It's memorable, hummable.

MAURA DOOLEY, Bloodaxe Books catalog, 1997

The ability of a poem to inhere in the memory over the years is one of the surest guarantees that it is going to inhere in the language.

SEAMUS HEANEY, introducing Richard Murphy, 13 October 2005

A poem begins as a list of things one might otherwise have forgotten; it ends as origami.

FINUALA DOWLING, *The Poetry Paper*, no. 3, 2006

You can't bring home a Matisse and hang it on the wall. If you want to hear a piece of music live, you've got to gather an orchestra. But bring a poem and you've got it in your head and it stays with you.

NIALL MACMONAGLE, RTÉ Radio I, January 1998

[T]here is one important thing to say about poetry: you don't need to know a lot of it for it to have value and meaning in your life or the life of your society. Two or three poems, even two or three bits of poems, known by heart and genuinely cherished can stand everybody in good stead.

SEAMUS HEANEY, Friends of Classics online, 13 January 2004

Poetry is the one art form where its memory and its acquisition are one and the same thing.

DON PATERSON,
Poetry Review,
Summer 2007

⸪

One of the major reasons some poets write is because they just can't remember any poems by anybody else, so they write them themselves.

THOMAS MCCARTHY, RTÉ Radio I,
February 2004

I tend to write poetry, principally because little I read in British poetry excites me, so I have to create it for myself.

JEREMY REED, *Poetry Writers' Yearbook 2007*

It is the duty of the poet to make his verse memorable long before it is the duty of the reader to remember it.

AUBERON WAUGH, *The Literary Review,*
November 1997

Just because something gets stuck in your head doesn't make it worth hearing. There are deeper patterns of recognition and pleasure than those of rote learning.

DAVID WHEATLEY, *Poetry Ireland Review,* October 2005

Not all memorable poems are good, but all good poems are memorable.

STEPHEN KNIGHT, *The Independent on Sunday,* 14 December 2003

What is not memorable, in either a deep or simple sense, is not poetry.

EDNA LONGLEY, *Princeton University Library Chronicle,* Spring 1998

My poems almost always start in some kind of memory... It's like a little beeper going off in your mind. Some little thing wakens excitement, and it gets connected with some other things. Ideally, it's like an avalanche—a little pebble begins to move, gathers a lot of energy and multiplies itself.

SEAMUS HEANEY, *The New Mexican,* 26 September 2003

THE AUDIENCE

Lovers of poetry may total a million people / on the whole planet. Fewer than the players of *skat*.

> LES MURRAY, *Conscious and Verbal*, 1999

The unpopularity of poetry at present... is in some ways an advantage both to poetry and to society as a whole. As poetry has exited from society, so to speak, it has acquired the right of hermits and other loners to be itself.

> DAVID PERKINS, *Harvard Review*, Fall 1995

If every person in the country was buying poetry and it was available on every street corner... poetry probably wouldn't be doing its job.

> SIMON ARMITAGE, *The Independent*, 13 March 2004

Poetry, like weeds, does seem to flourish in gaps: on the walls of Tube trains, in a couple of inches in a newspaper column, in the spaces between radio programmes.

> ALISON BRACKENBURY, *PN Review*, March–April 2000

Every poem implies its audience.

> JOHN BARR, *Poetry*, September 2006

Writing *for* any audience is the wrong way to win one... Rather, a poet should be writing *to* an audience—one listener or many—the poet's own soul, or an ideal reader, or a nation.

> A.E. STALLINGS, *Poetry*, April 2005

Art created to please an audience—whether the mass audience of television, the pocket-sized audience of the poetry workshop, or the clubby audience of the "poetry subculture"—will always lack the fine edge of necessity.

RICHARD TILLINGHAST, *AWP Chronicle,* March–April 1993

The point is to create something readers want even though they don't know that's what they want yet.

DAVID KIRBY, *Smartish Pace,* November 2000

Don't write the kind of poetry you think people want to publish. Write the kind of poetry you want to read.

MARK HADDON, *Poetry News,* Autumn 2005

Write poetry and, if you've a modicum of talent, it will end up out there. Slick, shiny and published, although maybe not all that often *read*.

PETER FINCH, *The Writer's Handbook 2007*

Poems can be remarkable, virtuoso performances, but if the author hasn't trembled before writing itself, hasn't been inspired by more than the desire to write something, the reader too will not tremble, will not be inspired, will not be tempted to place the book under her pillow.

TATYANA VOLTSKAIA, *Modern Poetry in Translation,* 2002

The poet needs to reach out to people he or she has not met. That someone will read your poem and say "Yes, that is right; I know that, I recognise that." I think poetry always has that interior communicable strength.

ANNE STEVENSON, *Poetry Ireland Review,* Summer 1989

Poetry is a solitary art, more now than ever, and its proper audience is the deeply educated, solitary reader, or that reader sitting within herself in a theater.

HAROLD BLOOM, *The Best of the Best American Poetry*, 1998

Unless the poets themselves become educators, there will never be a larger audience for poetry. Poetry requires a sophisticated level of learning. To get the nuances of poetry requires not only a high level of language learning, but also cultural learning.

JOSEPH PARISI, *Bookslut*, January 2006

A lot of poetry is a kind of soliloquy—and therefore one has no audience!

SORLEY MACLEAN, BBC Radio 4, September 1995

People who don't read poetry sniff something happening. This is one of the effects of a poet in a community. There is an audience for poetry which is small. There is a public for poetry which is a bit larger. Then outside the audience and the public there is the crowd listening or picking something up.

SEAMUS HEANEY, BBC Radio 4

The bottom-line test of whether poetry is any good can only be whether it gets read by people whose lives are about something other than poetry and who have no plans to make a niche for themselves in the identity-validating institutions of poetry-writing.

COLIN FALCK, *American and British Verse in the Twentieth Century*, 2003

Perhaps the key factor that has been missing for English poets since the war has been the

There is a wonderful, simple conversation encoded in all poems worthy of the name: "You've felt this, too, haven't you?"

CAROL RUMENS, *Brangle*, no. 3, 1999

꙳

audience; the kind of audience that has other things to do than to read poetry, and therefore comes to it with a direct expectation of usefulness.

FELICITY ROSSLYN, *PN Review,* November–December 1993

An artist needs not so much an audience, as to feel a need to answer, a promise to respond. The response may be a contradiction, it may be unwanted, it may go unheeded, it may be embraced but twisted... but it is owed, and the sense that it is owed is a basic requirement for the poet's good feeling about the art.

ROBERT PINSKY, *Poetry and the World,* 1988

Poetry—any art—has a psychic function, fulfilling a need in the individual artist, so that it would be produced even if there was no immediate audience.

THOMAS KINSELLA, *Poetry Ireland Review,* Winter 2002–03

Production is outstripping demand, and the market cannot sustain this. Just as we need forests to mop up the excess carbon dioxide in the atmosphere, so we need new readers to absorb all this verse.

ADAM NEWEY, *New Statesman,* July 2001

Like subsidized farming that grows food no one wants, a poetry industry has been created to serve the interests of the producers and not the consumers.

DANA GIOIA, *Can Poetry Matter?,* 1992

COMMUNALS AND LONERS

Reading poetry is mostly solitary, its effect is communal. It connects the reader, across gender, race, culture, time and space with other possible ways of being human; it does not fuse and merge us; on the contrary, on the ground of common humanity, it points up difference and variety.

DAVID CONSTANTINE, *Magma Poetry,* Summer 2004

Poetry is an endeavor so large and so deeply communal that if one person doesn't write a great poem, eventually somebody else will.

JANE HIRSHFIELD, RTÉ Lyric FM, October 2005

The word "communal" is treacherous when it comes to the enjoyment and appraisal of a work of poetry, in a way that it is not treacherous when used of a piece of orchestral music or a great religious or mural painting or a public sculpture.

MICHAEL SCHMIDT, *PN Review,* May–June 2005

Poets today... are afraid of revealing true individuality. They are communal, and careful about what readers or other poets might think. They are painfully self-conscious, and anxious to be and do the right thing.

JOHN BAYLEY, *Poetry Review,* Summer 1993

I am hostile to the very idea of poetry, so to speak, in the plural, as a collective mass or enterprise. Poetry as a certain good. The laureates in America and in England are busy promulgating something I wouldn't care to promulgate myself.

MICHAEL HOFMANN, *Poetry,* September 2005

I have no collective feelings. No one will ever catch sight of me in a crowd.

WISLAWA SZYMBORSKA, cited in *Parnassus* 28, nos. 1 & 2

Contact with other people does not lead to art; it leads to conversation.

ROBERT BLY, RTÉ Radio 1, June 2006

Community is the happy affirmation of the young writer; but solitude is the mature writer's dearest mate.

D.W. FENZA, *The Writer's Chronicle*, May–Summer 2006

Lots of things can be shared: a bed, a piece of bread, convictions, a mistress, but not a poem by, say, Rainer Maria Rilke. A work of art, of literature especially, and a poem in particular, addresses a man tête-à-tête, entering with him into direct—free of any go-betweens—relations.

JOSEPH BRODSKY, Nobel Lecture, 1987

If there is an audience for poetry, it is an audience of privacy. Who isn't appalled to find someone else standing in the poetry section of a bookstore?

DEAN YOUNG, *Poetry*, April 2005

❧

Whereas physics abstracts an experience in such a way that it holds for *anybody,* poetry can never have any other ambition than that it can hold for *somebody*... In real poetry there are no universal generalities... it is the subjective in the experience which must achieve a sort of objectivity.

LARS GUSTAFSSON, Rotterdam Poetry Festival, 2005

First and foremost, art of any kind enters the individual consciousness, and unless it has a purchase at that authentic, original, personal level, I don't think it can spread outwards. If you've got one person responding to poetry, you have an autobiography; if you have 20 people, you have the beginning of a culture.

SEAMUS HEANEY, *ThisWeek Community Newspapers*, 15 April 2004

The culture of the West puts a premium on individualism. In Africa, the individual is only a part of the whole. To define an individual, an understanding of the whole is required.

GBANABOM HALLOWELL, *The Writer's Chronicle*, December 2005

Poetry, like crime, can only be accomplished in absolute privacy and secrecy.

FRANZ WRIGHT, *Contemporary Poetry Review*, September 2006

We're never alone when writing a poem. Pick up your pen, and you're in dialogue with all the writing you've been touched by.

PHILIP GROSS, *Magma Poetry*, Winter 2005

THE WHOLE TRUTH

Poets deal in truths. They lure them, like so many silk ribbons, out of secret pockets, leaving the rest of us to shudder in recognition.

EILEEN BATTERSBY, *The Irish Times,* 29 March 2006

If you're not going to be honest as a writer, there's no point in starting.

HUGO WILLIAMS, *The Guardian,* 4 June 2005

When a poem doesn't work, the first question to ask yourself is "Am I telling the truth?"

WENDY COPE, BBC Radio 3, July 1995

No amount of "poetry" will make wrong ideas right.

DAVID CONSTANTINE, *A Living Language,* 2004

Could a way of life be built around truth? It sure could. Does poetry tell truth? It can and sometimes does. But to conclude from that that a way of life could be built around poetry is to jump into myth.

CARL RAKOSI, *The American Poetry Review,* January-February 1997

If poetry breaks its covenant with truth and justice, it has failed.

SEAMUS HEANEY, *The Sunday Tribune,* 7 April 1996

The truth of poetry is not a party truth, not even a moral truth, but a truth about the real nature of existence. Furthermore it is a discovered truth, a truth discovered through the truth of language, a truth the writer does not fully know at the time of writing.

GEORGE SZIRTES online, 25 April 2005

There are degrees of fidelity to the actual. I don't know a single poet who would hesitate at locating, say, a spousal argument in Paramus instead of Princeton if that change better served the poem's sonics.

STEPHEN DUNN, *After Confession*, 2001

A lyric poem, typically, expresses an intense feeling of the moment, and the truth of the poem consists of its truth to that moment. It is all about the subjective, all about the here and now. It is not—alas for the loved one—a contract, or a prenuptial agreement.

JAMES FENTON, *The New Faber Book of Love Poems*, 2006

Poetry doesn't have exclusive access to the truth; it's just that certain poems express the truth in ways that encapsulate and preserve it in memory, while also (another happy paradox) giving pleasure.

RACHEL HADAS, *Literary Imagination*, Spring 2006

It's important that it's clear that the poet is not *inventing* the value of something ordinary or unexceptional but *revealing* the value.

EAVAN BOLAND, *Irish Literary Supplement*, Fall 1988

Poems know something that we as the creators of poems don't know. This may just be the force of a thing that is finished compared to one that is still developing, the force of order in contrast to disorder, the force of something elevated out of time compared to the casual.

ÁGNES NEMES NAGY, *A Hungarian Perspective*, 1998

One of the great things about being a writer is the extent to which it allows us to invent ourselves. It's like being in a witness-protection program.

PAUL MULDOON, *The Paris Review*, Spring 2004

A bitter truth is better than a sweet lie.

ZBIGNIEW HERBERT, *PN Review*, no. 26, 1982

I'm against lying in life, in principle, in any other activity except poetry.

CHARLES SIMIC,
The Irish Times,
23 July 2005

⌣.

Words have properties which even the best lexicographers limp after, or ignore; only in poetry do they have their full value.

JOHN DEVITT, *Cobweb*, Spring 1995

Being a poet means... to make an implicit vow that you will live more honestly. That's why it is called a vocation... People assume that you won't abuse it and that it should be pursued disinterestedly.

SEAMUS HEANEY, BBC 2, October 1997

Perhaps poetry *is* conservative (with a small and decidedly non-political "c") in that it is defending eternal pleasures and truths. To participate in an art that is devoted to such verities—even in a minor way—is an immense privilege, and a serious responsibility.

DOUGLAS DUNN, *The Poet's Voice and Craft*, 1994

The one persuasive charge against poetry would be that it doesn't seek the truth about human beings and the world, but confines itself instead to gathering pretty baubles on the world's beaches, pebbles and shells.

ADAM ZAGAJEWSKI, *A Defense of Ardor*, 2004

Perhaps, after all, poetry... is a particular sort of ignorance. And that is much harder to learn than knowing.

JAAN KAPLINSKI, *Through the Forest*, 1996

The making of poems is mysteriously tied up with not-knowing, with willing ignorance and an openness to mutation.

TONY HOAGLAND, *The American Poetry Review*, July-August 2003

Poems must have the ring of truth. If you hit them with a toffee hammer they must ring true, even if they're telling lies.

SIMON ARMITAGE, *Fulcrum*, no. 4, 2005

In Estonian, the lovely word for "poet"—*luuletaja*—also means "liar."

SALLY LAIRD, *The Observer,* 22 April 1990

When it comes to poetry, an art that relies so much on tone, imagination, and a peculiar cooperation of the two that might properly be called sleight of hand, the truer something sounds, the more guarded a consideration it deserves.

BENJAMIN PALOFF, *Michigan Quarterly Review,* Winter 2007

For every lie we're told by advertisers and politicians, we need one poem to balance it.

JORIE GRAHAM, cited in *Newsweek,* 12 April 2004

Poetry and advertising share a method—the minimum words for the maximum impact.

CRAIG RAINE, *The Guardian,* 5 February 2005

The problem of being a poet / Is the problem of being always right.

PAUL DURCAN, *Greetings to Our Friends in Brazil,* 1999

Once you've written a line on the page, that poem has its own lifeforce that needs to be realized. It now becomes utterly irrelevant what really happened.

CAMPBELL MCGRATH, *Sundog,* Fall 1999

Too often, the focus on literal truth presents us not with the essence or core of the poet's being, but with the patio furniture of his or her life.

DAVID ALPAUGH, *Poets & Writers,*
March–April 2003

Art should be fair in both senses of the word. Fair is the perfect word because it means both justice and beauty.

ALICE FULTON,
Atlantic Unbound,
13 July 2004

If... phrases such as "weapons of mass destruction" bleed language of its meaning, then poets must restore the blood to words.

MARTÍN ESPADA,
Poetry Foundation
online, 2006

༄

No other art form clings to representation—what we think of in fiction as "realism"—like mainstream poetry.

IRA SADOFF, *The American Poetry Review*,
November–December 2005

To me it's always open house; if you want it and it doesn't exist, just make it up.

PHILIP LEVINE, *So Ask*, 2002

I've adapted the principle of our legal system, of presuming innocent until proven guilty, to this: That we should presume that details in a poem are literal until proved figurative.

ALAN SHAPIRO, *Rattle*, Summer 2005

We may become so used to thinking poems mean more than they say that we forget they... mean exactly what they say.

W.D. SNODGRASS, *The Southern Review*, Spring 1995

A writer who keeps a personal diary uses it to record what he knows. In his poems or stories he sets down what he doesn't know.

ADAM ZAGAJEWSKI, *Another Beauty*, 2000

Truth is not exclusive to poetry, of course, but there is no poem which does not engage with truth.

KATHLEEN JAMIE, *Strong Words*, 2000

Everything I commit to paper is part of a lifelong process of making myself at home in a mysterious and deceptive world. To tell a deliberate lie in building this metaphysical home would be as grievous an error as using bad mortar or unseasoned timbers in the construction of a house.

JOHN BURNSIDE, *The Daily Telegraph*, 4 March 2006

[Poetry] is against lying, against evasion and shoddiness of speech. Against all the ways of speaking and writing which reduce our humanity, narrow our sympathies, wither our ability to think and feel. Against all the forces of cretinization. Poetry is an intrinsic fight-back against all that.

DAVID CONSTANTINE, T.S. Eliot Prize adjudication, 16 January 2006

One of the most revealing questions you can ask about any poet has to do with his sense of responsibility. To whom or what does he hold himself responsible in his writing? The poet who replies "Nothing"—who believes that the concept of responsibility is foreign to the totally free realm of art—is likely to be a bad poet.

ADAM KIRSCH, *Harvard Magazine*, November–December 2006

AMONG WOMEN

When the history of poetry in our time is written—I have no doubt about this—women poets will be seen to have re-written not just the poem, not just the image... They will have altered the cartography of the poem. The map will look different.

EAVAN BOLAND, *Irish University Review,* Spring-Summer 1993

Women's poetry tends to be less formally constructed in order to give freer rein or freer expression to the flow of the subconscious and the depiction of women's lives which tend not to have boundaries like men's lives.

DOROTHY HEWETT, *A Woman's Voice,* 1996

Perhaps style in art is a male thing, as a substitute for pregnancy and childbirth. Women seem to be more interested in what the content of the work is.

CAROL ANN DUFFY, BBC Radio 4, August 1997

I had two children... It is the greatest act of creativity and the one which is most likely to make you question other forms of creativity.

EAVAN BOLAND, *Irish Tatler,* 1999

I write about things in which women are interested: childbirth, family life, relationships from a woman's view, women's histories, women's health and social questions to do with women. That's what the function of a female poet is. But I don't think you address yourself exclusively to women.

FLEUR ADCOCK, *Thumbscrew,* Winter 2000-01

It is the job of women poets to describe men's bodies, every single bit of them.

> MOLLY PEACOCK, cited in *PN Review,* January–February 2004

Divisions according to gender should apply only to changing-rooms and public toilets—because of natural bashfulness. In poetry, there is nothing to be ashamed of.

> ALEKSEI ALEKHIN, *Modern Poetry in Translation,* no. 20, 2002

I've always believed that men who recite poetry, who are the most magnificently attentive, are also the most callous.

> CHRISSY ILEY, *The Sunday Times,* 24 September 1995

A man pays court with his poems. / A woman dismisses him with hers.

> JIM HARRISON AND TED KOOSER, *Braided Creek,* 2003

The working conditions for young women poets are infinitely poorer than the conviviality and congratulations that surround their male counterparts.

> EAVAN BOLAND, *Irish Literary Supplement,* Spring 1991

I was (and still am) in no way conscious that a woman poet's task, with respect to skill, differs in any way from a man's.

> ANNE STEVENSON, *Poetry Wales,* June 1991

Poetry is erotically charged language in which gender is a very fluid concept. All really good poets of either sex fuse and subvert conventional ideas of masculine and feminine.

> ALISON CROGGON, *Salt,* no. 12, 2000

Men's poetry seems to be more about words. As intimate as cross-words or lectures.

> SELIMA HILL, *Contemporary Women's Poetry,* 2000

The gender of the poets from whom you learn is the least significant thing about them, not nearly as important as how they use the word "and," or whether they put a comma between two adjectives.

CAROL RUMENS,
Poetry Ireland Review,
Autumn 1992

⌣∴

At its deepest level—you may say at the level of ontological underpinning—the Irish poetic tradition is sexist and masculinist to the core.

NUALA NÍ DHOMHNAILL, RTÉ Radio 1,
December 1993

It is a sad truth—the anthologies and scholarly journals of the last fifteen years are evidence—that established Irish male poets, some with international reputations, were unhelpful and even obstructive in their attitude to the emergence of poetry by women.

EAVAN BOLAND, *Seneca Review,* Winter 1993

All male poets are amazingly opinionated; I have never met one who wasn't.

WENDY COPE, *The Times,* 20 April 1994

No woman has ever written an epic poem nor ever will. They have certain minor gifts. The great gift of woman is being a woman.

KATHLEEN RAINE, *Acumen,* April 1988

A woman is so naturally fluid and her mind is so dominated by her body, that for a woman to write real poetry—as men traditionally have been able to do—is difficult.

MEDBH McGUCKIAN, *Irish Literary Supplement,* Spring 1997

Must it be said that, for all the trumpeting about [American] women poets, the empress has no clothes? That she is a Lady Godiva after all?

DEREK MAHON, *The Irish Times,* 5 June 1993

Women's creativity does not demand the right to build monuments that will loom in the minds of people yet unborn. Women's art is traditionally biodegradable, and women's poetry may be no exception.

GERMAINE GREER, *Times Literary Supplement,* 30 June 1995

There seems to be a confidence issue in being a woman poet that is different to men. It's a more difficult identity to claim for yourself, if you're a woman. Being the object of poetry for so many years, women will naturally find it harder than men to be the subject of their work. It's very unfeminine to be a poet.

SARAH MAGUIRE, *The Wolf,* April 2004

If my women friends had been aware that I was writing poetry, they would have made fun of me, and no young man would want to approach me, not even to dance.

CLARIBEL ALEGRÍA, *World Literature Today,* May–June 2007

Feminism remains a superb tool of analysis for discovering why a woman did not write a poem. It is of no value whatsoever in judging the poem that she wrote.

EAVAN BOLAND, *Verse* 13, no. 1, 1996

Pregnancy and motherhood is like *being* the poem, like the word made flesh.

CAROL ANN DUFFY, BBC Radio 4, August 1997

One female poet comments: "Men, relative to women, often seem to move twice as fast and

I don't think poetry is gendered... but I think the politics of poetry are gendered.

PAULA MEEHAN,
RTÉ Lyric FM,
January 2002

~

go twice as far, based on having done about half the amount of work, that is—half the writing, half the schmoozing, half the experience."
    SUZI FEAY, *The Independent on Sunday,* 7 March 2004

The women poets writing today are stronger than the men. This just seems so obvious. We men have written ourselves into a little narrative corner, where we write very confident, professional poems with all the effects of poetry, but the reader feels no explosion of consciousness.
    HENRI COLE, *The American Poetry Review,* May–June 2004

In the 1970s, when I started on the circuit, I was called a poetess. Older male poets, the Larkin generation, were both incredibly patronising and incredibly randy. If they weren't patting you on the head, they were patting you on the bum... There are a lot of women poets now, and their work is accepted and respected.
    CAROL ANN DUFFY, *The Times,* 3 September 2005

INTERVIEWER: Does it make any difference to you being a woman poet?
LIZ LOCHHEAD: I don't know. I've never tried being a man poet!
    BBC RADIO 4, May 1992

SEX, LOVE, AND MARRIAGE

Poetry is absolutely the same process as falling in love... You suddenly feel very excited and very cold, happiness together with some kind of fear.
YEHUDA AMICHAI, Lannan Literary Videos, 1991

The best love poems confirm something we secretly felt but never said.
TESS GALLAGHER, *The Observer,* 11 February 1996

The poem that says "I love you" is the little black cocktail dress, the classic thing that everyone would like to have written one of.
JAMES FENTON, BBC Radio 4, October 1994

This is the true function of the love poem: to remind us of who we are, and who we are capable of being: while our everyday social roles define us as persons, love reminds us that we are also spirits.
JOHN BURNSIDE, *Strong Words,* 2000

The trouble with love poems is that the emotion reflects too much credit on the poet.
ANTHONY CRONIN, *The Sunday Independent,* 22 February 2004

The test of a desirable poem is not that one wants to marry it immediately but that one wants to meet it again—soon.
KEVAN JOHNSON, *Poetry Review,* Autumn 1993

In a good poem as in a good marriage not everything is said.
DAVID BURNETT, *Quoins for the Chase,* 2003

In all literate societies, the idea of poetry has been inextricable from the idea of love. It is almost as if that particular kind of patterned utterance is a mating call of some kind.

GERMAINE GREER,
Channel 4,
December 1992

⌇

Verbalising love makes it self-conscious, dead. It's as self-defeating as retaining moonlight in a casket.

JAMES HARPUR, *The Guardian,* 13 February 1999

A love poem that blindly praises the beloved... can be about as sexy as a letter of reference.

DAVID BIESPIEL, *The Oregonian,*
5 February 2006

Valentiners require simple declarations of love, and actually great poetry is not the place to go for these. Great poets know that the truth is always complex, but the last thing people want on Valentine's Day is complexity.

DAVID BADDIEL, *The Times,* 11 February 2006

The trouble with much modern poetry is that it's nothing but sex chopped up on the page.

UNATTRIBUTED, *Acumen,* October 1993

I think all poetry is erotic. It's the Pleasure Principle. You could spend the afternoon in bed with your mistress or writing the poem and it would use the same sort of energy.

MEDBH MCGUCKIAN, *The Irish Review,* Autumn–Winter 1994

There's a surge of pleasure when you're writing a poem that's akin to physical eroticism.

CAROL ANN DUFFY, *The Guardian,* 25 September 1999

Mastery of verbal expression is usually a very satisfying sexual experience.

RICHARD HOWARD, *Five Points* 10, no. 3, 2006

Erotic poetry makes its own strategic use of the emotional tactics that lovers have always employed on each other. Poetry enacts a simultaneously frustrating and engaging dance of intimacy: hurry and delay; contact and distance; love and hate; pleasure and pain.

ANN TOWNSEND, *Radiant Lyre,* 2007

A poet without a strong libido almost inevitably belongs to the weaker category; such a poet can carry off a technical effect with a degree of flourish, but the poem does not embody the dominant emotive element in the life process.

STANLEY KUNITZ, *The Wild Braid,* 2005

Intercourse also means communication; words are a crucial part of lovemaking. That's why half the tradition of poetry consists of love poems.

JOHN POCH, *The Writer's Chronicle,* May–Summer 2005

Sex is as mysterious as poetry, when it comes down to it. With one, as with the other, all the parts may seem to fit together perfectly well, and yet it often isn't right. When it *is*—well, something unsurpassable takes over: call it energy, inspiration or what you will.

PATRICIA CRAIG, *New Statesman,* 28 February 1992

Most of my poetry is post-coital. People should make love a great deal and direct the feelings they get into creative work.

PETER REDGROVE, *Staple*

Poems about sex face the same (if greater) challenge as poems about fine meals or the Grand Canyon: since the experience in question

A thousand naked fornicating couples with their moans and contortions are nothing compared to a good metaphor.

CHARLES SIMIC,
The Gettysburg Review,
Winter 1995

❧

Having breakfast with poets is often like breakfasting at the zoo—with the added excitement of not knowing whether you're going to eat with the friendly chimpanzees or grizzly bears with sore heads!

PATRICIA OXLEY,
Acumen, October 1994

⌣

doesn't require special verbal skill to make it pleasurable or interesting, the plain style can seem pointless, while elaborate metaphors risk comic overkill.

STEPHEN BURT, *The New York Times,*
15 December 2002

Fulfilment in love is its own best poem; why go on about it in ecstatic verse when the moment of triumph has already been joyously experienced in mind and body, and in bed?

BRENDAN KENNELLY, *The Sunday Tribune*

Poetry is language articulating itself at its most acute. To quicken language to that pitch of arousal you have to be in bed with the Muse of that language.

CATHAL Ó SEARCAIGH, *The Honest Ulsterman,*
Winter 1999–2000

Metaphor sleeps around.

ALFRED CORN, *Salmagundi,* Fall 1995

Every new poem is like finding a new bride. Words are so erotic, they never tire of their coupling.

STANLEY KUNITZ, *The Language of Life,* 1995

Sometimes I am tempted even to describe poets as "matchmakers" between words that have been kept apart, but which now, in a poem, consummate their festive union.

ERIC ORMSBY, *Facsimiles of Time,* 2001

The best love poems are those in which we can watch the poet being seduced by the poem.

LAVINIA GREENLAW, *Times Literary Supplement*, 24 November 2006

Some readers of my poems think I don't like sex because I have criticised various points of technique. That's as absurd as accusing a literary critic of not liking books.

FIONA PITT-KETHLEY, *She*

The borderline between the sexes is where art is born.

MICHAEL LONGLEY, *The Observer*, 24 March 1991

In his teens he was oblivious to everything for poetry and love, though his reading list was considerably longer than his list of conquests.

SERGEI DAVYDOV, on Vladimir Nabokov, *The New York Times*

For a chap with a face like a butternut squash, the voice of a clinically depressed I-Speak-Your-Weight machine, the *joie de vivre* of a Southend clam and the swashbuckling sex appeal of Lord Irvine of Lairg, the late Philip Larkin still manages to generate excitement.

JOHN WALSH, *The Independent*, 24 April 2001

Women flew to Los Angeles from around the world to bed him, ignoring (or digging) his beer-belly and pockmarked simian face that "hung down between his shoulders, giving him the appearance of a massive troglodyte," as one acquaintance described him.

RON POWERS, on Charles Bukowski,
The New York Times, 19 November 2006

Love is the charge behind the lyric, technical mastery its muscle.

JOHN MONTAGUE,
Fortnight,
February 1999

⸙

A lot of poets' wives are not very happy because they suspect that the poems are not about them.

STEPHEN SPENDER, *The Daily Telegraph*, 22 October 1994

⌣

Much of Robert Burns's thinking was done below the neckline, and a good deal of it below the waist.

IAN MCINTYRE, *The Times*, 14 November 2001

A successful happy marriage poem, like a happy marriage itself, is a triumph over the unlikely. You must write it with the inventive care with which you would write science fiction.

STEPHEN DUNN, *Seneca Review* 21, no. 2

In the history of literature there have occasionally been "poetic couples" like the Brownings, where both man and wife wrote poetry. They rarely equal each other in talent, but the lesser partner often plays an important, supportive role which sustains the more outstanding, but often vulnerable, person.

GEORGE GÖMÖRI, *The Independent*, 15 July 2003

I think it's natural for poets to become friends, but I also think, after a certain time, it's very difficult for poets to keep a friendship alive—for example, I've always felt that if two poets marry, the marriage has to be almost impossible.

YEHUDA AMICHAI, *The Paris Review*, Spring 1992

The marriage of any two strong poets is bound to be rocky; they're competing for the same muse-time, the same stardom, the same booty.

J.D. MCCLATCHY, *Poetry*, June 1998

You can't have two poets living together—it doesn't work. There's only a certain amount of creative energy available in the household.

FLEUR ADCOCK, RTÉ Radio 1, February 1994

A trembling hypersensitivity is hell to live with. I feel for my husband.

HEATHER MCHUGH, *Seattle Post-Intelligencer,* 20 April 2000

Only another poet understands the overwhelming need to write, to devote much time and energy to the process; only another poet understands the emotional and intellectual struggles and rewards of writing. Ideally then poets are on the same side.

PENELOPE SHUTTLE, on marriage to Peter Redgrove, *The Wolf,* Summer 2005

The longer she was married to Donald Hall, the better her poems became.

ROBERT BLY, on Jane Kenyon, *The Telegraph,* 8 May 2005

To write love poetry some kind of tension is needed. If a relationship or marriage has no hidden drama, then the poetry will tend to be dull.

MICHAEL ARMSTRONG, *Acumen,* September 1995

I always felt I wrote best when things were breaking up. I wrote my best collection just as my marriage was coming apart... Some people need instability and I think a threatened stability was the ideal situation for me.

MICHAEL SCHMIDT, *The Irish Times,* 28 January 1999

When I said I wanted to marry a poet, I saw it as living in this marvellous harmonious meeting-of-two-minds way, but I didn't think about having children or doing the ironing or any of that sort of stuff.

ELSPETH BARKER, on marriage to George Barker, *The Independent on Sunday,* 26 July 1992

Of course I've read all his work and, although I like the prose, I find the poetry very hard to relate to, especially the love poems because I know the women they're addressed to and that turns me off.

WILLIAM GRAVES, on Robert Graves, *The Sunday Times*

A good erotic poem will express desire; incite desire.

SMITA AGARWAL, *Poetry Review,* Winter 2000-01

Love poetry is not dead, it is in a state of arousal.

CRAIG RAINE,
The Guardian,
13 February 1999

⁌

Keats was the first poet I got really excited about. In fact, I was rather in love with him until I found out how tall he was.

WENDY COPE, cited in *The Daily Telegraph,*
28 October 1995

Professional artists and poets have about twice as many partners as other people, British psychologists have found. Their creativity seems to act like a sexual magnet.

UNATTRIBUTED, Reuters, 29 November 2005

I sleep easy in the knowledge that I have never been so naïve or stooped so low as to sleep with a poet. Yet attend any reading at the Poetry Society and you'll spot a dozen intense young women in lumpen cardigans trying to seduce a man with dandruff and a beard.

ROWAN PELLING, *The Independent on Sunday,* 4 December 2005

Who wouldn't want to fall in love with a poet, with someone with all those fine phrases to use up?

RACHEL CAMPBELL-JOHNSTON, *Tatler,* February 2000

Of course girls fall for poets—it's false modesty to say they don't.

HUGO WILLIAMS, *The Observer,* 20 November 1994

For me, the girls have given rise to the poetry—the poetry hasn't brought in the girls.

ADRIAN HENRI, *The Observer,* 20 November 1994

If you're a man and you want to really please a woman, do you necessarily write a poem? I'm not convinced... There are other things I should do—and maybe cleaning the kitchen floor is one of them.

IAN DUHIG, BBC 2, December 1992

In modern times, poets write parodies about love. They send themselves up. Love poetry has become a form of retaliating first.

E.A. MARKHAM, *The Guardian,* 13 February 1999

Love these days usually comes dressed in inverted commas.

SUE HUBBARD, *Poetry London,* Spring 2001

Generally I approach love poetry as another way of looking at the wide world. The "you" and "I" are like two posts holding up a clothes-line. Any image can be hung out there to dry—everything except your dirty washing.

MICHAEL LONGLEY, *In the Chair,* 2002

Poets make notoriously dicey lovers, prone as they are to fusty classical allusions, a documentary impulse in the bedroom, ego, overweening love of nature and—in the case of middle-aged male poets—the hazardous tutoring of young female students.

EMILY NUSSBAUM, *The New York Times,* 30 December 2001

[Robert] Lowell's decline begins shortly after *Near the Ocean,* whose opening poem also contains the dated and sexist couplet "All life's grandeur / is something with a girl in summer."

TOM PAULIN, *The Observer,* 3 August 2003

[Robert Lowell] knew a lot about both grandeur and girls, but only he would have thought to link the two words in a line of verse, capturing thereby not only the *tendresse* of a sunlit affair, but also the way in which even the most frivolous, the most laughable, loves can make life seem a noble venture.

JOHN BANVILLE, *The Irish Times,* 9 August 2003

The best love poems are known / as such to the lovers alone.

LES MURRAY,
The New Yorker,
19 May 2003

⌣

A naïve reader always assumes that a love poem is necessarily addressed to a person (either openly, or in secret). Yet this is rarely the case, even when the poet says it is: it is love that the poem loves, not the seeming object of that love.

JOHN BURNSIDE, *La Traductière,* no. 17, 1999

Prose and Cons

"Poetic" is usually a compliment; "prosaic" is always an insult.

ERIC McHENRY, *The New York Times,* 9 January 2005

if you dribble past five defenders, it isn't called sheer prose

TOM LEONARD, *access to the silence,* 2004

Prose is walking; poetry is flying.

GALWAY KINNELL, KQED Radio, January 1997

Prose is inclusive; poetry is exclusive... Poetry by its nature reduces, sharpens, distills, compresses.

MICHAEL HOFMANN, introducing *Robert Lowell,* 2001

The poem is an escalator. The novel is a racing car. It has to go quicker and it eats up the road.

CRAIG RAINE, *Thumbscrew,* nos. 20-21, 2002

The novel's timespan is different to that of the poem: a poem may infold or implode, a novel stretches out.

VONA GROARKE, *The Irish Times,* 21 September 2002

Prose is like TV and poetry is like radio.

SIMON ARMITAGE, *Times Educational Supplement,* 2002

The novel relates; the poem tries to leave unsaid as much as possible.

CHARLES SIMIC, *Harvard Review,* Spring 1996

Prose is for the sun and the day—poetry is for the moon and the stars and night.

GEORGE MACKAY BROWN, *Poetry Wales,* September 1991

Under certain concentration, any piece of prose becomes what poetry is.

RICHARD HOWARD,
Five Points 10, no. 3,
2006

⌣

In prose, the connective tissue is allowed to show; in poetry it is subverted, subtracted, made invisible, suggested.

STANLEY PLUMLY, *Atlantic Unbound,*
8 January 2003

What good poetry and good prose have in common is vitality of rhythm.

MICHAEL LONGLEY, *Poetry Ireland Review,*
Winter 1993-94

Theirs is a heterotextual romance.

CAMPBELL MCGRATH, on poetry and fiction,
Poetry, July-August 2007

Surely there is nothing—*nothing*—that poetry can do that prose cannot do, *except* to the extent that its effect has to do with measure.

STEPHEN YENSER, *The Southern Review,* Winter 1994

People in love or in mourning do feel that they must rise to a big occasion, when they must use the best language there is. Ordinary prose, which is used for instructions on how to clean the cooker and so forth, won't do.

U.A. FANTHORPE, *The Guardian,* 13 February 1999

The thing about poetry is that you can write a poem for somebody. But with fiction, you wind up writing it *about* someone.

CLAIRE KEEGAN, *The Irish Times,* 12 May 2007

If literature is food for the mind, then a poem is a banquet, according to research by Scottish scientists which shows poetry is better for the brain than prose.

RICHARD GRAY, *Scotland on Sunday,* 3 April 2005

The main difference nowadays between poetry and prose is that, dreadful though it is, poetry doesn't go on for nearly so long.

"Bookworm," *Private Eye*, 3 December 1993

Narrative writing helps to develop logical thinking, poetic writing to enhance analogical thinking.

Eduardo Jaramillo Muñoz, *Reading and Writing Poetry*, 2005

Compared to ordinary language, poetry can be like ice-skating compared to walking.

Robert Pinsky,
The New York Times,
19 March 1995

Poetry is a different area of the brain [from prose]—much closer to music and mathematics.

Margaret Atwood, BBC Radio 3, June 1995

A poem is an interruption of silence, whereas prose is a continuation of noise.

Billy Collins, *The Paris Review*, Fall 2001

Poetry [is]... a sculpture of silence. It is precisely this inclusion of silence in words that distinguishes the poem from prose. The difficult thing is making the silence be heard, making it be felt.

Eugène Guillevic, *Living in Poetry*, 1999

Poetry requires a kind of exalted indolence, the touch of the gods, pure gift. Prose demands a certain earthbound sobriety, the will of a mule, and *work*.

Christian Wiman, *The New York Times*, 21 November 2004

Prose evokes; the well-chosen word describes the thing. But poetry *invokes;* the memorable word conjures its subject from the air.

Don Paterson, T.S. Eliot Lecture, October 2004

Poets tend to sit by the window while novelists choose the aisle. Novels are social, inclusive, open forms. Poetry has to be a bit more restrictive about the baggage allowance.

NICK LAIRD, *The Irish Times*, 8 January 2005

ﻌ

People would rather read my prose because they don't know that it's writing—it doesn't bother them. Poetry always says that it's writing.

CLIVE JAMES, *New Straits Times*, 3 March 2004

you can talk about prose without mentioning school

TOM LEONARD, *access to the silence*, 2004

Poetry is in some ways lordly or aristocratic: It gets bored more easily than prose, it likes to skip steps, and it is very interested in pleasure. The rectangular blocks of print embodying its young, middle-class nephew, the novel, seem too confining for poetry, which prefers speed and glamour.

ROBERT PINSKY, *The Washington Post*, 26 June 2005

[P]oetry is something that takes place after prose has been exhausted.

BILLY COLLINS, *Connect Savannah*, November 2006

Whereas a poet may get away with being still a child, on the page as elsewhere, one has to at least behave as though one were a grown-up in order to write acceptable prose.

AMY CLAMPITT, *Predecessors, Et Cetera*, 1991

As long as a poet sticks to the writing of poems, he is socially harmless. But the volatility of the poetic mind expressing itself in prose, with its dangerous social dimension, threatens everyone.

HARRY CLIFTON, *The Irish Times*, 11 January 2003

Prose may be the more difficult art, but poetry is the higher, the only discipline that can really save language from corruption and misuse. Poets are indeed the unacknowledged legislators of mankind, since poetry offers the only language that can in the end reshape the world.

> PETER ACKROYD, *The Times*

Why has the experimentalism of the avant-garde, which has failed in the novel, succeeded in poetry? Because poetry is *always* experimental; while the novel, on the contrary, by its nature, cannot be... Which is to say that experimentalism is synonymous with poetry and that, applied to the novel, it leads simply to the substitution of the novel with poetry.

> ALBERTO MORAVIA, *The Threepenny Review*

Poetry can come from anywhere—unlike the novel, unlike drama, which require perhaps human experience; poetry has in it a kind of child wonder.

> BRENDAN KENNELLY, RTÉ Radio 1, September 1995

Poetry's essence is not to show or to tell as we say of fiction, but to reveal.

> PATRICIA HAMPL, *The Iowa Review,* Winter 1995

Fiction requires willpower; poetry requires the abdication of willpower.

> MARGARET ATWOOD, BBC Radio 3, August 1995

The dud poet may fool us for a while, but not the dud novelist.

> GABRIEL JOSIPOVICI, *Times Literary Supplement*

Don't steal ground from the poor fiction-writers—they have so much more typing to do.

> ROY FISHER, *Poetry News,* Spring 1998

I think of poetry as being audible. One of the differences between prose and poetry is that you *have* to hear poetry.

> W.S. MERWIN, Lannan Readings & Conversations, 26 October 2005

Prose adds. A poem multiplies.

DAVID BURNETT,
Quoins for the Chase,
2003

૮

Fourteen lines of a sonnet can bring you to the point of feeling that takes a novelist 70,000 words.

STANLEY COOK, *Cambridge Contemporary Poets 2,* 1992

I often think of my novels as sonnet sequences.

JOHN BANVILLE, RTÉ 1 television, June 1992

One of the differences between prose and poetry is that in poetry there is no second order... There's no beginner's luck, no first, second and third league. There's only one league and we wish to be in that one league of poetry which inheres in the language and stays.

SEAMUS HEANEY, RTÉ Radio 1, October 1995

If, God forbid, I had to define the difference between prose and poetry, I think I'd say it was the difference between what things are made of and what they are.

SHEENAGH PUGH, *Poetry Review,* Winter 1997–98

When I can't write poetry, which I find difficult, I write prose. I find I write poetry uphill and write prose downhill.

DANNIE ABSE, *The Guardian,* 29 September 2001

A poet's job is to write poetry and you are rather going to exhaust the Muse if you write too much prose... It is a betrayal for a poet to adopt prose.

R.S. THOMAS, BBC Radio 4, September 1994

Poetry was magic and prose paid the school fees and bills. Any money from poetry was used on antiques, plates, beautiful things; writing prose was treated like a craft.

TOMÁS GRAVES, on Robert Graves, *The Daily Telegraph,* 1 January 2005

If poetry was a physical ailment it would more likely be hay fever: sharp, serial, sometimes colourful, not life-threatening. (Novels would be a cluster headache, requiring a dark room and a lie down.)

DAVID McCOOEY, *The Age,* 8 January 2005

All creative writing is storytelling... Fiction describes what it means, and poetry becomes what it means in images. Fiction is a linear art made of time, poetry is childishly timeless and circular.

RUSSELL EDSON, *Double Room,* Spring-Summer 2004

A prose poem is essentially a shortish piece of imagistic, lyrically written prose that employs poetic structural strategies, in particular poetic closure. It is like a building sheathed in the smooth glass of prose, whose inner workings remain poetry.

CAMPBELL McGRATH, *Smartish Pace*

Just as free verse did away with meter and rhyme, the prose poem does away with the line as the unit of composition. It uses the means of prose toward the ends of poetry.

DAVID LEHMAN, *The American Poetry Review,* March-April 2003

The prose poem is the result of two contradictory impulses, prose and poetry, and therefore cannot exist, but it does. This is the sole instance we have of squaring the circle.

CHARLES SIMIC, *The Unemployed Fortune-Teller,* 1994

A poem without lines, without metre of some kind is the literary equivalent of a vegeburger.

JOHN GREENING, *Poetry Review,* Summer 1995

With a lyric poem, you look, and meditate, and put the rock back. With fiction you poke things with a stick to see what will happen.

MARGARET ATWOOD, *The New York Times,* 18 May 1997

If poetry should be as well written as prose, then prose poetry has one more, not one less, master to serve.

D.H. TRACY, *Poetry,* January 2006

ᕦ

The prose poem is a pure literary creation, the monster child of two incompatible strategies, the lyric and the narrative. On one hand, there's the lyric's wish to make the time stop around an image, and on the other hand, one wants to tell a little story.

CHARLES SIMIC, *Verse* 13, no. 1

There's an idea that the prose poem is just a weak-minded regular poem, a poem that didn't work hard enough to get itself into lines... that it's a moral weakness to write a prose poem.

CAMPBELL MCGRATH, *Sycamore Review,* Winter–Spring 1998

A prose poem walks into a bar, and the bartender says, "What'll you have? The usual paragraph?" A flash fiction walks into the doctor's office and the doctor says, "How's that stanza feeling?" There may be a difference between flash fiction and prose poems, but I believe the researchers still haven't found the genes that differentiate them.

DENISE DUHAMEL, *Double Room,* Fall 2002–Winter 2003

Poetic prose—or even poetic poetry—makes English-speakers giggle.

EDMUND WHITE, *London Review of Books,* 22 August 1996

When I was a student of Classics at Trinity College Dublin, the Professor of Greek... asked us to bring to the next seminar our own definitions of poetry. Mine was (and is): "If prose is a river, poetry is a fountain."

MICHAEL LONGLEY, *Poetry Ireland Review,* Summer 1999

It sounds like a publisher's nightmare: too long and prosaic for poetry fans, but too concerned with its own form and music for readers to dip into on the train. The verse novel (like the rock opera or the sound sculpture) is the awkward child of successful parents, destined to disappoint both of them.

MICHAEL SYMMONS ROBERTS, *Guardian Unlimited,* March 2006

The difference between a book of poems and a novel is around £5,000.

DERMOT BOLGER, *The Irish Times*

She had the largest poetry advance ever on her last book—£10,000.

OLIVE PITT-KETHLEY, on Fiona Pitt-Kethley, *The Sunday Times*

Visualizing a Poem

Poems-about-paintings stretch to the horizon on all sides, a fine excuse for polymorphic musings in lieu of poetic invention.

William Scammell, *The London Magazine*, December 1991–January 1992

I am inclined to see poems-about-paintings as easy poems, or exercises, or trainer poems... The artwork is already there; all the poet has to do is dance around in front of something both fixed and culturally valuable. One feels a sense of pre-approval if one writes about Great Art.

Kay Ryan, Poetry Foundation online, 5 December 2006

It sometimes seems that anyone can come up with a string of images. It's the structure that's hard to produce, some reason that these particular images appear together in this particular order or constellation.

Reginald Shepherd, Reginald Shepherd's Blog, 19 February 2007

Poetry is the only way to fight television, because we make our pictures with poetry.

Kostis Gimosoulis, BBC Radio 3, April 1994

Poetry and cinema can both be said to share a syntax and grammar of close up, jump cut, slow dissolve and flashback.

Paul Farley, *The Guardian*, 5 February 2005

Poems are other people's snapshots in which we recognize ourselves.

Charles Simic, *The Unemployed Fortune-Teller*, 1994

As a general rule, it is best to avoid books in which poems and photographs are put together. The poems will be thin, the pictures flashy, the whole an exercise in artifartiness.

ROBERT NYE, *The Times,* 5 December 1991

The trouble with much so-called "experimental" poetry is that it looks exciting and "new" simply because of its arresting appearance on the page: read it out and it sounds quite flat.

N.S. THOMPSON, *PN Review,* November–December 2003

Poetry's very shape puts us in a receptive mood.

CON HOULIHAN, *Evening Press,* 21 April 1993

On occasion I feel a charge from a poem before I start reading... I'd suggest it is an effect of claritas, the "radiance" a poem has because of its formal completeness. Sometimes the very look of a poem on the page causes it to jump towards one, as the moon does when it emerges from behind thin cloud.

MAURICE RIORDAN, *Poetry London,* Autumn 2005

A poem almost exists because of the pattern of space around it.

FAY WELDON, BBC 2, January 1992

For me, writing a poem and drawing are like crossing the same terrain by different forms of transport.

IMTIAZ DHARKER, *Kee Magazine,* Winter 2005

ALL white space in and around a poem is silence, not paper.

JORIE GRAHAM, *Smartish Pace,* 2004

Only Joking

Whether it's a question of can't or won't, few poets are funny on the page. Poets who do entertain are in danger of being considered light-weight, as if humor and seriousness were mutually exclusive.

ALICE FULTON, *Poetry,* October 1991

In academic America the prejudice against humor in poetry is matched only by the bias in favor of the sincere autobiographical utterance.

DAVID LEHMAN, *The American Poetry Review,* November–December 1995

We are a country of millions of fools, who believe the most imbecile things about ourselves and the world, but when it comes to poetry only solemnity counts and joking is un-American.

CHARLES SIMIC, *The Paris Review,* Spring 2005

A joke is like an explosion—there's just this little smoke and it's gone. A poem is like a much, much richer joke.

ADAM ZAGAJEWSKI, *AGNI* online, 2004

The solemnity of so much contemporary verse may rest on the fallacious expectation that poetry should dispense wisdom. Wisdom being scarce, we get platitudes.

PHILLIP LOPATE, *The New York Times,* 8 September 1996

I sometimes make little jokes and I do, quite often, engage in lead-ing people on, gently, into little situations by assuring them that all's well and then—this sounds awfully manipulative, but part of writing is about manipulation—leaving them high and dry, in some corner at a terrible party, where I've nipped out through the bathroom window.

PAUL MULDOON, *Oxford Poetry,* Winter 1986-87

The trouble with frivolity, at least in poetry, is not that it is irresponsible, but that it is *unfeeling.*

DONALD DAVIE, *PN Review*

Good light verse is harder to write well than more serious poetry; so much depends on technique and careful craftsmanship.

ELIZABETH JENNINGS, *The Daily Telegraph,* 28 March 1992

In the worlds of alcohol and yoghurt, the word "Light" (or Lite) is used to indicate that the product is good for you but not much fun. In the world of poetry, the word "Light" (or Comic) is used to suggest that the product is fun but not much good for you.

MARK LAWSON, *The Independent,* 9 March 1992

Conventional metres and conventional rhyme schemes, as far as I am concerned, can nowadays only be used for light and occasional verse.

JOHN HEATH-STUBBS, Poetry Book Society *Bulletin*

Trying to print light verse in this country [the United States] nowadays is like trying to peddle mink coats at a convention of militant ecologists.

X.J. KENNEDY, *Parnassus* 21, nos. 1 & 2

Humor is like a disobedient dog. You call its name and it runs in the other direction.

BILLY COLLINS, *The New York Times,* 7 October 2004

⌣:

By the third stanza, the dark side of the mind has to come in—or it's not a poem. So, light verse is not poetry at all. Cheerful poetry is not poetry at all.

ROBERT BLY, RTÉ Radio 1, June 2006

Lightness and play are no longer at odds with "poetry": these days they inhabit the same territory.

BILL MANHIRE, *Doubtful Sounds,* 2000

All poems about cats are essentially cute and lightweight, even those about trying to murder them.

DON PATERSON, *Times Literary Supplement,* 26 May 1995

POETIC DRIVE

Poets are known for being non-drivers, and it seems that many also have difficulty in using their telephone-answering machines (not to mention speaking into other people's).

JAMES CAMPBELL, *Times Literary Supplement,* 21 November 1998

My haphazard survey of male poets reveals a species that cannot drive and, mainly, cannot swim.

EVA SALZMAN, *The Times,* 28 January 1998

Trains are the best places to write. There is something about the rhythm of a train that helps you to write, especially poetry.

IAN MCMILLAN, *The Times,* 15 July 1999

Most of the poets I know don't drive. They go by train. Then you can get your work done. You can't work when you drive.

U.A. FANTHORPE, *The Guardian,* 14 December 1998

I find driving a wonderful time for drifting into composition or revision... If it's iambic pentameter or whatever, I would count it on the steering wheel.

SEAMUS HEANEY, BBC Radio 4, September 1998

If you're alone, bumper-to-bumper traffic jams leading to or from New York City allow for plenty of time and opportunity to write a poem.

DAVID LEHMAN, Edifice Rex blog, 12 April 2000

I often write in the car, while my husband drives.

ANNE STEVENSON, *Ready Steady Book,* 2006

The poet is the perpetual passenger, the perpetual gazer out of windows. Keats would not have had a 4×4.

IAN MCMILLAN,
BBC Radio 4,
November 2006

⤴

The car has become as well as a fact of modern life a potent symbol for several Irish poets, and indeed for contemporary poetry in general.

MEDBH MCGUCKIAN, *Metre*, Autumn 1997

Auden was a poor driver, but a great poet.

JOHN FULLER, *W.H. Auden: A Commentary*, 1998

One of my favourite pastimes is listening to poetry on cassette in the car while driving. God help the poor sod who steals my car, and cranks up the stereo and gets Ezra Pound at full tilt.

SIMON ARMITAGE, *Verse*, Spring 1991

What destroys the poetry of a city? Automobiles destroy it, and they destroy more than the poetry.

LAWRENCE FERLINGHETTI, *Poetry Flash*, November 1998

Language is like a car able to go two hundred miles an hour but which is restricted by the traffic laws of prose to a reasonable speed. Poets are fond of accelerating.

KENNETH KOCH, *The New York Review of Books*, 14 May 1998

The slower the imagination, the faster the car.

ROGER MCGOUGH, BBC Radio 4, November 2006

I suspect many writers read books the way mechanics look at cars, with an eye to what is going on under the bonnet.

PAUL MULDOON, *The Sunday Times*, 4 October 1998

Readings

Reading poetry to strangers is a very intimate act. It's kind of like a poetic lap dance.

Billeh Nickerson, *The Globe and Mail*, 25 October 2004

Poems take on a much fuller human character when read aloud; they are contextualised, humanised, demystified.

Michael Glover, *The Independent*, 6 March 1999

Three questions that turn bowels to sorbet: / Would you like to try some Japanese whiskey? / Would you like to see my earwax candles? / Would you like to hear my new sestina?

Ian Duhig, *The Writer Fellow*, 2004

We've all been there. Right at the front of that poetry reading where the flannel-trousered bard, half-way through the sixty-seventh section of his Norse epic in pararhymed quatrains, is prefacing the next section with its full progenitive details, while beyond the darkening windows of the Community Centre gather the glum clouds of late *late* evening, the incipient rumblings of thunder and that thrashing against glass of the first handfuls of hail-seed and rain to wash away any last tatters of hope for your last bus home.

Annabel Gage, *Acumen*, January 2005

That's one reason I never go to poetry readings—poems are always over before I've cottoned on to them.

Charles Causley, cited in *Financial Times*, 23 November 1991

I often quit a poetry reading feeling like a one-pint measure into which the poet has tried to dump ten gallons.

X.J. KENNEDY,
Poets & Writers,
September–October
1997

❧

I've always found most poetry readings comparable to jazz: I don't see the point of either. Both involve a small group of people making a lot of noise, and then, just when you think it's all over, it carries on.

JACI STEPHEN, *Daily Mirror,* 3 October 1994

The reading of poetry in public is a largely perfunctory act. You learn the mannerisms, the gimmicks, the over-emphasis of certain words—just like actors do.

R.S. THOMAS, *The Independent,* 29 June 1994

By and large, audiences respond to performances, not to poems.

DONALD HALL, *The American Poetry Review,*
March–April 2005

For the "audience," listening to poets, rather than reading poems, prevents a full experience of the complexity, the substance, the music of verse. The poem is always only what the poet wrote down on the page. Everything else is show business.

ADAM KIRSCH, *Slate,* 4 December 2001

Aren't the persuasions of poetry private? To my mind, the right sized room to hear poetry is my head, the words speaking from the page.

KAY RYAN, *Poetry,* July–August 2005

I loathe any kind of verse that is aimed at stock responses in poetry audiences, quite especially what... I have come to call the titter of recognition.

MICHAEL HAMBURGER, *Testimonies,* 1989

Anything will do [in performance poetry], so long as it is properly signalled and allows the poem to go up in a puff of laughter. After a while you don't care what you say so long as it gets that little orgasmic squirt.

HUGO WILLIAMS, *Times Literary Supplement,* 20 January 2006

While an audience can laugh if amused, there are no conventional noises for being moved or provoked to thought.

TOM LUBBOCK, *The Independent,* 3 June 1989

Listen out for it at readings: that faintly precious, slightly mesmerised, dreamy-sweet intonation many poets audibly "put on" whenever they slip from introduction into poem: like a decaf cappuccino with too much froth.

MARIO PETRUCCI, *Poetry Writers' Yearbook 2007*

When people read poetry out loud... they always use a version of the poetry voice. It's that slightly reverential voice, slightly slowed down from real life, slightly too ponderous to get the rhythms going... The only good thing about the poetry voice is that it lets you know that what is being read is meant to be poetry, and nowadays it is not always easy to tell.

MILES KINGTON, *The Independent,* 4 October 2001

The poetry voice? It's sing-songy without being musical. It's incantatory without being hypnotic. It's slow, it's monotone, it's somewhat self-important and it's always slightly reverential. It's not unlike the voice of a

It's *never* good for the ego to travel two thousand miles to give a reading to seven people. I have a keen enough sense of my own irrelevance; I don't need to have it dramatized to me by having no one show up to hear me read.

ALAN SHAPIRO,
Rattle, Summer 2005

⌣

If half the poets out there reading their old poems would stay home and write some new ones, our literature would be vastly enriched.

ROBERT PHILLIPS,
The New York Times,
12 February 1995

∵

clergyman who... wants to sound a bit like God without actually giving himself airs.

MILES KINGTON, *The Independent,* 8 March 2005

The voice we want to hear is that of the poem in its polytonality: what we get at a reading is the poem filtered by the timbre of the author's social performance.

PAMELA COREN, *PN Review,* May-June 2007

Listening to a series of shorter poems read aloud allows the mind to concentrate, while refreshing it through the change of theme, tone and rhythm.

JEANETTE WINTERSON, *The Times,*
19 November 2005

When you meet the usual haunted-looking individuals who organise readings—men with eyes red from crying, women with garlands in their hair—they have either just taken over from someone who committed suicide, or are trying to pass the job on to someone whose sanity is still intact.

HUGO WILLIAMS, *Times Literary Supplement,* 20 November 1992

A major promotion may bring crowds to your readings but for most practitioners it is still twenty stragglers, no lectern because the organiser thought you wouldn't need one, and three sales of your new pamphlet at the door.

PETER FINCH, *The Writer's Handbook 1995*

Certain readings can still look and feel like the last meeting of the most eccentric followers of some obscure, dwindling and discredited religious movement.

SIMON ARMITAGE, *Poetry Review,* Spring 1993

It is interesting and exciting that, as poetry once more becomes a performance art, women poets are now far more successful than they were, for instance, in the mid-twentieth century when the density of interlocking and abstruse allusions was the true note by which to know a poet.

GERMAINE GREER, *The Observer,* 4 November 2001

Some poets make bad performers because they are more concerned with presenting themselves than their poems.

MICHAEL GLOVER, *The Independent,* 29 June 1994

Most poets read badly, perhaps from a sense that all their labour has gone into composition, and someone else must master the almost equally tricky art of reciting it.

JOHN BAYLEY, *Poetry Review,* Spring 1995

Surely poets who offer themselves as readers should be auditioned in the usual way?

CHRISTOPHER LOGUE, *Thumbscrew,*
Winter 1994-95

There are writers of verse—now, more than ever—who, before an audience, chant or drone or strut or mince or yammer or harangue, but very few can read their work so as to keep their listeners constantly aware of the beauty of sense, however complex, and the sense of

For poetry readings the general rule is that if the poet is outnumbered it is a success. If outnumbered by a dozen or more, it is a huge success.

THOMAS LYNCH,
*Bodies in Motion and
at Rest,* 2000

೨:

> There's no such thing as a short poetry reading.
>
> MARIE HEANEY, cited in *Metre*, Autumn 2003
>
> ⌣

beauty arising from the powerful, delicate, and compelling ways in which that sense is made by poetry.

JOHN HOLLANDER, *Poetry*, September 1995

We have poets who read better than their poems, and at the other extreme poets who do their own work no service at all. We have poets who shout and poets who prefer a dramatic monotone; poets who seem to be declaiming for more hours than they spend actually writing the stuff.

RITA DOVE, *The Writer's Chronicle*, October–November 2005

Even an otherwise undemanding poem by a poet today will be muddled up in the reading. The poet very often recites with a slight trailing up at the end of the otherwise randomly broken line, in a pompous, breathy seriousness that hardly befits the slightness of the poetry itself.

ERNEST HILBERT, *Contemporary Poetry Review*, May 2005

Poets know their own poems in a way and to a depth that is unique... In this respect, it's difficult to say a poet ever reads his or her work entirely "badly." Even if they mumble a bit, or read ponderously, or at too great a lick, their delivery will still have important things to tell us.

ANDREW MOTION, *Times Literary Supplement*, 25 November 2005

The very best readings are pheromonal—when the room fills with the sweet subliminal scent of aroused communication.

MARIO PETRUCCI, WriteWords online community, 2005

My great happiness about poetry readings is that they're a mechanism for widening the circle—ten times as many people will come to a reading as will buy a book. You're reading over the heads of the elite.

LES MURRAY, *PN Review*, July–August 1996

I love being on the road. One night you read to 1,000 people. Next night you change trains three times to get to a little place where you hear a church bell chiming the hour, and walk up the street to the pub and have a fabulous half of ale, and an unusual stranger fetches you to read to 12 people who've prepared a huge buffet, and they are all having affairs with each other's husbands and write verses themselves.

CAROL ANN DUFFY, *The Times*, 16 October 2004

Slams are a long way from the older idea of poetry readings, often in a draughty library, where an intense soul in corduroy trousers is whispering his free translations of Rilke's sonnets.

TOM PAYNE, *The Daily Telegraph*, 10 April 2004

Sooner or later every wannabe versifier will turn up at an open poetry night to vomit spiritually over the other would-be poets in the crowd. And be under no illusion, the entire audience is sitting on a sonnet; there would be no one there otherwise.

PATRICK HUSSEY, *The Independent on Sunday*, 18 April 2004

It's a sad fact that many of those who attend readings are there primarily for the "open mike"... It would be like attending a concert where everyone in the audience was carrying a violin and hoping to get onstage at the end of the symphony to play a little tune they've been working on.

BILLY COLLINS, Barnes & Noble online, April 2000

Fundamentally, poetry is a performance medium. Look at the way we teach poetry. We talk about onomatopoeia, about metre, about rhyme, about voice— it's all oral.

KWAME DAWES, *The Independent on Sunday*, 23 August 1998

⁓

In a culture that places tremendous, even worshipful emphasis on performance and performers, it is inevitable that... there will be forms that ape the successful, mass-media, corporate product. And performances that create a hybrid of poetry with stand-up or rock music or rap music will get a certain number of people interested in poetry itself.

ROBERT PINSKY, *The Ann Arbor News,* 13 March 2006

I contend that "performance poet" is nearly always an insult in the mouth of a published poet who reads their own work badly. It is a smear, implying that you are a showoff, using the cheap trick of impressive presentation to pass off substandard work to an unsuspecting public.

ROS BARBER, Shallowlands blog, 21 March 2006

No matter what degree of pleasure you give an audience, there's no pleasure greater than the pleasure you give them when you shut up.

BILLY COLLINS, *The Poetry Paper,* no. 3, 2006

No, Thanks

I don't mind poetry so long as I don't have to read it.

LYNN BARBER, *The Daily Telegraph,* 22 October 1994

I hate everything about writing except doing it.

TONY HARRISON, *The Independent,* 5 August 1995

To write poetry you don't have to like it.

JOHN KINSELLA, *Agenda,* Summer 2003

In his more curmudgeonly mode John Hewitt once said to me: "If you write poetry, it's your own fault."

MICHAEL LONGLEY, *Mortification,* 2003

You're a poet or you're not (and if you're not, count your blessings).

FRANZ WRIGHT, *Contemporary Poetry Review,* September 2006

The cultural dynamism of any community is probably in inverse relationship to the number of self-styled "poets" it contains. The more the "poets," the lower the overall cultural values, the less demanding the criticism, the less rigorous the personal discipline, the greater the self-indulgence, and worst of all, the more insufferably boring the society will be.

KEVIN MYERS, *The Irish Times,* 2 April 2002

It is the legend of the life of John Keats we must blame for the fact that poetry is not an acceptable topic of conversation among grown men in public houses.

MICHAEL GLOVER, *The Independent,* 31 October 1995

No one writes
without being
aware that readers
come to any new
text, as it were,
with pistol cocked
and an interroga-
tor's scowl: "Does
this bard have
anything to say
that I have to
listen to, or can
I just terminate
proceedings
right now?"

ALFRED CORN,
Poetry, February 1993

⌣

Englishmen first started blushing in the
proximity of verse between 1890 and 1910. We
must blame the pre-Raphaelites, Swinburne,
Rossetti and Co. At this time we developed our
national image of the poet as a vague, hyper-
sensitive, unpunctual, sexually ambiguous drip
who is always in love, drunk, drugged to the
eye-balls and perpetually unable to cope with
the world.

STEPHEN PILE, *The Sunday Times*

You may have noticed that poetry is dead. The
obituary has already been written. It has a
ghoulish afterlife in readings and poetry slams...
Reading a poem involves self-examination...
we don't have the time or the inclination.

MARTIN AMIS, cited in *The Guardian*, 9 June 2007

People are afraid to read 20th century poetry.
It is too compacted, too intense, too uncom-
promising. It never allows you to relax into it.
It seems to be a cerebral pact between the poet
and a small, devoted audience of initiates; and
the understanding and, God forbid, the enjoyment of poetry can only be
the consequence of strenuous intellectual effort.

MICHAEL GLOVER, *Financial Times*

I don't think poetry is a popular sport. Poetry requires a certain amount
of solitude and silence and those are not the activities most people are
interested in.

RICHARD HOWARD, cited in *The Salt Lake Tribune*, 4 January 2004

Maybe the so-called contemporary indifference to poetry is nothing more than dread, dread that poetry is so penetrated by silence.

FORREST GANDER, *A Faithful Existence,* 2005

Why is poetry so scary? One answer is that it mobilises the full resources of human language, and this is clearly not something we do every day.

TERRY EAGLETON, *The Times,* 20 January 2007

People are completely justified in their fears or their antipathy toward poetry, because much of it is emotionally serious but also emotionally miserable as well as being incomprehensible, and that's a kind of a deadly combination.

BILLY COLLINS, *Planet Jackson Hole* online, 29 May 2007

Speaking from my small experience of teaching, aversion to poetry doesn't need to be created; it is genetic.

ALAN JENKINS, *The Guardian,* 9 October 1997

There are a million poets that write interesting verse, but I can't think of a single one that I would think of getting up in the morning and going to to find my life profoundly changed and enlightened and deepened by.

A.R. AMMONS, *Michigan Quarterly Review,* Winter 1989

I realize, increasingly, that I sit down to a new book of poems much in the same way I take my place in the dentist's chair: I may benefit from the experience but it won't be a pleasure.

STEPHEN DOBYNS, *The New York Times,* 13 December 1992

Like priests in a town of agnostics, poets still command a certain residual prestige. But as individual artists they are almost invisible.

DANA GIOIA, *Can Poetry Matter?,* 1992

⌣

In the course of my lifetime, poets have ceased to be seen as masters of a great art, speaking in the name of some vision of beauty or wisdom. Poetry is something everybody writes, interchangeable, demotic, involving neither skill nor knowledge but only a sufficiently strong urge to write it.

KATHLEEN RAINE, *PN Review,* November–December 2000

Usually, I think there's nothing to be said about mediocre poetry. It's like being a talent scout for an opera company, when all you can say about the voice you hear is, "No, it has no carrying power, it hasn't any capacity to stay on pitch, it hasn't any sense of innate rhythm, it hasn't any expressive color, it hasn't interpretive power... it's just no, no, no."

HELEN VENDLER, *The Paris Review,* Winter 1996

I do not give the honorific name of "poetry" to the primitive and the unaccomplished.

HELEN VENDLER, *The New York Times,* 19 February 1995

Much poetry of the moment... is clever, modish, desiccated—and I would rather eat dry coconut than read it.

KATE KELLAWAY, *The Observer,* 27 February 2000

Poetry... has outsourced ambition to the novel, thought to philosophy and conceptual art, political analysis to the press, introspection to psychology, and feeling to Hallmark and the music and movie industries.

TREVOR JOYCE, RTÉ Lyric FM, June 2007

Too many contemporary poems start small and end smaller. They don't bite off more than they can chew—they bite off so little they don't need to chew.

WILLIAM LOGAN, *Contemporary Poetry Review,* August 2002

ON THE CONTRARY

If poetry retrospectively appears prophetic, this is because it looks in more than one direction or in unexpected directions.

EDNA LONGLEY, *Poetry & Posterity,* 2000

One of the laws of poetry seems to be that there can be no good poem of unalloyed happiness, that good poems always pull in two directions.

JANE HIRSHFIELD, *The American Poetry Review,* September-October 1995

Poems are never made out of 100% good will and good tidings. There is always a little cold wind in a good poem.

GEORGE SZIRTES online, 25 December 2005

Even in the poetry of the most profound sorrow and lament, if the work is of the highest order, there is always somewhere—if you look for it—a lift in the words, an element of praise, a singing line.

PAUL MURRAY, *Logos,* Summer 2005

A poem's every line conceals the sufferings of Cambodia and Auschwitz... Every line also holds a spring day's joy. Tragedy and joy collide in every line.

ADAM ZAGAJEWSKI, *A Defense of Ardor,* 2004

Poetry provides a safe home for ambiguity and ambivalence. Any poem which sets out to be merely amusing or merely sincere fails to take advantage of poetry's strange duplicity.

BILLY COLLINS, Poetry Book Society *Bulletin,* Spring 2003

Poetry's there with these ordering principles and you as a person bring your disorder to poetry. And you meet and any really exciting poem has got both that disorder and the order in it.

GREGORY ORR,
Rattle, Winter 2005

᷍

This is why lyric poems are so rife with irony—good poems undercut their own yearning to say one thing well, because to say one thing is simply not to say enough.

JANE HIRSHFIELD, *The American Poetry Review,*
November–December 2005

Poetry requires us to hear in its musical system, to see from its imagery, to know from its sentences that we always inhabit a place of overlapping emotions, the place where the shine in your eyes is from tears and those tears come from *both* laughing and crying, the shimmering verge.

MOLLY PEACOCK, *How to Read a Poem,* 1999

Poetry can have it both ways; that is why it is poetry. It enchants and disenchants at the same time.

BARON WORMSER, *The Sewanee Review,*
Fall 2006

Poetry teaches us that it is possible to have two opposing thoughts at once, which our master cultural narratives seem to deny.

EDWARD HIRSCH, *Five Points* 2, no. 2, 2003

A poem that does its work must stand on the knife edge of yes and no. The last line of a poem should have both the yes and the no in it; that's what makes it complex.

DORIANNE LAUX, *The Kansas City Star,* 28 January 2001

Paradox... is the smile of truth.

ALICIA OSTRIKER, *The Writer's Chronicle,* December 2006

A good poem is almost always about something else, which is why they are hard to write.

CHARLES CAUSLEY, *Poetry News,* Winter 1998

What a poem should do is present something in order to convey the feeling. It should be precise about the something and reticent about the feeling.

DORIS CORTI, *Writers' News*

We look to poetry for the thisness that it encapsulates, and the otherness that it evokes.

PETER JAY, *The Spaces of Hope,* 1998

Poetic manifestos invariably say "yes" and "no," but poetry itself "maybe" and "perhaps."

ANDREW MOTION, *Strong Words,* 2000

A poem needs nervous tension, like an arrow needs a bowstring.

A.B. JACKSON, *Poetry News,* Winter 2003-04

Often a poet's strength seems to result from, or at any rate to accompany, the reconciliation of two opposing qualities.

ANNIE FINCH, *The Kenyon Review,* Winter 2003

In trying to portray the world as it is, poetry reveals the seeds of paradox wherever two words clash. Its truth is to show where and in what manner the dimension of contradiction begins.

RAOUL SCHROTT, Rotterdam Poetry Festival, 2003

Poetic language is essentially oxymoronic, a coinage stamped on two sides with logically irreconcilable messages.

ANNE STEVENSON, *Contemporary Women's Poetry,* 2000

A poem without internal contradiction is not a poem.

DONALD HALL, *The American Poetry Review,* January–February 2002

Ambiguity stops the flow of language, charging each word with tension and scruple. It forces words to play double and triple roles in the line and the sentence, demanding that the reader puzzle out what is ordinarily obvious. It is, in short, the music of doubt and self-doubt.

ADAM KIRSCH, *Contemporary Poetry Review,* March 2006

Openness to plural meanings in words implies a liberal openness to plural values.

MARK THOMPSON, *Literary Imagination,* Winter 2006

IN AND OUT OF FASHION

Most literary reputation is fragile and fleeting, and the reputation of poets especially so. Their stock is traded on a Nasdaq of singular cruelty and volatility.

CHARLES MCGRATH, *The New York Times*, 15 June 2003

Various generations of writers have always competed to clear a space of attention for themselves. Today's period style soon becomes the barricade where the next generation of poets will protest.

D.W. FENZA, *The Writer's Chronicle*, December 2006

To write in a fashionable style is not necessarily a sign of possessing no talent; it is after all what almost all poets have always done. The problem for the modern poet is simply that the fashions succeed each other so quickly that to adopt all of them looks like spineless simplemindedness. Nothing looks as stale as yesterday's chic.

DICK DAVIS, *Times Literary Supplement*

Poets used to flake out in foreign parts from an excess of emotion and TB. Not any more—now the complaint might be poetry circuit fatigue. Too many readings, TV appearances, book signings. For poetry is Fashionable.

JANE SPEED, *Elle*

Poetry has almost ceased to be the subject of comment amongst the lettered classes, and every announcement of its revival is little more than a publicity stunt above a mouldering corpse.

TONY FRAZER, *Poetry Ireland Review*, Summer 2002

Most poetry eventually joins the vast shelves of the unread and most readers of poetry follow a beaten track. Time, which is said to be the mother of truth, can all too easily confirm habit and lay its slow dust on the unclamorous.

JOHN FULLER, *The Forward Book of Poetry 1998*

Poems, one realizes, depend so much on whatever contemporary notion of the "poetic" was fashionable at the time that reading them years later one cannot escape being struck by how much they sound alike.

CHARLES SIMIC, *The New York Review of Books,* 3 July 2003

One of the few attractive things about poetry is that it's too small to be picked up in any style radar.

ROBIN ROBERTSON, *The Guardian,* 7 November 2006

YOUTH AND AGE

Randall Jarrell wrote that "Poets are in the beginning hypotheses, in the middle facts, and in the end values," which may be another way of saying that poets begin as question marks, become exclamation points, and end as ellipses.

WILLIAM LOGAN, Poetry Foundation online, 30 October 2006

Poets grow older; verse turns from passion into habit: but only the first condition is inevitable.

SEAN O'BRIEN, *Times Literary Supplement,* 28 October 2005

Louis MacNeice said the middle stretch is bad for poets and I think that is right. If you can get through that without going mad or dying of alcoholism or committing suicide, there is a rich seam waiting for you, which is what happened to me in my 50s and 60s. The muse came back.

MICHAEL LONGLEY, *The Belfast Telegraph,* 2 November 2006

Poets have always been young men in a hurry, desperately seeking to establish a poetic reputation before being prematurely swept away by death in the form of bizarre boating accidents, duels, battlefield mishaps, bottles of arsenic or one of the traditional picturesque illnesses such as consumption or syphilis.

SUZI FEAY, *The Independent on Sunday,* 24 August 2003

Teenagers are interesting for many reasons—for their sex lives, their music, their unshakeable belief in the suitability of jeans for every social occasion—but the one thing you pass on, politely but firmly, is their poetry.

TOM SHONE, *The Sunday Times,* 1 September 1996

After a certain age, a poet's main rival is the poet he used to be.

WILLIAM LOGAN,
Parnassus 27,
nos. 1 & 2

∽

This new enthusiasm for poetry among the young, if it exists, has another, sadder explanation: they have lost the ability to communicate in prose.

AUBERON WAUGH, *The Literary Review,* June 1994

There's a huge premium attached to being a young poet. The critical culture has collapsed and been replaced by a fast-food one.

MICHAEL SCHMIDT, *The Independent on Sunday,*
8 October 1995

Assimilating a new poet is like learning a new language. It takes time.

JONATHAN SKINNER, Here Comes Everybody blog, 21 December 2005

During more than thirty years of observation, I've seen many talents flare only to fizzle out; and some few continue to hold public attention. The readership tends to place its highest hopes on unfamiliar figures, greeting them with a messianic fervor hard to sustain when a second or third book appears.

ALFRED CORN, *Contemporary Poetry Review,* May 2004

Too often you get the impression that poets' first books are either their best, or the one in which they satisfied the taste of their time, and that the subsequent work is a gradually diminishing set of variations on the same themes or poses.

W.N. HERBERT, *Poetry London,* Spring 2004

First books by young poets can be dreary, especially if they focus on deceased kin. Usually the poet zeroes in on a fetish object (such as Grandpa's photo album), swaddling it in layers of ambivalent nostalgia and relinquishing it after experiencing a tiny epiphany.

JOHN PALATTELLA, *The Nation,* 9 May 2005

I started writing when I was 28. I don't think people really write anything worth reading before that. You have to be a grown-up to write poetry, and you have to have read quite a lot of poems too.

KATE CLANCHY, *The Daily Telegraph*, 13 March 2004

Poets produce twice as much of their lifetime output in their 20s as novelists do. A great novelist or non-fiction writer who dies at 28 may not have yet produced her or his magnum opus.

JAMES KAUFMAN, *The Guardian*, 23 April 2004

I'm 28 right now and I guess that's young by today's standards for poets but Keats had written his great odes long before he was my age.

SHARA MCCALLUM, *Smartish Pace*

When you're engaged in the actual excitement of writing a poem, there isn't that much difference between being thirty-five or fifty-five.

SEAMUS HEANEY, *The Paris Review*, Fall 1997

Poets can love their early efforts—in not a few instances those pieces will be their best—but prose goes off quickly.

JOHN BANVILLE, *The Irish Times*, 21 February 2004

Sometimes you read your old work and you find you really don't like the person that wrote it.

DON PATERSON, *Scotland on Sunday*, 25 January 2004

By and large I prefer not to tinker with past efforts: this resembles denting cold metal that was red-hot in another life.

MICHAEL LONGLEY, *Collected Poems*, 2006

In youth, poems come to you out of the blue. They're delivered at your doorstep like the morning news. But at this age, one has to dig.

STANLEY KUNITZ, *The New York Times*, 30 November 1995

The greatest artists grow into the knowledge of good and evil while somehow managing to keep alive the child inside.

ROBERT B. SHAW, *Poetry,* May 1998

Poets, because they should never completely grow up, must continually come of age.

MICHAEL LONGLEY, *Irish University Review,* Spring–Summer 1994

We could almost define poets as needing controlled immaturity to secure their poetry.

DEAN JUNIPER, *London Magazine,* August–September 1998

There is something beyond Craft where poetry is concerned. Has to be. Otherwise a mastery of craft would mean a mastery of the poem. We'd expect a mature poet with control over "the principles of craft" to never write poorly. With the exception of Stanley Kunitz, most poets seem to get worse as they "mature," not better.

TERRANCE HAYES, Poetry Foundation online, 5 June 2006

Given the increased longevity which the demographers and doctors promise us, there comes the prospect of a growing army of pensioner poets, all rhythmically tapping their feet and demanding attention, their mutual envy sharpened by a diminishing number of publishers and readers.

LAWRENCE SAIL, *PN Review,* January–February 2001

Poets *always* dry up... It demands a concentration that you are no longer able to give—a combination of concentration and energy.

THOM GUNN, *The Georgia Review,* Spring 2005

A Selected Poems is like a clock awarded by an affable but faintly impatient employer. It means it's later than you think.

SEAN O'BRIEN, Poetry Book Society *Bulletin,* Winter 2002

PUSHY POETS

Allegedly we are surrounded by geniuses. Everybody is becoming more proficient. *Everybody* is a poet. People use with ease big words like Art and Culture. It's *frightening.*

LAWRENCE DURRELL, *The Sunday Times*

The example of Larkin and Eliot, severe critics of their own work, seems alien to our Thatcherite enterprise culture, where Creative Writing Fellowships have created a new breed of eager-beaver writing fellows and where everyone must be seen to be hustling their product up and down... the country.

BLAKE MORRISON, *London Review of Books*

Today the wannabe poet progresses like the academic, the civil servant, the manager, up a series of marked steps to become a member of the fraternity and sorority of Published Poets. The *obedience* such an ascent requires can be at odds with the very principles of the art. It is an art of speculation not in the old sense but entirely in the new: speculating on the prize, the publisher, the public—poetry has become as keen to embrace the main chance as the basest prose.

MICHAEL SCHMIDT, StAnza lecture, March 2006

Of course, very little poetry would be written without any ambition at all, but I have long been haunted by the words of Henri Michaux, who said that the mere ambition to write a poem is enough to kill it.

RICHARD MURPHY, *Books Ireland,* Summer 2002

I see no reason to spend your life writing poems unless your goal is to write great poems. An ambitious project—but sensible, I think. And it seems to me that contemporary American poetry is afflicted by modesty of ambition.

DONALD HALL,
Poetry and Ambition,
1988

⌣.

More bilge, to put it politely, gets written with and through ambition than perhaps any other quality... You need a pure heart, a good ear, and a wicked vocabulary. That's my prescription.

MICHAEL HOFMANN, *Poetry*, June-July 2004

Oracular spontaneity is rare these days, and heartfelt, inspired sloppiness underrated. The poets are pros now, like the software coders, and they function smoothly as nodes in the great network.

WALTER KIRN, *The New York Times*,
19 November 2006

Those encouraged to describe themselves as poets nowadays may not be much good at writing poetry, but they are brilliant at public relations.

AUBERON WAUGH, *The Literary Review*,
April 1999

People wish to be poets more than they wish to write poetry, and that's a mistake. One should wish to celebrate more than one wishes to be celebrated.

LUCILLE CLIFTON, cited in *Poets & Writers*,
January-February 1992

You take your poems seriously, but you don't take yourself seriously. What the muse hates more than anything is self-importance.

MICHAEL LONGLEY, *The Observer*, 29 October 2006

To promote the poet rather than the poem is to sin against the muse.
Revenge is likely to take the shape of writer's block!

BIDDY JENKINSON, *The Leonard L. Milberg Collection of Irish Poetry*, 1998

Promotion violates the innocence and defencelessness of poetry.

MICHAEL HOFMANN, *The Times*, 4 October 1997

The ethic we should associate with poetry—a lack of egotism; a painful
sympathy for the common plight of common humanity; revulsion at the
human cost of commerce; a concern, negatively or positively, with the
spiritual—is difficult to reconcile with the competitive urge to best one's
contemporaries, to carry off the glittering prizes, and to concentrate so
much acclaim on one's own figure that shadows fall across all else.

ROBERT POTTS, *New Statesman*, 1 April 2002

Publishers should scrap the corrupt practice
of solicited pre-publication blurbs, and the
shot in the arm they provide to debutant writers who don't deserve to be in print anyway.

DAVID WHEATLEY, *Poetry Ireland Review*,
September 2004

There is a disgraceful abdication from truth in
the words that are wrapped around books.

SEAMUS HEANEY, *Salmagundi*, Fall 1988

Among the foremost repositories of demented
prose today are fashion magazines, art journals—and the back covers of poetry books.

JOSEPH PARISI, *MPA Newsletter*, Fall 1996

What I sense in many poems I read are risks
fabricated for the purposes of getting a

Poetry is not an
ego trip that pre-
serves your ego
in the amber of
the poem, but
rather that you've
made your own
ego transparent,
conquered it.

ALLEN GINSBERG,
cited in *The Paris
Review*, Summer 1995

⁓

This is what I feel a poet has to do with his life: not expose it, not confess it, not present it literally, but convert it into legend.

STANLEY KUNITZ, *The American Poetry Review*, March–April 1998

⌒·

poem—consumer risks to awaken consumer desire.

JORIE GRAHAM, *Denver Quarterly*, Spring 1992

You can generate a certain amount of self-importance in the poetry world, as if there were no world outside the poetry world, or as if the poetry world mattered to anything but the poetry world. Whether or not you're invited to that festival or to this reading, can keep you going and persuade you that you're engaged in some important activity.

IAN HAMILTON, *The Dark Horse*, 1996

The great enemy of art is the ego. It keeps getting in the way. One needs the ego to disappear so that I become you; I become the people walking up and down the street.

PAUL DURCAN, *Oxford Poetry*, Spring 1988

A work of art is simultaneously a search of the ego and an abandonment of the ego; and the only way to abandon the ego is to let the instruments that you are using almost perform themselves.

JOHN F. DEANE, RTÉ Radio 1, January 2006

The command which is unspoken but deep in the mystery of poetry is to somehow abdicate from audience, from self-promotion or self-alignment, and to go towards the subject, to give yourself over and disappear.

SEAMUS HEANEY, RTÉ Radio 1, November 1994

The only reason you write about yourself is that this is what you know best... And if you knew anybody else as well as you know yourself, you would write about that other.

STANLEY KUNITZ, *Interviews and Encounters with Stanley Kunitz*, 1993

We are all interested in our own poems, just as we are interested in the smell of our own armpits, because they are uniquely redolent of ourselves. We are not, for converse reasons, much interested, as a rule, in the slapdash maunderings of other people.

EDITORIAL, *The Spectator*, 23 September 2000

The difference between the kind of poetry in which an "I" tells about itself and a poetry which "sings gods and heroes" is not great, since in both cases the object of description is mythologized.

CZESLAW MILOSZ, *Road-side Dog*, 1998

Getting into Difficulty

In the hands of any real poet, poetry exists at the very heart of the language. It is always "difficult" because, by its very nature, it is saying things that verge on the unsayable.

BRYAN APPLEYARD, *The Sunday Times*

Poetry is meant to be difficult like any interesting and enduring art form. If people want their art to be like a pop song with a hook then they should look elsewhere.

ROBIN ROBERTSON, *The Globe and Mail,* 2 February 2002

Why does music, why does poetry have to address us in simplified terms, when, if such simplification were applied to a description of our own inner selves, we would find it demeaning? I think art has a right—not an obligation—to be difficult if it wishes.

GEOFFREY HILL, *The Paris Review,* Spring 2000

Poetry is, for good or ill, a highly specialized use of language, and the news it offers requires, beyond intelligence and sensitivity, a good deal of concentrated effort, patience and time, qualities our frenetic, hyper-specialized culture keeps in short supply.

ALAN SHAPIRO, *The American Poetry Review,* March–April 1992

Many weak poems substitute vagueness for mystery.

STEPHEN DOBYNS, *Best Words, Best Order,* 1996

Poetry can be reticent without being obscure.

DANA GIOIA, *Poems of Love,* 1990

Making up a poem is a way to share a secret without telling it.

KATE GREENSTREET, Here Comes Everybody blog, 17 September 2005

There's a balance to be struck between being mystified and being intrigued.

MICHAEL LASKEY, *Poetry Ireland Review*, Autumn 1999

Any fool can write an obscure poem... To write clearly and still express interesting things is fiendishly difficult.

NORMAN MacCAIG, *The Sunday Tribune*, 17 January 1988

The ground is currently thick with poets dropping obliquities like phone numbers on napkins, in part because of the ease with which this method can be adopted.

DAVID ORR, *Poetry*, June 2003

The poem is the solution to a problem only it has raised, and our reading of it necessarily entails determining what that problem was.

PAUL MULDOON, cited in *Poetry*, December 2006

It's true that a good many poems deliberately resemble puzzles or riddles... but the most accomplished poets in that vein have the knack for getting readers to enter into the spirit of the game.

DAVID BARBER, *The Atlantic* online, 25 July 2006

Poetry is like solving a crossword puzzle in which you are also the compiler.

DON PATERSON, *The Observer*, 20 March 1994

Finally, I don't believe in poetry as crossword puzzle, as being necessarily difficult.

PAUL MULDOON, BBC Radio 3, June 1994

Let poetry be difficult, very difficult, the difficulty of a deep ocean, but not obscure, the obscurity of a muddy shallow little lake.

PETER VIERECK,
Parnassus 17, no. 2

I don't think that all poetry has to be accessible. There's a lot of things in life that we get pleasure from without understanding. Sex comes to mind.

ALAN SHAPIRO,
Rattle, Summer 2005

∴

Some poets are writing crosswords and more poets are writing algebra. I was never any good at crosswords and I'm hopeless at algebra. I'm not into the popular argument of saying that poetry must be the lowest common denominator; let's have it the highest common multiple perhaps.

GABRIEL FITZMAURICE, RTÉ Radio 1, June 1993

Obscurity must be a tool. It works to force the reader to ask questions that will direct him or her to an understanding of the poem. Any question that does not increase our understanding detracts from it.

STEPHEN DOBYNS, *Best Words, Best Order,* 1996

After a whole Romantic era, and a straining academic era after it, can any poet still write truly straight and plain?

LES MURRAY, *Times Literary Supplement,* 3 December 1993

Poetry has to be brave enough to risk the chance of death by mediocrity when the alternative is certain extinction through wilful academic obscurity.

NEIL POWELL, *PN Review*

There are many obscure poets whose work I love, adore even, but they will only ever be "great" in the university cafeteria or in the minds of other poets, never in the world.

SIMON ARMITAGE, *Fulcrum,* no. 4, 2005

There is more, not less intensity in plainness, because simple stuff operates without the safety net of the poetical.

HUGO WILLIAMS, *Strong Words,* 2000

A plain style can be a way of disguising what has not been explored.

MICHAEL KINSELLA, *Poetry Ireland Review,* December 2004

The most difficult thing in the world is to be clear.

PAUL MULDOON, *The Independent on Sunday*

All the best poets are capable of thinking, and thinking straight, and probably intend to do so most of the time, although they do not always manage to stick to the plan.

DONALD JUSTICE, *The New Criterion,* February 1997

Obscurity can be a compliment when young; when old it is merely another disease.

WILLIAM LOGAN, *Poetry*

I am bored by poems that are transparent from beginning to end, but I am quick to put down poems whose opening lines make me feel I have walked in on the middle of a Swedish movie being run backwards with no subtitles.

BILLY COLLINS, *The Writer's Chronicle,* September 2006

When that faintly desperate adjective "accessible" appears in a review, the book in question is sure to be poetry.

STEPHEN KNIGHT, *The Independent on Sunday,* 1 October 2006

As far as I can tell, there are two kinds of poets: those who want to tell stories and sing songs, and those who want to work out the chemical equation for language and pass on their experiments as poetry.

SIMON ARMITAGE, *Short and Sweet,* 1999

To the familiar complaint that poetry is too difficult and elitist and should adapt itself to

No audience member at a concert or a dance performance is challenged to imaginatively contribute to the performance in the way that a reader of a good poem visualizes an image made with words, draws on his own life experience to decipher meaning, or alertly registers subtext.

Catherine Brady,
Critical Mass,
26 April 2007

its potential audience, it must be replied that when poetry makes overtures to populism it ceases to be itself.

Sean O'Brien, *The Printer's Devil*

It is no denigration of a poem to say that it resists its audience for a while.

Seamus Heaney, RTÉ Radio 1

People talk a lot about clarity as one of the goals of poetry—but if writers aren't finding their way into mystery, even as they try to clarify something for themselves, then they might as well forget the whole deal.

Bill Manhire, *Doubtful Sounds,* 2000

Poems are suggestive, dense and intimate; they are meant to resonate on the page; television is literal, fluid and accessible. Poetry is Marianne Moore and Wallace Stevens; television is Judy Woodruff and Mister Rogers. Putting it bluntly, when you read a poem, you aren't supposed to get it right away; with TV, getting it fast is the whole game.

Ed Sikov, *Connoisseur*

Most people reading a poem (as in watching a TV ad) value resistance... Working out, using your own imagination to go deeper, is part of the joy. For then *you* have a stake in the meaning you find, in the relationships of rhythm and consonant, feeling and thought.

Ruth Padel, *PN Review,* May-June 2005

Readers *like* some puzzlement, some baroque, perhaps, and certainly some material that doesn't release all its savor at a first lick. Really, writers and readers alike, we work beyond our own intelligence; necessarily so. That's the raison d'être, the road to the trance which art exists to provide.

LES MURRAY, *The Paris Review,* Spring 2005

Who wants to read a poem that is too easily understood? Such poems are like easily grasped gods, capable of carrying a message, perhaps, but not capable of pointing toward the truth. It seems to me that the beauty of the form is all tied up with a poem's refusal to be completely known.

MATT FITZGERALD, *Poetry,* November 2006

So much of the energy of the poem comes from the secrets it folds into what we would call, in a flower, its crown. The height of the beauty of a bloom is its folded state, rather than when it's fully opened.

STANLEY KUNITZ, *The Wild Braid,* 2005

Since the mass scale of journalism and movies and pop music undermine the criteria of evaluation in our culture, it's important to emphasize that a singular value of poetry is the freedom, complexity, and depth that derives from its small scale, the fact that it has few readers, that it is difficult to access, that it's *not* a mass art form.

CHARLES BERNSTEIN, *The Argotist* online, 2005

A friend once borrowed [my early poems], and when he gave them back he asked "When are you publishing the answers?"

NORMAN MACCAIG, *The Independent*

⌣

We are beginning to lay too much emphasis on accessibility in the wrong way. Of course, it should be accessible, but it might be accessible

The reason modern poetry is difficult is so that the poet's wife can't understand it.

WENDY COPE, *The Sunday Times,* 1998

⸪

through the feelings it arouses rather than through the actual act of mental comprehension.

ANTHONY CRONIN, RTÉ Radio 1, January 1987

It is perfectly right to demand accessibility when you are designing a public lavatory... But what is a proper term in civics and in architecture is not necessarily a proper term in literature or painting or music.

GEOFFREY HILL, BBC Radio 3, January 1999

Whenever an undeniably original poet appears—Mallarmé, Eliot, Moore, Milosz, Ashbery—no matter how alien the content, or how allusive the lines, readers flock to the poems. "Accessibility" needs to be dropped from the American vocabulary of aesthetic judgment if we are not to appear fools in the eyes of the world.

HELEN VENDLER, *The New Republic,* 28 February 2005

Alas, the world is full of poets who are accessible... and yet nobody reads them either. Could it be because they insist on telling the reader something he or she already knows?

JOHN ASHBERY, cited in *The New Republic,* 28 February 2005

Language that excites the reader's interest is accessible, however much resistance it may offer to understanding; dull poetry is inaccessible poetry.

KIT FRYATT, *Metre,* Autumn 2002

"I find poetry difficult," some people say. My response to this remark is: "Yes. And that is only one of the good things about it." Difficulty, after all, is magnetic, much desired: hence the video game, the crossword puzzle, golf. They are reliable, packaged forms of difficulty.

ROBERT PINSKY, *The Washington Post,* 31 July 2005

One could argue that poetry's difficulty for some readers stems from the very source of its incredible power: the merging of its irrational procedures with the rational nature of language.

JORIE GRAHAM, *The Best American Poetry 1990*

So-called difficult poetry is often very rude. It ignores the presence of the reader. It wants to be an act of writing taking place in front of you, but it doesn't want to address you.

BILLY COLLINS, *Portsmouth Herald*, 23 January 2005

Poetry in our century has made a virtue of ambiguity, intellectual strenuousness and a kind of proud, reader-repellent costiveness: it is reaping the miserable rewards now.

MICHAEL GLOVER, *The Independent*, 12 January 1999

Part of the problem is that people are afraid they're not going to understand poetry. So they *don't* understand it because they're paralysed by the actual act of apprehension. They're apprehensive rather than apprehending.

CRAIG RAINE, *The Sunday Tribune*

Poetry is an artificial language, a language of artifice, and most contemporary poetry aspires to idealized speech. In some of it, however, communication is not a goal and clarity is not a virtue; this sort of poetry keeps critics employed.

STEPHEN DOBYNS, *The New York Times*

Difficult poetry is the most democratic, because you are doing your audience the honour of supposing that they are intelligent human beings.

GEOFFREY HILL,
The Guardian,
10 August 2002

༦

The charge frequently levelled against poetry nowadays of being difficult, obscure, hermetic, and whatnot indicates not the state of poetry but, frankly, the rung of the evolutionary ladder on which society got stuck.

JOSEPH BRODSKY,
Poetry Review,
Winter 1991–92

༈

Poetry complicates us, it doesn't "soothe"; it helps us to our paradoxical natures, it doesn't simplify us.

JORIE GRAHAM, *The Paris Review,* Spring 2003

If you write whatever it is well enough—Wallace Stevens is a good author to demonstrate this with—the reader will put up with quite a lot of incomprehension.

ROBERT PINSKY, cited in *Contemporary Poetry Review,* October 2003

Almost everyone who at some time or other has uttered "Sheer poetry!," or simply gasped "Wow!" at a bird soaring, a footballer swerving or any act that seems perfect in itself, understands poetry in the most visceral sense.

GEORGE SZIRTES, *Poetry Writers' Yearbook 2007*

The best poets are communicators—they need to make themselves heard... Modernists and theorists are always seeking to lure this ancient art form away from its roots and strengths towards some intellectually fortified bunker on the outskirts of obscurity.

SIMON ARMITAGE, *The Independent,*
24 October 2003

With many poetry editors paying more heed to peer approval than reader response, and poetry's sly spin doctors trying to foist their academically distorted version of contemporary poetry on baffled readers, it's not surprising that bookshops see poetry as a minority interest.

NEIL ASTLEY, *Bloodaxe Poems of the Year,* 2003

A lot of young poets these days are being educated into a state of hysterical aesthetic complexity. I saw poetry worksheets from the University of Iowa this year and what I saw was a widespread terror of not being smart, and a compensating effort to intimidate the reader.

Tony Hoagland, *Fence,* Fall 2000-Winter 2001

It's more difficult to read than Dante in the original—even if you don't know Italian!

Tom Phillips, on Dorothy L. Sayers's translation of Dante, BBC Radio 3, November 1993

Some modern poetry has become so "difficult" that it is incomprehensible to many intelligent, well-read people who are quite capable of understanding sophisticated works of fiction, philosophy and science.

Peter Reading, *The Sunday Times,* 8 November 1992

Reading the most respected modern poetry, you are immediately confronted by problems of comprehension which it takes another book to resolve.

Hugo Williams, *The Guardian,* 25 February 2006

What It All Means

Meaning in metrical poetry is everything so long as it both confirms and (sometimes) deliberately conflicts with the pulse beat that gives it life.
> ANNE STEVENSON, *Contemporary Women's Poetry*, 2000

"What does this line mean?" is the most intelligent question you can ask of a poem.
> CRAIG RAINE, cited in *The Guardian*, 23 August 2003

A poem becomes alive at just that point when it escapes what it was "meant" to be.
> BRUCE MURPHY, *Poetry*, December 1995

If poems had meanings they would not need to be poems.
> ADAM PHILLIPS, *London Review of Books*, 18 June 1998

Poetry is to a large degree sound. The sound pattern emerges first, then the words, then the meaning, in that order.
> NUALA NÍ DHOMHNAILL, *Fortnight*, September 2004

Poetic language... can be defined first as a language in which the sound of the words is raised to an importance equal to that of their meaning, and also equal to the importance of grammar and syntax.
> KENNETH KOCH, *Making Your Own Days*, 1998

The folly of the rage for meaning is to treat a poem like a locked box to be broken into for its contents, then thrown away.
> THEODORE WEISS, *The American Poetry Review*, May–June 1995

What makes poetry reach beyond prose is its joyful recognition that there is more to words than meaning alone.

> FRANCIS R. JONES, *Comparative Criticism,*
> no. 16, 1994

I asked John Ashbery once in a mutual interview, "Is there a hidden meaning in any of your poems?" and he said, "No, I wouldn't put one out there because the reader might find it."

> KENNETH KOCH, cited in *Poets & Writers,*
> September–October 2002

Too many poems are all meaning and no reserve.

> MEDBH
> MCGUCKIAN,
> *Irish Literary*
> *Supplement,*
> Fall 1990

A writer is not interested in explaining reality; he's interested in capturing it.

> BRENDAN KENNELLY, RTÉ Radio 1, February 1997

Reading a poem is like taking a boat ride. The words are what you feel as you ride across the water, and when you look at the wake behind you, that's the meaning of the poem.

> MAXWELL CORYDON WHEAT JR., *The New York Times,* 24 June 2007

POETRY IN EMOTION

A poem calls forth emotion in its recipient as air calls forth breathing, or a crossroads creates a town. Suddenly there's something that wasn't there before.

ÁGNES NEMES NAGY, *A Hungarian Perspective,* 1998

Poetry... is a hotline to the emotions.

ANDREW MOTION, *The Times*

Sometimes poetry is emotion recollected in a highly emotional state.

WENDY COPE, *Serious Concerns,* 1992

Post-modernism has been a rocky road for poets. It is hard to mix emotion and sincerity with irony and distance.

STEPHEN DOBYNS, *The New York Times,* 21 August 1994

Good poems resolve emotions; bad ones provoke them.

PETER ROBINSON, *Untitled Deeds,* 2004

There's too much lukewarm irony, too much sophisticated indulgence. The tragic dimension disappears in this intellectual environment. That's why ardor is to be defended.

ADAM ZAGAJEWSKI, *Poets & Writers* online, August 2004

Somehow in writing about extreme emotional states your craft develops; you've got to play your technique against something extremely important.

DOUGLAS DUNN, *The Independent,* 8 August 1992

The poet is a specialist in emotions... One of the poet's duties is to obtain the rights of a citizen for as many of the nameless emotions as she or he can.

ÁGNES NEMES NAGY, *A Hungarian Perspective*, 1998

For the poetry reader... there are certain emotions you are allowed to feel—sadness, love—but this is such a miserable choice of all the emotions one feels. One feels anger, boredom, chilliness—quite strong emotions, but they don't get much of a run in poetry, and I think they should.

CRAIG RAINE, *The English Review*

One wonders how it is that English poets ever manage to make great poetry out of a language that can sound as emotionally shy as ours.

MICHAEL GLOVER, *Financial Times*, 7 November 1992

English... is a language easily embarrassed.

KATHLEEN JAMIE, *Modern Poetry in Translation*, 3rd ser., no. 3, 2005

Embarrassment at being human may be a deeper provocation to artistic production than we usually think.

KAY RYAN, *The Yale Review*, April 2004

Lyric poetry neither stands nor falls on its themes; it stands or falls on the accuracy of language with which it reports the author's emotional responses to the life around him.

HELEN VENDLER, *Seamus Heaney*, 1998

Intimate revelations may be a kind of literary credit card today, but they don't help us out of emotional overdraft, they mostly recycle the same emotions over and over.

ADRIENNE RICH, *The Best American Poetry 1996*

✿

We are driven to write by fire and then must distance ourselves to a cool dispassion in order to make those flames burn for anyone else.

MARK DOTY,
Poetry Foundation
online, 2006

Poetry... is a series of intense moments—its power is not in narrative. I'm not dealing with facts, I'm dealing with emotion.

CAROL ANN DUFFY, *The Times*,
3 September 2005

People find poetry difficult because they're looking for hidden ideas in it but the real purpose of a poem is emotional resonance. If poetry wasn't fundamentally emotion then it wouldn't need to be written in rhythm and with imagery. It's in the wrong form if you're writing basically about ideas.

ROBERT GRAY, *The Age*, 25 August 2002

Certainly one can make good poems without feeling much or discovering anything new. You can produce fine poems without believing anything, but it corrodes the spirit and eventually rots the seed corn of the heart. Writing becomes manufacturing instead of giving birth.

LINDA GREGG, *American Poet*, Spring 2001

All good poetry enacts an interplay between thought and feeling, challenging the intellect at the same time as it draws on emotion.

NEIL ASTLEY, *Staying Alive*, 2002

While poetry can accommodate abstraction to some degree, a poem fails when thought masters feeling.

DANIELLE CHAPMAN, *Poetry*, January 2005

When contemporary poets are praised for their objectivity, all too often this means that they have excluded emotion from their work.

JOAN ALESHIRE, *After Confession*, 2001

It is the job of the poet to make the reader cry.

MICHAEL S. HARPER, *The Language of Life,* 1995

Contemporary poets no longer cry, they simply endure in a chilly, elegant despair, interrupted from time to time by an outburst of morose laughter.

ADAM ZAGAJEWSKI, *A Defense of Ardor,* 2004

Nostalgia is a tricky matter in poetry, in life. If it does not have an almost visionary intensity, the feeling can seem too easy.

ROBERT HASS, *The Washington Post,* 5 October 1997

It's the cancer of poetry, sentimentality. It's being in love with your own sensitivity as opposed to actually feeling anything.

DON PATERSON, *Verse* 20, nos. 2 & 3, 2004

The poem that refuses to risk sentimentality, that refuses to risk making a statement, is probably a poem that is going to feel lukewarm. So I'm in favor of work that if it fails, fails on the side of boldness, passion, intensity.

MARK DOTY, *The Charlotte Observer,* 14 March 2003

The problem with sentimentality is that if it is not risked then the poem can entirely lose emotional register.

CAITRÍONA O'REILLY, *Poetry Review,* Autumn 2004

WORD COUNT

Most poetry is shorter and goes further than prose because it can dispense with "That's the reason why," and "And I suppose I ought to say."

PETER FORBES, *The Guardian*, 27 October 1992

How does a reader deal with 120 pages of poetry written over a two- to three-year period? When I read Amy Clampitt or Derek Walcott in large doses, I hear Elias Canetti whispering "One should fear words more." It is as if they wanted language to take the place of the world.

MARK RUDMAN, *The New York Times*

Why, in the 21st century, would anyone tell a long story in verse? Not only are you likely to get more readers (and money) if you turn your material into a novel or screenplay, but even in the narrow world of poetry the highest praise usually goes to work that is lyrical, personal and short.

CHRISTIAN WIMAN, *The New York Times*, 4 September 2005

If any kind of poetry merits that standard accolade of blurb-writers, "risk-taking," it must be book-length narrative verse—the risk being the number of eggs in a single basket, the size of the basket, and the knowledge that almost everyone these days lives in fear of cholesterol.

THOMAS M. DISCH, *Parnassus* 17, no. 2

Russell Edson once said to me that the problem with most poems is that there is too much language chasing too little of an idea. Every poet, especially every prose poet, should have that taped over his desk.

PETER JOHNSON, *Another Chicago Magazine*, 2004

Short poems are not fragments but miniatures, *multum in parvo,* lyrical DNA. Like short letters, they can be harder to write.

EDNA LONGLEY, *Princeton University Library Chronicle,* Spring 1998

Short poem: be brief and tell us everything.

CHARLES SIMIC, *London Review of Books,* 10 May 2007

The tiny oeuvre is a courtesy to the reader and a bribe to posterity.

DON PATERSON, *Oxford Poetry,* Summer 2001

Pope and Yeats wrote too much, keeping the bed aired for when the muse would deign to visit. They were too promiscuous.

A. ALVAREZ, *The Sunday Telegraph,* 16 January 2005

Some of our finest poets are unreliable judges of their own work, publishing too much of what they write (perhaps some publish more than they write).

STEVEN CRAMER, *Poetry,* July 2003

Most poets write and publish far too much. They forget the agricultural good sense of the fallow period. The Muse despises whingers who bellyache about "writer's block" and related ailments.

MICHAEL LONGLEY, *Colby Quarterly,* September 2003

A poet who publishes many books of poems— seven, nine, eleven books—seems to say *I am special in fresh ways, cornucopically, every year, every month. Deeply revealing apprehensions of the*

The more one reads poetry, the less tolerant one becomes of any sort of verbosity, be that in political or philosophical discourse, be that in history, social studies or the art of fiction.

JOSEPH BRODSKY, *The New York Times,* 12 June 1988

❧

*great truths of life come to me so often—much more often than they came to
Hopkins or Eliot—that I astound myself.*

MARK HALLIDAY, *The Georgia Review*, Summer 2003

Two or three lyrics can make a poet immortal, but to build a readership
during your lifetime—especially these days, when the media-saturated
collective memory is so short—it is wise to be steadily productive.

JOHN KERRIGAN, *Metre*, no. 9, 2001

He had for the past two decades lived an ascetic existence in Japan, with
little interest in winning greater reward for his own poems. Of these,
some 80,000 remain unpublished. Until he slipped into a coma on
December 31 last year, he was still writing the equivalent of a small book
of poetry every day.

OBITUARY OF CID CORMAN, *The Times*, 29 March 2004

I keep saying next time I'm going to write a poem that is only nine lines
long, but I think I have an *all you can eat* personality and it doesn't work
out.

SYDNEY LEA, *The Writer's Chronicle*, September 2004

Poetry is the art of saying in two words what is better said in ten.

BRIAN SEWELL, *Evening Standard*, March 1994

Life is short and so, thank God, are most poems.

CHRISTINA PATTERSON, *The Independent*, 5 December 2003

ORIGINAL ANGLES

Poetry: words which can only be used once.

MIGUEL CASADO, *Agenda,* Summer 1997

The task of the artist at any time is uncompromisingly simple—to discover what has not yet been done and to do it. To do it, moreover, in a way which not only breaks with, but is also a logical extension of, the past.

CRAIG RAINE, *The Guardian*

"Make it new"—Pound's old command—is still as talismanic as ever. Yet the trouble with superficial ways of making new is that they leave out the old.

HELEN VENDLER, *The New Republic,* 28 February 2005

If poetry grows out of the dialectic between innovation and emulation, our literature has always prized originality over continuity. Originality is, after all, America's one strict tradition.

DANA GIOIA, *Can Poetry Matter?,* 1992

Most writing has only a tiny quotient of "originality." We are mostly writing out of what we have read. That's not a bad thing. That's an acknowledgement of filiation.

ROSANNA WARREN, *Full Circle,* 2002-03

If a poem, piano concerto, or painting does not feel alive and pressing, demanding from us the attention of fresh discovery, it is not, at that moment, fully art—only something travelling under art's name which we happen to share a room with... Art lives in what it awakens in us.

JANE HIRSHFIELD, Napa Valley Writers' Conference, July 2005

Originality is a new amalgam of influences.

MARVIN BELL,
Poet's Market, 2004

The excitement of poetry for me is doing something that hasn't been done before by someone else or even by yourself—especially by yourself.

LOUIS SIMPSON, *Poetry Ireland Review,*
Summer 1990

Poetry resides in the unrepeatable perfection of its original articulation.

SEAMUS HEANEY, *The Sunday Tribune,* 7 April 1996

To put it crassly, in order to make his work sell, as well as to avoid cliché, our poet continually has to get where nobody has ever been before—mentally, psychologically or lexically.

JOSEPH BRODSKY, *Times Literary Supplement,* 26 October 1990

Alienation is... the necessary consequence of originality, and originality is the only prize worth striving for.

ADAM CZERNIAWSKI, *Poetry Review*

Every distinctive poet notices something new about the language.

ADAM PHILLIPS, *London Review of Books,* 4 March 2004

Every poem requires a new language.

PAUL HOOVER, *The American Poetry Review,* March-April 2005

Poetry is a battle against the prompter, which can only give us someone else's lines to say. The poet has to speak his own lines, be in his own play.

CRAIG RAINE, *Gown,* Spring-Summer 1990

A good poem has the inevitability of truth, and it's hard to conceive of the world having ever been without it—which is why we so often suspect our best lines of having already been written by someone else.

DON PATERSON, *Poetry Review,* Summer 2007

My greatest fear is that I'll discover—or, worse, that someone else will point out to me—that I've stolen another man's words, thinking them my own.

THOM GUNN, cited in *The Economist*, 5 April 1997

Poets are, and always have been, plunderers of other poets: the true patron of poetry is Hermes, the god of thieves.

J.G. NICHOLS, *The Reader*, Autumn 2004

"Inimitable" is one of those off-the-shelf, unhelpful epithets that get loosely tossed in the direction of mastery, but in poetry the test of true originality is to be eminently imitable—it's doing it first and registering the trademark that counts.

PETER FORBES, *The Independent*

It's a theory of mine that the more you admire a person, the less likely you are to imitate them, mainly because you know the tricks of their trade so well that blood rushes into your cheeks when you find yourself passing them off as your own.

SIMON ARMITAGE, *New Statesman*, 25 April 1997

Critics will often try to find your poems like someone else's because it makes their job easier—that's lazy and frequently false. They make similarity sound like plagiarism.

MICK IMLAH, *Oxford Poetry*, Autumn 1983

Masterworks, those rare pieces of writing held in practically universal regard, regularly develop a thin coating of dust derived from precisely that regard: considered, praised and appraised, they seem gradually obscured by all that handling.

MARK DOTY, *The Guardian*, 11 November 2006

Poems are mutts. There is a lot of cross-breeding.

BILLY COLLINS, *The Exeter News*, 6 May 2005

⁕

Most poets learn and perfect one type of poem and then fill book upon book with its clones.

Brian Henry,
PN Review,
July-August 1998

☙

Time, familiarity and imitation are the implacable enemies of artistic originality. Who now is jolted by the surprise in Haydn's "Surprise" symphony?... Perhaps nowhere in English literature have time, familiarity and imitation played greater havoc with original work than with Wordsworth's.

Norman Fruman, *Times Literary Supplement,*
27 August 1993

One is always surprised by the drumstroke in Haydn's "Surprise" symphony, no matter how many times one has heard it, and one is always interested by a poem that genuinely contains a mystery.

T.J.G. Harris, *PN Review,*
September–October 1993

Unless a poem surprises you a little bit, some little gate is opened by the words within themselves, then the poem could be perfectly okay, but it won't hold you forever.

Seamus Heaney, *The Sunday Times,* 8 October 1995

Who hasn't felt that subtle, sometimes violent shift in estimation upon seeing a poet repeat himself? If the greatest sin is being boring, then surely a close second is dulling some past excitement by revisiting it again and again.

Peter Richards, *Verse* 17, nos. 2 & 3, 2001

A poem should take you somewhere different. Of all people, you might say, a poet should be the one least likely to step into the same river twice.

Seamus Heaney, BBC 1, March 1998

Trying to write another good poem by recreating the circumstances and repeating the techniques that allowed you to write the last one is as daft as making love in the same situation, at the same time and in the same position, in the hope that you might recreate a child with the same physique and personality as the last.

DON PATERSON, *How Poets Work*, 1996

A poet must strive to avoid repetition... It is easy to become bored by the near-formulaic approach which is so seductive, when a poet has settled into his own voice as into a warm pair of slippers.

PETER JAY, *The Spaces of Hope*, 1998

We all know poets who won't surprise us with a different sound because they've become habituated to a manner and the critical attention the manner attracts. If there's restlessness in such work, it's only wind rippling a pond—it doesn't kick up bottom sand.

W.S. DI PIERO, *Poetry*, January 2006

Having a "style" for so many artists is like having a chronic condition whose symptoms crop up predictably, season to season, year to year.

DAN CHIASSON, *Ploughshares*, Winter 2006-07

In cooking, to follow the advice of an expert closely—so closely that one reproduces their work exactly—may be a triumph. In poetry, it is a disaster. Successful poets produce their own recipes, and only use them once.

JOHN REDMOND, *How to Write a Poem*, 2006

All poets, if they are any good, tend to stand apart from their literary age. They either linger in the past, advance into some imaginary future, or live in some version of the present that is altogether their own.

CHARLES SIMIC, *The New York Review of Books*, 7 April 2005

THE POETRY CURE

Writing poetry gives you energy. There is a great restoration of yourself spiritually after writing a poem.

ELAINE FEINSTEIN, BBC Radio 4, October 2001

People read poetry to bathe their forehead in the well of reality. To refresh themselves.

PAUL DURCAN, *The Sunday Independent*, 3 December 1995

Poetry itself—a way of preventing something or other you can't defeat from getting the better of you.

D.J. ENRIGHT, *Play Resumed*, 1999

The moment something real happens to you, whether good or bad, you don't *need* poetry. Either you don't need it or it doesn't help you... Poetry starts only after the climax. It's one of the first signs that you have *overcome* something.

YEHUDA AMICHAI, *The American Poetry Review*, November–December 1987

We are lonely for where we are. Poetry helps us cope.

TIM LILBURN, *Poetry International*, nos. 7 & 8, 2003–04

I don't need yoga, valium, or any other relaxant. When necessary I recite the first few verses [of Gray's "Elegy"] and I feel the better for it.

MIKE MURPHY, *Lifelines II*, 1988

As the aeroplane takes off, or the dentist drills into my tooth, I close my eyes and silently recite something by Shakespeare, Housman or Emily Dickinson. It doesn't banish fear but it helps prevent total panic.

WENDY COPE, *Poem for the Day*, 1994

Writing poetry is the best way I know of untying the knot of obsession. It's cheaper than therapy and better for you than getting drunk.

GWYNETH LEWIS, Poetry Book Society *Bulletin,* Summer 2003

For me the private act of writing poetry is songwriting, confessional, diary-keeping, speculation, problem-solving, storytelling, therapy, anger management, craftsmanship, relaxation, concentration and spiritual adventure all in one inexpensive package.

STEPHEN FRY, *The Ode Less Travelled,* 2005

Poetry is often something unexpected in the therapeutic context. It's newer and more conspicuous than a chat with the social worker. It's more permanent than a conversation with another user at the drop-in. It's more public than a diary and more attractive than a feedback form.

FIONA SAMPSON, *The Healing Word,* 1999

Whenever we shape our disorder into poetry or song, we've taken control of what had the power to control or overwhelm us.

GREGORY ORR, *The Writer's Chronicle,* October–November 2006

One of the hardest things about being unwell is feeling disempowered and out of control. Writing poetry can make you feel in charge again.

JULIA DARLING, *The Poetry Cure,* 2005

Poetry can work as the highest form of talking cure, but you have to tell the absolute truth, so far as you can dredge that up. I'd always disapproved of the idea of poetry as therapy; but get sick enough and you'll shed any such

Poetry... can be a direct transfusion of hope or calm or compassion— a sort of I.V. for the soul.

RITA DOVE,
The Washington Post,
30 January 2000

Poetic language is different from ordinary language, different to the point of strangeness, even, yet poetic language is absolutely essential to our mental and emotional well-being. How else are you going to get your Vitamin P?

DAVID KIRBY, *What Is a Book?*, 2002

᷎

snobberies! I said to the Black Dog: "You bastard, you make me cry, I'll make you sing."

LES MURRAY, *The Paris Review,* Spring 2005

Next time you feel a bit under the weather, give the pills and potions a miss and try reading—or writing—some poetry. That is the advice of doctors who are taking part in a Bristol University study which shows that sometimes a few lines of Wordsworth, Keats or Browning can overcome a patient's need for minor tranquillisers.

PAUL STOKES, *The Daily Telegraph,* 15 February 1994

If you are not reading and writing poetry, you are suffering from linguistic malnutrition.

PHILIP HOWARD, *The Times*

So many people claim poetry solaces them that it must be true. But so do sex, wine, wasabi peas, Italian *Vogue,* shopping, and Pilates.

DAISY FRIED, *Poetry,* March 2005

The point of poetry is to be acutely *dis*comforting, to prod and provoke, to poke us in the eye, to punch us in the nose, to knock us off our feet, to take our breath away.

PAUL MULDOON, *Princeton University Library Chronicle,* Spring 1998

I sort of believe in pushing people around a little with my poems. I want my audience a little scared or alarmed or shocked, it's a way of getting them to pay attention. It's my way of poking a finger in someone's chest.

TONY HOAGLAND, *Winston-Salem Journal,* 12 April 2007

Writing a good poem about how bad you feel doesn't protect you from that feeling or release you from it.

ALAN SHAPIRO, *The Virginia Quarterly Review,* Fall 2006

However depressing the content of the poem, if you've managed to write one, and get it published, then you are going to be in a good mood (at the very least about that one important thing). So it is that a last line, expressing the deepest spirit of depression, may be written in a mood of complete professional elation.

JAMES FENTON, *The Guardian,* 6 January 2007

Poetry is not written out of despair, which in its pure form is absolutely mute. The poetry that *seems* to come out of despair—Larkin's "Aubade," for instance, or late Plath—is actually a means of staving it off.

CHRISTIAN WIMAN, *Poetry Review,* Summer 2007

To bind up a problem in a particular form of memorable words is not to solve it, but it does confer a certain power: the primitive, magical power of naming, which is at the root of all poetry.

PETER FORBES, *We Have Come Through,* 2003

For the serious poet, art is anything but therapeutic. Sylvia Plath's poetry did not alleviate her tragic illness... Dylan Thomas's fluid outpourings of words did not cure his alcoholism.

LEAH FRITZ, *Acumen,* May 1995

Poets continue to write of their experiences of mental illness. If poetry is some kind of wonder-drug, it sure ain't working for them.

CHRISTINA PATTERSON, *The Independent,* 27 January 2006

Poetry has always attracted more than its fair share of the seriously unhinged.

CHRISTINA PATTERSON, *The Independent,* 10 May 2003

⌣

Maybe more poets have been driven mad by trying to get a line right, than the mad have been driven well by writing a good line.

JOHN HERSCHEL,
Rattle, Summer 2006

⌣̇

A lot of the writing that's going on at present, far from being therapeutic, is an essay towards a collective nervous breakdown.

CIARAN O'DRISCOLL, *Cyphers*, Winter 1993

Is it part of the poetic vocation to pick and worry at one's psychic scars until they turn septic and poison you?

JOHN WALSH, *The Independent*, 19 January 1998

Writing a poem can help you find what needs to be healed... But there's always a risk that you will end up picking at old sores.

KEVIN HART, *Verse* 20, nos. 2 & 3, 2004

Ko Un hugged all the germs of Korean society with his entire body, and contracted its diseases.

KIM SEUNG-HEE, *The Korea Times*, 14 October 2005

The dog needs its fleas, the poet his miseries.

DAVID BURNETT, *Quoins for the Chase*, 2003

Successful poets are magnets for unhinged people with swivelly eyes and large, unpublished manuscripts.

MARK HADDON, *The Sunday Telegraph*, 2 October 2005

I think I am too normal to be a "real" poet.

MIROSLAV HOLUB, *Poetry Review*, Summer 1994

Among poets there are probably higher than average rates of clutch burnout, job turnover, rooting about, sleep apnea, noncompliance, nervous leg syndrome, depression, litigation, black clothing, and so forth, but this is where we live.

C.D. WRIGHT, *Cooling Time*, 2005

Twenty-seven poets had nervous breakdowns, fifteen committed suicide, and fifteen were/are diagnosed as alcoholic. Nineteen served time in jail, fourteen died in battle, three were murdered, one executed. Zany professions include lumberjack, tax inspector, furniture remover, carpet salesman, and policeman.

IAN HAMILTON, on poets in *The Oxford Companion to Twentieth-Century Poetry,* 1994

Of an average sample of 200 nursery rhymes, at least half contain incidents we might find unsavory, to say the least, including 15 maimings, nine abandoned children, eight murders, seven severed limbs, one case of the *desire* to have a limb severed, and one rather perplexing "death by shriveling."

JULIA WALLACE, *The Yale Review of Books,* Winter 2005

Robert Louis Stevenson finished *A Child's Garden of Verses* writing with his left hand, with his right arm bound to his body against haemorrhages, lying in a darkened room to save his eyesight.

CAROLINE MOORE, *The Sunday Telegraph,* 23 January 2005

Quite apart from measles, mumps, chickenpox and scarlet fever, the family was abnormally prone to fevers, ingrown toenails, sprained or broken bones, sinister rashes, infected jaws, bronchial troubles, septicemia and throat bugs.

HILARY SPURLING, on W.B. Yeats's family,
The New York Times, 20 October 2002

Poetry is not a painkiller; it is a cure. Where there is no cure, poetry helps us to live with the problem.

JEANETTE WINTERSON,
The Times,
19 November 2005

Poetry can be a kind of beautiful tyranny that eats your life away. It's more predatory than it's usually given credit for. It forces you to look at your obsessive dreams and voices, to listen to them, to write them down as they bid you.

BRENDAN KENNELLY, *Begin,* 1999

Poetry can be therapeutic for its readers, by articulating for them what they cannot say for themselves, and enabling them to understand their experience as belonging to a larger pattern. But not for the poet... You might say that poetry is diagnostic, rather than therapeutic.

ALICIA OSTRIKER,
The American Voice,
no. 45, 1998

༜

Poetry is dangerous because it probes deeply into the psyche. It's an enchantment that puts you in touch with darker, more unconscious and irrational feelings, and that can be shocking... Poetry gets under the skin: it makes it harder to avoid some unpleasant truths about ourselves. It sinks anchor at sea bottom.

EDWARD HIRSCH, *Five Points* 4, no. 2

The systematic interrogation of the unconscious, which is part of the serious practice of poetry, is the worst form of self-help you could possibly devise. There is a reason why poets enjoy the highest statistical incidence of mental illness among all the professions... Then again I think maybe 5 percent of folk who write poetry really want to write poetry; the other 95 [percent] are quite safe, and just want to be a poet.

DON PATERSON, T.S. Eliot Lecture, October 2004

Would you let a poet take your pulse or read your X-ray? Probably not, if you hoped to recover. While I'm still breathing I wouldn't even let one push my bath chair.

ROSEMARY GORING, *The Herald*, 20 June 2005

If I break my leg, I'll go to a doctor. If I break my heart or if the world breaks my spirit, I'll go to a poet.

JEANETTE WINTERSON, *The Times*, 13 January 2007

Writing a poem is a bit like being sick. It is quick and efficient and you always feel better afterwards.

SARAH-JANE LOVETT, *The Sunday Times,* 2 October 1994

Poetry wants to be contagious, to be a contagion. Its syntax wants to pass something on to an other in the way that you can, for example, pass laughter on. It's different from being persuasive and making an argument. That's why great poems have so few arguments in them.

JORIE GRAHAM, *The Paris Review,* Spring 2003

It's like knowing you're going to get a cold or feeling a headache coming on, except that it's a good deal more pleasurable.

ANDREW MOTION, on writing poetry, BBC Radio 4, March 1998

Poet Laureate Andrew Motion has admitted to using chemical stimulation to help him write poetry—a daily cup of cold remedy Lemsip... A spokesman for Lemsip manufacturer Reckitt Benckiser reassured users: "It is fair to say that it doesn't cause poetry in most people."

UNATTRIBUTED, BBC News online, 15 October 2002

POETRY POLITICS

Poetry in my view is a defense of the individual against all the forces arrayed against him.

CHARLES SIMIC, *The Paris Review,* Spring 2005

By means of such a funny thing as writing poetry, I am trying to defend the matters that are significant to me... I know that I am unable to save my nation or the occupants in my block of flats, but I must act in such a way as though it were possible. Just try. There is no government on earth which could deprive me of that struggle.

ZBIGNIEW HERBERT, *PN Review,* no. 26, 1982

[P]oetry below a certain level of awareness is not good poetry and cannot save people... So it's a question of awareness that shapes our poetry, even if poetry doesn't deal with direct political topics or historical topics.

CZESLAW MILOSZ, *Poets & Writers,* November–December 1993

Historically, dissident political poetry does not age well. On the contrary, some pieces we may describe as sycophantic have a better chance of surviving. One could list examples almost to infinity, such as Virgil's famous Eclogue IV.

ALEXEI TSVETKOV, *Fulcrum,* no. 4, 2005

A society and a country stand to gain so much from having the most inclusive poem they can.

EAVAN BOLAND, RTÉ Radio 1, 18 August 2003

Our tendency to judge poets and poems by what side of a controversy they take, or by their efficacy in moving an audience towards one or another side, makes the most depressing feature of the discussion of poetry now, especially inside the academy.

STEPHEN BURT, *Contemporary Poetry Review*, August 2003

There is a political poetry only in a very simplistic sense... protest poetry in which everyone protests about the same thing, so that there is safety in numbers.

ANTHONY CRONIN, *Journal of Irish Studies* 21, 2006

There's no point in writing poems on political subjects simply to go on record on the right side. Poetry had better be interesting always, it had better be fresh always, and so the sort of poem that simply says "don't drop the bomb" is of no interest to me.

RICHARD WILBUR, *The American Poetry Review*, May-June 1991

What we want from poetry is to be moved, to be moved from where we now stand. We don't just want to have our ideas or emotions confirmed. Or if we do, then we turn to lesser poems, poems which are happy to tell you killing children is bad, chopping down the rainforest is bad, dying is sad.

JAMES TATE, *The American Poetry Review*, September-October 1996

I would never tell students "Don't write about a political issue, or a disaster in the world, or evil." But I would say let's be aware that everyone in this room is against torture, everyone in this room is against the molestation of children—so to write expressing that moral view is going to be very boring.

MARK HALLIDAY, *The Sycamore Review*, Spring 2004

Poetry is a cure for ideology.

YVES BONNEFOY,
BBC Radio 3,
September 1999

∴

Irony and satire are such a good antidote to oppression because oppression needs to be earnest (or at least look earnest) in order to be feared by those it seeks to cow.

MATTHEW ROHRER,
*National Poetry
Almanac,*
2 January 2005

A great danger we encounter, as poets away from direct participation in the affairs of the community, is that we take ourselves easily as the guardians of moral purity. I can always proclaim: Politics is dirty and the government is corrupt, but I as a poet am clean; my aims are beyond reproach. This... leads to a sort of vanity in the poet, an arrogance.

JAYANTA MAHAPATRA, *Contemporary Poetry Review,* April 2004

You can't write a political poem if it's just about politics.

NICK LAIRD, *The Irish Times,* 16 April 2005

If you're going to write a poem of political protest... you have to be sure that it's *your* subject, that it's *your* anger, not somebody else's anger.

SEAMUS HEANEY, *Between the Lines,* 2000

Politicians deal with issues; poets deal with epiphanies.

JOHN AGARD, BBC 2, October 1993

I am a poetician, not a politician.

YEVGENY YEVTUSHENKO, cited in *Financial Times,* 13 March 1993

Not many of our politicians are poets, though all of our poets are politicians.

STAN GEBLER DAVIES, *The Independent,* 26 June 1993

There is an element of almost complete freedom and frankness that can be experienced in a poem—not always the case in the political world.

JIMMY CARTER, *Interview,* December 1994

I like the company of poets. They take you away from the boring realities of life, if you like, and open up all sorts of new exciting things, sometimes quite startling.

CHARLES J. HAUGHEY, Irish prime minister, *The Irish Times*, 31 December 1990

He admired action-man/woman politics. Mrs. Thatcher was a big enthusiasm... He liked Mrs T's belligerent business sense, her militarism, patriotism and all-round impatience with slackers. These were traits he shared and was proud of.

HORATIO MORPURGO, on Ted Hughes, *Areté*, Autumn 2001

Politics is a local, transient business in which a week is a long time, whereas poetry, or at least the better sort, is universal and enduring.

TERRY EAGLETON, *The Irish Times*, 2 August 1996

The poet who elects to write about political reality is no different from the poet who chooses love, landscape or a painting by Cézanne as the subject for a poem. The choice of a political subject entails no necessary or complete commitment to an ideology.

TOM PAULIN, *The Faber Book of Political Verse*, 1986

I consider the division often made between politics and poetry to be thin and contrived... Separating them is a luxury. Literature is about life.

JACK MAPANJE,
The Scotsman,
5 August 2003

༚

The term "political poetry" posits a sort of detention area in which a certain sort of poetry is carefully segregated from other sorts of poetry. The implication is that the political nature of life, the fact that human beings live in societies and that political decisions are being made daily in those societies, in war and in peace, is not part of poetry per se.

BARON WORMSER, *The Manhattan Review*

In the area of politics, there are two things in which the poet is an expert. Human suffering and human dialogue.

STANISLAW BARANCZAK, *Partisan Review,* Fall 1992

༄

I was brought up in a world where, when top writers took supposed apolitical and universal themes and said they dealt with "Man," that category didn't include black men or women.

JAMES BERRY, *Oxford Poetry,* Autumn 1984

The great majority of poets published in literary magazines are white, yet relationships of race and power exist in their poems most often as silence or muffled subtext if not as cliché.

ADRIENNE RICH, *The Best American Poetry 1996*

Poetry can only generalise through the particular. It affirms and extends community by being true to what is individual and peculiar. Its politics, you might say, are ideally democratic.

DAVID CONSTANTINE, *Strong Words,* 2000

The language generated by poetry is the last hope for political possibility, because it's a language of affirmation, understanding, accommodation.

EAMON GRENNAN, Lannan Literary Videos, 1997

A bad poem is bad enough, but a bad poem about something as big as the [Ulster] Troubles is an impertinence and an offence.

MICHAEL LONGLEY, BBC Radio 3

I'm not a political writer and I don't see literature as a way of solving political problems.

SEAMUS HEANEY, *The Irish Times*

I'm not interested in party politics. I'm very much against that in a writer—the world is never as simple as party politics would suggest.

PAUL MULDOON, *The Literary Review,* June 1986

Joseph Stalin was a poet... Fluffy verses of the "Hello, Sun! Hello, Sky" variety that would shame even Fotherington-Thomas poured from his pen when he was 16 and 17, before he embarked on his better known careers of revolution and genocide.

ANDREW ROBERTS, *The Daily Telegraph,* 9 October 2004

I heard that Saddam Hussein, in solitary confinement, was spending his time writing poetry, reading the Koran, eating cookies and muffins, and taking care of some bushes and shrubs.

ELIOT WEINBERGER, *London Review of Books,* 3 February 2005

People in the West don't know me. Their image of me is distorted. They don't know that I am a poet, for example.

MU'AMMAR AL-GADHAFI, Libyan president, *Newsweek,* 4 April 1994

There is a peculiar link between frustrated poetic ambition and tyranny: Hitler, Goebbels, Stalin, Castro, Mao Zedong and Ho Chi Minh all wrote poetry. Radovan Karadzic, fugitive former leader of the Bosnian Serbs, once won the Russian Writers' Union Mikhail Sholokhov Prize for his poems. On the whole, you do not want a poet at the helm.

BEN MACINTYRE, *The Times,* 4 June 2005

Poetry has in it, in its rhythms, its variousness, its contradictoriness, indeed in its beauty, an intrinsic power of revolt, which the poet forfeits if he reduces the poem to the expression of a cause.

DAVID CONSTANTINE, *Poetry London,* Spring 2007

⌣⋮

It's all too typical for contemporary poets to write as if they assume that the social importance of what they advocate—justice for women, the environment, the poor, etc.—gives importance to the self-identity of the poet, as if suffering can be "borrowed."

JUDITH KITCHEN,
The Georgia Review,
Winter 1995

Violent movements which contain poets are more dangerous than ones which don't.

CONOR CRUISE O'BRIEN, RTÉ I

Shelley would have dearly loved to sway the hearts of the leaders of the Britain of his day; but then, as now, the politician's heart contained only a picture of himself, the gunman's that of his next victim.

MICHAEL HARTNETT, *Poetry Ireland Review,*
Winter 1993-94

By going to floodlit places, like the Berlin Wall, a poet may share in the floodlighting, but by staying at home and illuminating obscure lives he can floodlight the dim suburbs, or the wilderness.

ANNA ADAMS, *Acumen*

Language is not neutral. It's very much a political tool. It's charged with prejudices. So a poet who says "I'm not in politics" is not being realistic.

CHINUA ACHEBE, *The Sunday Tribune*

It is the duty of all poets, everywhere and at all times, to be dissident members of the permanent opposition.

THEO DORGAN, *Poetry Ireland Review,* Winter 1993-94

At all its great moments in modern history, poetry reveals that it is less the reflection, the mirror-image, of a time, than a rebellion against it. Poetry is the consequence of its own lack.

YVES BONNEFOY, *Modern Poetry in Translation,* Summer 1992

The difference between a politician and a poet is that a politician uses words to improve his career whereas a poet uses his career to improve his words.

RICHARD MURPHY, cited in *Poetry Ireland Review,* December 2006

The difference between political poetry and propaganda is that political poetry gives the reader the sense that the poet could have argued the opposite case and still been compelling, though perhaps not convincing.

DAVID ORR, *Poetry,* December 2005

You start from the wrong place with political poetry, because you start by knowing too much, and so what you're likely to write is propaganda.

W.S. MERWIN, *The Irish Times,* 20 March 2004

My sense of poems, be they anti-war or pro-diversity, is that the poem's motive is not something I can often know in advance if it's going to be any good. The poem needs to find its own way, it needs to take me along toward where it wants to go.

ROBERT WRIGLEY, *Sou'wester,* Fall 2003

There is no use coming to poets, either in Soviet Russia or Northern Ireland, and expecting or ordering them to deliver a certain product to fit a certain agenda, for although they must feel answerable to the world they inhabit, poets, if they are to do their proper work, must also feel free.

SEAMUS HEANEY, cited in *The Irish Times,* 23 August 1993

A poem or short story or novel is not necessarily impelled by the most apocalyptic events

As far as politics is concerned, the poet's most important work is to fiddle while Rome burns.

ROBERT CRAWFORD, *Times Literary Supplement,* 14 April 1995

available. Sometimes a poem will arise if you just stumble going down the stairs.

DENIS DONOGHUE, RTÉ Radio 1, February 2004

You can spend a lifetime, twenty-five years, in a concentration camp or you can survive a bombardment of Hiroshima and yet not produce a single line, whereas a one-night stand gives birth to an immortal lyric.

JOSEPH BRODSKY, *Poetry Ireland Review,* Winter 1992–93

Often, the best poem about a momentous event may be written long before the event happens.

ROBERT PINSKY, *The Washington Post,* 10 September 2006

It would be foolish for a poet to attach his poems to the impermanence of a cause when what he wishes is that his poems transcend the political and social climate in which they were born. To have written something that history cannot account for or that his own time cannot take credit for is the poet's deepest wish.

MARK STRAND, Rotterdam Poetry Festival, 2001

Poetry is a pre-requisite for political thinking but it's not [a] sufficient form of action. Poetry is not the end of politics. It's the beginning of politics.

CHARLES BERNSTEIN, *Green Integer Review,* January–February 2006

Of course poetry is irrelevant to the "real" world of power and politics, but so is philosophy, painting, music and any other human activity where something genuine can be found.

CHARLES SIMIC, *The Age,* 9 March 2003

Poetry does not court relevance, except to life's permanent conditions.

SEAN O'BRIEN, *The Sunday Times,* 10 August 2003

Making Nothing Happen

Auden's conviction that poetry makes nothing happen was inexact. *Bad* poetry makes nothing happen, largely because bad poets make nothing happen to poetry—they cannot excite the form, so the form can hardly be expected to excite the world.

JAMES WOOD, *The Sunday Correspondent*

Auden's famous assertion that "poetry makes nothing happen" is usually taken to be a statement about the ineffectual nature of the poetic enterprise. This view presupposes that making *something* happen is better than making *nothing* happen. But is this true?

JOHN BREHM, *Good Times,* 11 August 2005

It's almost a great thing that a poem doesn't make things happen—it may prevent things from happening. It's a place where something is finally crystallised which loose in the world might be more dangerous.

LES MURRAY, BBC Radio 4

Poetry is not about making things happen. That's what language does. Poetry is about making language happen.

DONALD REVELL, *The American Poetry Review,* July–August 1996

You cannot earn your living at poetry; it makes nothing happen; the audience is tiny and as often as not composed of fellow-aspirants seeing whether you are up to something they should take into account; you are reviewed among a clutch of your fellows at a length even a crime novelist might resent. The reward is that elusive, extraordinary rightness no other art achieves, the aesthetic equivalent of the hole-in-one.

GREY GOWRIE, *The Daily Telegraph*

If we look at this century, an extremely small part of human experience
has been fixed in language and literature. We may wonder how small a
percentage of what mankind has lived remains in the language.

CZESLAW MILOSZ, *Partisan Review,* Summer 1996

The very multiplicity of definitions about the Function of Poetry
proves, does it not, that most people are suspicious that poetry has no
function?

DANNIE ABSE, *Intermittent Journals,* 1994

Poetry is aimless, not purposeful. The poem is dancing with itself.

BILLY COLLINS, *Fulcrum,* no. 4, 2005

We have had poets addressing the so called socio-political ills since
Nigeria's independence, yet nothing has changed.

OBAKANSE LAKANSE, *Vanguard,* 29 August 2004

Poetry makes nothing happen—would that this were true of Religion.

PETER PORTER, *Afterburner,* 2004

Making Something Happen

Poetry is the only thing that makes anything happen. Everything else is paralysis.

PAUL DURCAN, *Poetry News,* Spring 1999

Poetry is a practical art. It is as good as a knife for cutting through the day's rubbish, and better than a folding umbrella for those sudden bouts of private rain that douse a body out of nowhere.

JEANETTE WINTERSON, *The Times,* 13 January 2007

Sometimes poetry makes things happen. In a large, resonant example, a poem by Osip Mandelstam about Stalin caused the poet's imprisonment in 1934.

ROBERT PINSKY, *The Washington Post,* 29 April 2007

One of the strongest ingredients in the collapse of the Soviet system was the poetry written in Eastern Europe and in Russia.

TED HUGHES, BBC Radio 4, March 1992

When poetry lays its hand on our shoulder we are, to an almost physical degree, touched and moved. The imagination's roads open before us, giving the lie to that brute dictum, "There is no alternative."

ADRIENNE RICH, National Book Awards speech, 15 November 2006

Each person is on Earth to make sense of themselves and for themselves and to bring the inchoateness of this self into an expressible state. These are the essential and redemptive steps of poetry.

SEAMUS HEANEY, *Salon*

Unless we read poetry, we'll never have our hearts broken by language, which is an indispensable preliminary to a civilized life.

ANATOLE BROYARD,
The New York Times

◡:

At present, only some forms of advanced science—particle physics for example—allow a young mind to experience the paradox, ambiguity, irrational thought, associative "leaping" any good poem teaches us to think and feel in. It opens those synapses in the brain. It always has. Once open, such minds can think differently in any field.

JORIE GRAHAM, *American Poet*, Fall 1996

Poetry makes something happen. The eloquence, the brilliant language, the musical sounds turn out to be going somewhere, toward some discovery or action—sometimes even toward the action of tossing the eloquence or images aside, like a raft that has served its purpose.

ROBERT PINSKY, *The Washington Post*,
13 February 2005

Poetry will not teach us how to live well, but it will incite in us the wish to.

DAVID CONSTANTINE, *Poetry Review*

Every poet, in every line, makes two things clear: how to write; how to live.

GLYN MAXWELL, *Reading Douglas Dunn*, 1992

When we think about Goethe—as when we consider any major writer—we are looking for hints on how to live. Keeping the house clean, arranging the kitchen cupboards and balancing the books, all have their real dignity illuminated by Goethe's loving regard.

ASTRIDA ORLE TANTILLO, *Chicago Tribune*, 28 January 2007

Poetry, being about everything, is an education in everything.

COLETTE BRYCE, *Poetry Writers' Yearbook 2007*

One of the things about which poetry can nudge people is matters of ecological consciousness and conscience. Because poetry has traditionally dealt with "Nature" anyway (especially in English), it is well placed to do so.

DENISE LEVERTOV, *Meaning & Memory,* 2001

If a poem, or any other art-work, is successful it is because it makes better (more interesting, more nuanced, more many-sided, more flexible) persons of us. Poems, like experiences, can be good or bad but they cannot be right or wrong.

JOHN REDMOND, *The Reader,* 14 May 2004

Poetry constitutes for a group, for a culture, the fundamental values of the spirit in that group. If you take it into yourself it founds your values for you.

SEAMUS HEANEY, *Reading the Future,* 2000

Sometimes a poem can change people's lives, strengthen and focus people's beliefs. And if people can change, that can change the world.

ADRIAN MITCHELL, *Poetry Review,* Autumn 1997

We are, when we read poetry, during the reading of the poem and lingeringly for some while

A good poem can give us words for what we feel and rescue us from the inarticulate. It can embolden us by giving names to our fears. It can state matters with a lasting clarity so that certain questions can't arise without some line or phrase of it coming to mind. It can subtly change us: a contagious sensibility can dispose us to think or live in one way or another.

RICHARD WILBUR, *The Missouri Review* 27, no. 3, 2004

after, more wakeful, alert and various in our humanity than in our practical lives we are mostly allowed to be.

DAVID CONSTANTINE, *A Living Language,* 2004

I believe very strongly that a poem should be a disturbing unit; that, when one goes into that force field, one will come out the other end a changed person.

PAUL MULDOON, BBC Radio 4, 2001

Writing poetry always involves an exposure to risk. You chance encountering feelings and thoughts that could change you. You chance becoming a slightly different person, precisely the one who will have written the poem in hand.

KEVIN HART, *Verse* 20, nos. 2 & 3, 2004

Who says that writing doesn't have any effect? I had a bucket of excrement dumped on my head for daring to criticise the North-East.

SEAN O'BRIEN, cited in *The Independent,* 1 December 1995

Scotland's national bard, Robert Burns, brings more than £157m a year into the country... The biggest single source of income is Burns-related tourism... Spending in the Burns supper season on haggis, shortbread and other edible delights equals £1.2m. Another £300,000 comes from other spending like paying pipers and kilt hire.

UNATTRIBUTED, BBC News online, 24 January 2003

Nobody enjoys a sunrise, or a sunset, without being tangentially influenced by the notions of Wordsworth.

PETER ACKROYD, *The Times,* 14 January 2006

MUSICAL ARRANGEMENTS

When you are writing a poem, you are setting it to music at the same time.
DON PATERSON, *The Independent,* 28 March 1998

Poetry is born of speech and silence. So it is a form of music.
PAUL DURCAN, *In Dublin,* 8 November 1990

Poetry, like traditional music, is a product of, and a repayment to, community.
BERNARD O'DONOGHUE, Poetry Book Society *Bulletin,* Autumn 1995

Although we are taught and encouraged to listen to music, very few of us are encouraged—and quite rightly so—to compose it... It has been assumed for too long, however, that the writing of poetry is something that almost anyone can do. If you can talk, it seems to be felt, you can write poetry.
DAVID LIGHTFOOT, *Sunk Island Review,* no. 10, 1995

It would be very odd to go to a concert hall and discover that the pianist on offer *wasn't any good at all,* in the sense that he couldn't actually play the piano. But in poetry this is an experience we have learned to take in our stride.
JAMES FENTON, Ronald Duncan Lecture, 1992

If only poets and novelists could be translated into *musicianhood,* even for a few seconds; then we'd see the vast majority, after only a few notes, revealed as a bunch of desperate scrapers and parpers without a tune in their heads or the rudiments of technique. God, the *time* we would save.
DON PATERSON, *The Book of Shadows,* 2004

For me, poetry is very much the time that it takes to unroll, the way music does... it's not a static, contemplatable thing like a painting or a piece of sculpture.

JOHN ASHBERY,
Oxford Poetry,
Winter–Spring 1992

⌁

There have always been different kinds of poetry written at any given moment—what I refer to, sometimes, as an AM track and an FM track—and a culture needs the variety. Some poets are writing an easy-listening kind of poem... And those poetries shouldn't be constantly compared to poetries that have other aims, other ambitions. No one accuses rock music of not being jazz, or opera.

JORIE GRAHAM, *American Poet,* Fall 1996

Reading many poets, one gets the impression of the lyre having been plucked so fervently that only one string remains, with subject and manner constricted to the short range of tones it allows.

R.S. GWYNN, *The Hudson Review,* Spring 1998

The rhythms of music and the rhythms of poetry have little in common... In the end, the music of poetry must be understood as no more than a metaphor struck off in the heat of wishful thought.

DONALD JUSTICE, *Oblivion,* 1998

How many contemporary slim volumes would you hold on to over your favourite CDs?... Not too many, I hope, the one saving grace of real contemporary poetry being how precious little of it there is.

DAVID WHEATLEY, *Poetry Ireland Review,* September 2004

[H]is songs have meant far more to me / than most of the so-called "poems" I've read.

PAUL MULDOON, on Leonard Cohen, *Hay,* 1998

In jazz, as in poetry, there is always that play between what's regular and what's wild.

ROBERT PINSKY, *The Paris Review,* Fall 1997

The worlds of jazz music and poetry have this much in common: the acceptance-winning poet or jazz musician both have to be the best of their kind in an intensely competitive world, where nothing less than the highest order of technique and invention will do. The audience for this brilliance is small, fickle and intensely critical.

JOHN HARTLEY WILLIAMS, *Poetry Wales,* October 2003

Opera and poetry are elitist and obscure by nature, and ought to be sold on the joy of difficulty.

LAVINIA GREENLAW, *The Guardian,* 20 December 2003

How do you lead a doggedly resistant public to enjoy more modern poetry? One answer might be: return to where the art began, set it to music, and sing it.

BOYD TONKIN, *The Independent,* 11 November 2005

For a poet to forget about song would be like living in a house and forgetting ever to go upstairs, or not realising that the door at the end of the corridor led into the west wing, or strolling to the edge of your garden and thinking: there's a path over there leading down to the sea, but I'd better not take it.

JAMES FENTON, *The Guardian,* 31 March 2007

The suggestion should always be there, even in the most talky poem... that once upon a time this stuff was sung, not spoken.

DEREK MAHON, *The Paris Review,* Spring 2000

We read poetry on the printed page as fast as we like—faster than we should—whereas we listen to music in its own time.

J.M. COETZEE, *The New York Review of Books,* 1 February 1996

Poetry mistrusts language; song cosies up to it.

GEORGE SZIRTES online, 27 September 2005

A relatively small number of educated people read poetry, and written poetry affects songwriting, and songwriting affects masses of people. Poetry becomes an expression that filters into the world slowly.

ROBERT HASS, *Grist,* 13 October 2005

The concept of song has gone out of contemporary poetry for the time being, and has been out of contemporary poetry for a long while. And all those attributes, like rhyme, complexity, or rigidity of meter, have gone. If music goes out of language, then you are in bad trouble.

DEREK WALCOTT, *The New Yorker,* 9 February 2004

Rock 'n' roll is wonderful, and so is poetry; but they are not the same thing. You can't dance to poetry.

LEONTIA FLYNN, *The Independent,* 5 June 2004

Poetry is... speech with song in it, the song made by words made to dance.

ROBERT NYE, *Acumen,* January 2006

Poetry is the music in the lyrics, without the decibel-deafness.

PENNY DYER, *The Chattanooga Pulse,* 24 May 2006

U.S. POETRY

American poetry now belongs to a subculture. No longer part of the mainstream of artistic and intellectual life, it has become the specialized occupation of a relatively small and isolated group.

DANA GIOIA, *Can Poetry Matter?*, 1992

We're the most important nation on the earth right now, because, one: we have thermonuclear weapons, and two: because we have more talented poets than have ever existed on the face of the earth.

NORMAN DUBIE, *Poets & Writers,* November–December 2004

It's hard to maintain there was ever a public role for an American poet. Whitman and Dickinson were essentially unknown to their contemporaries, although Whitman claimed to be speaking for all of us. No one knew.

CHARLES SIMIC, *Newsday,* 25 October 2003

Poetry is in some sense the national art form of Ireland; America's national art form is the Hollywood blockbuster. While poetry is flourishing in America, I can't even imagine a scenario wherein it escapes the wings and seizes the cultural spotlight.

CAMPBELL MCGRATH, *Smartish Pace*

Our poetry covers a narrower path than it should and, consequently, it occupies a smaller niche in American culture than it should. Its specialized nature is the result of pruning away most everything that is unsightly and unruly, including the comedic.

WILLIAM WALTZ, *The Blade,* August 2003

Our poems, in their charming and interchangeable quantity, do not presume to the status of "Lycidas"—for that would be elitist and un-American. We write and publish the McPoem—*ten billion served*—which becomes our contribution to the history of literature.

Donald Hall,
Poetry and Ambition,
1988

✥

The standard awful poem of the past forty years has been a sort of artless diary entry in free verse.

Richard Wilbur, *Between the Lines,* 2000

There is very little real poetry coming out of America at the moment because they have tried to harness Pegasus to the university and have turned it into a carthorse just plodding along.

Les Murray, BBC Radio 3

At present, American poetry is a fractured discipline—part profession, part gaggle of coteries, part contest hustle. Its mind may dwell in the vale of soul-making, but its common sense is aiming for the Lorna Snootbat Second Book Prize.

David Orr, *The New York Times,* 24 April 2005

When I look at American poetry, it's the professionalism that bothers me, the endless networking, the clammy handshakes, the look over the shoulder.

William Logan, *Poetry,* June–July 2004

There are probably at this moment in this country more than a hundred lyric poets writing between the ages of 22 and 67 who are all capable of greatness and who have all written individual poems that are astonishing in their beauty and originality. So, I think, it's very possible that what we're experiencing is a Golden Age of American poetry.

Norman Dubie, *The American Poetry Review,* November–December 1989

Last year's edition of the *Directory of American Poets* included 4,672 poets, all of them published, and all of them, incredibly, approved by a committee which determines that they are, in fact, poets. To read only one book by every living American poet—at the rate of one book a day, with no weekends or holidays off—would take 13 years, during which time another few thousand poets would have appeared.

ELIOT WEINBERGER, *Index on Censorship,* January 1990

If each M.F.A. graduate wrote just one good poem a year for ten years, at the end of a decade we would have 24,750 good poems—not to mention 4,500 degree-bearing poets, each of whom was required to write a book-length manuscript in order to graduate. New poems, poets, and manuscripts are added to the inventory every year.

JOSEPH BEDNARIK, *Poets & Writers,* May–June 2006

Say that in three years, in a country of 300,000,000, a book of poetry sells 800 copies. You could search through five football stadiums, each seating 75,000, before you could find one buyer. If I'm correct that only about 100 of those buyers finish a book of poetry, you'd have to search through 40 stadiums to find even one person who had read the book.

WILLIAM LOGAN, Poetry Foundation online, 3 November 2006

In the last few decades, it has become clear that professorships are the only form of sustained

[M]y generation's jihad… goes something like this: New Left politics to drugs to rock 'n' roll to anthropology to poetry. Or Abbie Hoffman to chocolate mescaline to Dylan to shamanism to Merwin.

DAVID RIVARD,
Harvard Review,
Fall 1992

The possibility is that [John] Ashbery is a major writer, but other than that I don't know any major writers, except possibly myself.

A.R. AMMONS,
*Michigan Quarterly
Review,* Winter 1989

❧

economic patronage that America is willing to offer its poets. Even our poets laureate only serve two-year terms. So the future of American poetry is classrooms and lecture halls, search committees and MLA panels.

JAY LADIN, *Parnassus* 29, nos. 1 & 2

I no longer see black poets writing defensively, reacting to the mainstream—they're out there poking into every cranny that interests them.

RITA DOVE, *The Writer's Chronicle,*
October–November 2005

The black poetic tradition is defined, to a large extent, by the accomplishments of black women, accomplishments that never came to black men. Phillis Wheatley published the first book. Gwendolyn Brooks received the first Pulitzer. Rita Dove became the first Poet Laureate of the United States.

AFAA M. WEAVER, The Academy of American Poets online, August 2005

On the American poetry scene these days, the only thing rarer than a fine poem is a negative review.

BRUCE BAWER, *Verse,* Winter–Spring 1992

Most editors run poems and poetry reviews the way a prosperous Montana rancher might keep a few buffalo around—not to eat the endangered creatures but to display them for tradition's sake.

DANA GIOIA, *Can Poetry Matter?,* 1992

[Robert Lowell's] poems are not easy reading for the average American, who knows no poetry, no history, no theology, and no Latin roots.

HELEN VENDLER, *The New Republic,* 28 July 2003

American poetry is full of "Oh, poor me."

MARK STRAND, *The New Yorker,* 14 July 1997

American poetry—a world as fractious and as riven as any Trotskyist cell.

STEPHEN SCHIFF, *The New Yorker,* 14 July 1997

British Poetry

My argument with English poetry of the post–Philip Larkin era is the denigration of it to a sideline: when you're not being a civil servant, you write poetry at the weekends. I think poetry demands more than that; it demands a total sacrifice.

Jeremy Reed, RTÉ Radio 1

English poetry has nostalgic lament as its default setting.

Paul Batchelor, *Poetry Review,* Autumn 2006

The fact is that the British poetry scene is reactionary, nostalgic and prejudiced. The reputations of many of its star turns depend on an exclusivity that maintains an embargo on true diversity. Experimentalism is beyond the pale, as is pretty much anything that amounts to a conviction.

Gregory Woods, *Magma Poetry,* Autumn 2003

[T]he stylistic tics that have become a matter of course in the contemporary English lyric poem: the subdued humour that is at best fey, the understatement that is supposed to be subtle, the abstract anti-climax of closing lines attempting transcendence but hinting only at limitation.

Sarah Fulford, *Poetry Review,* Winter 2004–05

A visiting Antipodean poet recently remarked, at the end of a reading by six young British poets, "How obedient they all are." He was referring to the ways in which their verse conformed, in its anecdotal structure, its oblique political manifests, poised ironies, the strict limitation of intent, to the lessons of workshops, the expectations of taste-makers, the requirements of the reading circuit.

MICHAEL SCHMIDT, *PN Review,* January–February 2004

When one looks at the progress of post-war English poetry it is like watching a dinosaur take side-steps in wet concrete.

JEREMY REED, *Lipstick, Sex and Poetry,* 1991

The English-language poetic tradition is hemmed in by a distrust of anything obviously academic or "intellectual" but doesn't have any respect for the mystical, transcendent role of poetry either. So we've ended up with a middle-ground culture. That's not a bad thing, we do it very well.

PATRICK MCGUINNESS, *PN Review,* May–June 2005

English is a language suited to poetry like no other. The crunch and snap of Anglo-Saxon, the lyric romanticism of Latin and Greek, the comic, ironic fusion yielded when both are yoked together, the swing and jazz of slang.

STEPHEN FRY, *The Ode Less Travelled,* 2005

There's an extra loss for a Welsh poet writing in English, and that is the longing for Welsh, for the secret language, mother tongue of all the stories, of all the centuries of speech and song.

GILLIAN CLARKE, *Modern Women Poets,* 2005

At risk of too gross a simplification, one might say that a typical British poem of the last twenty years is either a work that takes for its subject nostalgic recollections of the poet's childhood (mostly rural), or a descriptive, impersonal genre-piece.

JERZY JARNIEWICZ, *Cambridge Quarterly* 17, no. 1, 1988

⌣∴

When people ask me why I write in this tiny language of Welsh, I want to say that my worldview and vocabulary aren't any smaller than anybody else's. It could be they are enlarged because I am aware of all the different tiny villages, tiny communities all over the world.

MENNA ELFYN, *Asheville Poetry Review* 9, no. 2, 2002

If you look at anthologies since 1945, you would think that Scottish poetry had had more renaissances than a phoenix on a trampoline, each with slightly less fire and bounce than the last. It's not an accurate picture.

ROBIN BELL, *The Best of Scottish Poetry,* 1989

Britain is a plural society. You can't surgically remove the black British contribution from what it means to be British.

FRED D'AGUIAR, *The Guardian,* 4 August 1993

They recorded numerous votes for a weird character called Lord Bryon, while other suspicious nominations included *Allergy in a Country Churchyard, Golchy et Gwackorum Est, The Rhubarb of O'Mark I Am,* A.A. Milne's *Vespas,* and *Not Wading but Drowning.*

MARIANNE MACDONALD, on transcriptions of phone-in nominations for Britain's favorite poem, *The Independent,* 13 October 1995

IRISH POETRY

Like everything else in Ireland, poetry is contentious. There is always an occasion of outrage.

DENIS DONOGHUE, *The New York Review of Books,* 26 May 1994

Irish poets today, whatever their local or religious affiliations, speak in more collective tones than other poets writing in English. They are Irish almost before they are poets.

JOHN BAYLEY, *The New York Review of Books,* 25 June 1992

How does one explain the recent flowering of poetry in Ireland, with a population one-fiftieth of ours and a literature easily the equivalent of our own? Is it the relative absence of television addiction in Ireland? The centrality of literature to the national culture? The open sore of the Northern Ireland conflict as a stimulus to national self-definition?

RICHARD TILLINGHAST, *The New York Times,* 30 August 1992

If you leave aside the handful of Irish poets that everyone has heard of, it's tempting to lump together the remainder as unmemorable. There they sit, all writing away, as though poetry had become a matter of lessons learned, influences assimilated and risks eschewed.

PATRICIA CRAIG, *Times Literary Supplement,* 6 March 1992

At any given time, anywhere, most poets are no good, and in Ireland most of the poets are no good.

THOMAS KINSELLA, *Poetry Ireland Review,* Winter 2002–03

I think it's
because of the
bardic tradition
that we in Ireland
don't have the
strength of the
non-communal
poet, which is
experimentalism.

EAVAN BOLAND,
Parnassus 23, no. 1

⌣:

In general, Irish poets have had, and continue
to have, a stereotypic notion of what a poem
is—the stereotype changes with the fashions—and their efforts are directed exclusively
to producing that *object*.

MICHAEL SMITH, *The Irish Times*, 20 April 1995

I wish I had a pound (or ten) for every time
I have read the words "one of Ireland's most
exciting young writers": it's inflationary, and
it's not fair on the writers because they might
start to believe it.

RODNEY PYBUS, *Stand*, Spring 1993

If English poets suffer from indifference,
Irish poets suffer from too much public
expectation.

THOMAS MCCARTHY, *Agenda*, Autumn 1989

Artistic ambition is usually seen in Ireland as pretentious; the common
touch a sign of real genius. We are to take our poetry neat, like our politics, undiluted by *criticism*.

GERALD DAWE, *False Faces*, 1994

Apparently no literary discipline gives rise to as much heated controversy and embittered mud-slinging when placed under any form of critical scrutiny as does contemporary Irish poetry. Often we are gripped by
what can be most charitably described as "poetry wars."

FRED JOHNSTON, *The Irish Times*, 10 September 1993

Dublin is a very powerful and intense and abrasive atmosphere for poets, and anyone who has lived there knows that it is as far as a poet can get from a flattering environment!

EAVAN BOLAND, *Poets & Writers*, November–December 1994

Though I'm ever wary of generalizations about national "literary traditions," the wistful family anecdote seems to claim a central position in Irish poetry. Even experimentalists are prone to the occasional yarn about "me auld Da."

RODDY LUMSDEN, *Poetry London*, Summer 2004

Literary piety has replaced religious piety and patriotic piety, and it is in general even less sincere than either of them. You can buy "quality heat-resistant placemats and coasters" with the faces of Yeats, Joyce, Synge and even, just to remind us why satire is dead, Swift.

FINTAN O'TOOLE, *The Irish Times*, 17 August 2004

I find that in English I'm more of a rational human being. When I'm writing or speaking Irish I behave more intuitively.

GABRIEL ROSENSTOCK, RTÉ Radio 1

While William Wordsworth was wandering lonely as a cloud it is unlikely that his stream of consciousness was diverted by the notion that in nearby Ireland a host of energetic women poets was busy composing verse a good deal livelier than his limp ode.

CLARE BOYLAN, *The Irish Times*, 30 November 1987

Irish women poets were publishing at a substantial rate during the nineteenth century. Contemporary women poets may be writing out of silence, but it is the silence of ignorance, brought about through the time's neglect of their maternal literary heritage.

ANNE COLMAN, *The Irish Review*, Winter–Spring 1997

Home and Abroad

If the poem has no obvious destination, there's a chance that we'll be all setting off on an interesting ride.

Paul Muldoon, *Harper's*, September 1999

If you're going somewhere new and undiscovered you have to trust the imagination, you have to truly believe the poem knows better than you and thus follow where it leads.

Philip Levine, *So Ask*, 2002

Good poets are the explorers of the world. Out on the frontiers, they send back bulletins.

Eamon Grennan, *The Irish Times*, 11 September 1999

The figure of the poet as 20th century jetlagged nomad is gaining ground.

Helen Dunmore, *Poetry Review*, Summer 1995

It's crazy, all this travelling people go in for... If you stay put, you can travel in your imagination.

George Mackay Brown, *The Sunday Telegraph*, 24 September 1995

Poets behave like conquistadors wherever they roam, picking up a new verse form, a lover, some inventive cursing, a disease. Would Byron have been Byron without Italy and Greece? What would Eliot and Pound have become without the hostility of London? Can we imagine Hart Crane without the Caribbean or Elizabeth Bishop without Rio?

William Logan, *The New York Times*, 8 April 2007

It is the business of poets to be neither here nor there.

ALAN COREN, *The Times,* 24 August 1995

It's not location that changes poems or poets. It's where they are in their own work, what impasse or forward movement is there, that makes the difference.

EAVAN BOLAND, *American Poet,* Spring 1997

Only poetry recognises and maintains the centrality of absolutely everywhere.

LES MURRAY, *Krino,* no. 18, 1995

All poets live abroad.

PETER SIRR, *Metre,* Autumn 1997

Poetry, perhaps more than any other literary form, expresses the desire and need to be at home in the universe; to belong.

G.J. FINCH, *Critical Survey* 3, no. 1

Writing poetry is like finding your way home and you didn't know you were lost.

DIANE LOCKWARD, *The Star-Ledger,* 26 April 2003

Poetry is at once the most and the least international of genres—being, at best, both universal and untranslatable.

TIMOTHY GARTON ASH, *Times Literary Supplement,* 2 December 1994

Because it is distilled emotion, the most personal of the arts, poetry is also the most local.

GREY GOWRIE, *The Daily Telegraph,* 22 August 1992

Being everywhere at once while going nowhere in particular is what poets do.

ADAM GOPNIK, *The New Yorker,* 23 September 2002

Sitting is for when you've got the poem going or you're revising it, trying to perfect it. But the original impulse needs to come out of movement.

FLEUR ADCOCK,
Acumen, April 1992

⌣

If travel broadens the mind, it also tends to diminish the self, and perhaps to diminish the introspection from which lyric poems usually grow.

STEPHEN BURT, *Times Literary Supplement,*
24 September 2004

Good poems come out of tensions; and by travelling you are deliberately putting yourself into a situation where there's a tension between the new and the old, where you are and where you've come from.

SINÉAD MORRISSEY, *Magma Poetry,*
Summer 2003

The space of a single sheet of airmail stationery becomes a poetic form in itself when James Wright turns to describe cities and landscapes... the travel letters reveal a compelling mastery and clarity.

JONATHAN BLUNK, *The Georgia Review,* Spring 2005

That poets today can form a *confraternitas* transcending distances and language differences may be one of the few encouraging signs in the current chaotic world order.

CZESLAW MILOSZ, *The New York Review of Books,* 15 February 1996

As the poetry world has become more professionalized, our tastes have grown narrower, more sectarian; we like only poets who publish in the journal edited by our friend, or only avant-gardists from our particular block in lower Manhattan, or only the poets who've attended the institution where we received our M.F.A.

VERNON SHETLEY, *The Yale Review,* October 1993

We learned from him that poetry, like charity, begins at home; that if you enjoy a vivid inner life and are alert to people and places, your home ground may prove to be a gold mine.

MICHAEL LONGLEY, on John Hewitt, cited in *The Irish Times*

I often write on the subway or in buses or in planes and in transit lounges. I do not know why I feel safe when I am in motion, moving, traveling—and the where to is not as important as the act of moving, some fissure in my internal geography compels me to it.

MEENA ALEXANDER, *World Literature Today,* January–February 2006

PRIZE POETRY

The poet hardly exists who doesn't think himself cock of the walk, an emperor with clothes, deserving to be bemedaled until he can scarcely stand upright. There are not enough weavers to dress the legion of such poets.

> WILLIAM LOGAN, *The Undiscovered Country,* 2005

The kinds of savage attacks poets turned on their rivals in the eighteenth century are understandably out of fashion in a world where you never know who's going to be on the next grant panel or prize committee.

> VERNON SHETLEY, *Metre,* Autumn 2001

In the poetry business, the prize-giving process is usually so tainted by conflicts of interest that only the uninitiated and the naive can possibly be impressed.

> ROBERT MCDOWELL, *The Hudson Review,* Winter 1999

Prizes, in and of themselves, are baloney... The work of an artist ultimately survives or not, depending on what that work means to artists who come afterwards.

> ROBERT PINSKY, *Partisan Review,* Winter 1999

As feel-good events go, the ceremony for the T.S. Eliot poetry prize ranked just above a tussle with your online tax return, but probably below a Thai takeaway in front of Celebrity Big Brother. It was, of course, not fair of Cyril Connolly to describe poets as "jackals fighting over an empty well," but it is true that £10,000 prizes do not, on the whole, boost the health and happiness of those who don't win.

CHRISTINA PATTERSON, *The Independent,* 27 January 2006

Poetry prizes are now the vehicle of literary reception. Control the prizes, and you control the culture of reception.

MICHAEL SCHMIDT, *PN Review,* September–October 2002

Poets go crazy when somebody else wins an award.

GERALD STERN, *Rattle,* Summer 2003

Any prize tends to legitimize one. A friend of mine once said, "The fear of failure is the common cold of the artistic personality." Once you win a prize, it puts a dent in that—at least for a few hours.

C.K. WILLIAMS, RTÉ Radio 1, March 2005

My self-esteem is so low that getting the Pulitzer Prize just made me break even.

FRANZ WRIGHT, *Image,* Fall 2006

Nobel is one of the few magic words in the world. It blesses the art of poetry.

SEAMUS HEANEY, *The Times,* 13 October 1995

Bellaghy Celebrates as Farmer's Son Wins Top Literary Award

Irish Farmers Journal, headlining Seamus Heaney's Nobel Prize, 14 October 1995

Contemporary poets, alas, have prizes instead of readers. The number of poetry prizes in the land is astonishing… Such is their plenitude that one is almost inclined to think contemporary poetry less an art than a charity in need of constant donations.

JOSEPH EPSTEIN, *Poetry,* September 2004

You cannot possibly begin a sentence, "I have won," which ends with "Nobel Prize." It's against all decorum.

SEAMUS HEANEY, *The New York Times,* 29 March 2000

There is no such thing as a free Nobel Prize.

MARIE HEANEY, RTÉ I television, October 1995

In Critical Mood

Reading reviews of modern poetry is like attending prize-giving in a small, caring primary school: everyone has done terribly well, it's all absolutely marvellous.

HARVEY PORLOCK, *The Sunday Times*, 24 July 1994

An honest, descriptive, detailed, clarifying criticism keeps poetry healthy—it's poetry's weedkiller and, to the extent it encourages what's best in writing, it can nourish poetry too. No good growth without good gardeners.

DOUGLAS DUNN, *Acumen*, April 1991

[T]he little world of poetry has thousands of inhabitants, each of them convinced that someone who dislikes or reprehends their work must be motivated by a personal vendetta or a deep-rooted enmity toward what is true and beautiful.

THOMAS M. DISCH, *The Castle of Indolence*, 1995

You can't review a book if you're not prepared to be rude about it if you don't like it.

WENDY COPE, *The Dark Horse*, no.2, 1995

Only weak poetry is explicable; only over weak poems can criticism achieve its jealous mastery.

GEORGE STEINER, *The Sunday Times*

Criticism often anaesthetizes the lion with which the poet struggled.

ROGER LITTLE, *PN Review*, May–June 1993

Discrimination is needed. Without it, art succumbs to the randomness of commercialism, in which the shoddy product can displace the well-made and durable simply by being more effectively marketed.

MICHAEL HAMBURGER, *Testimonies*, 1989

⌣∴

Criticism is our jailer. Poetry should be sprung from it so that it is as natural a form of reading as a novel.

LES MURRAY, *The Independent*, 11 May 1994

A poem has far more power to show up a critic than the other way round.

RUTH PADEL, *PN Review*, May–June 2005

We suffer from a lack of intelligent talk about poetry... Many young poets if they criticize poetry at all adhere to the philosophy of the booster club, Boost don't Knock.

DONALD HALL, *The American Poetry Review*

If a critic gets ten books sent to him for review, and he finds six or seven of them are excellent, then he is either the luckiest poetry reviewer on the planet, or he has no taste.

CHRISTIAN WIMAN, *Poetry*, September 2005

A critic who does his job must be a good hater if he's to be a good lover, because if he likes everything he reads he likes nothing well enough.

WILLIAM LOGAN, *Poetry*, February 2006

The horrible truth is that very few people in today's literary world have the capacity to make an independent judgement about poetry. They pay lip-service to the great poets of the past whose stature was established by discrimination of the kind they lack, and today they rely, if they bother at all, on publicists' hype.

PETER FORBES, *Poetry Review*, Summer 1989

Gossip is the highest form of criticism many writers will venture.

WILLIAM LOGAN, *The Virginia Quarterly Review,* Fall 2005

Burdensome artistically, exhausting over time, damaging to one's poetic reputation, and the source of rebuffs both private and professional... poetry reviewing is an enterprise only a few people ever do credibly or well, and then rarely for long periods.

MARY KINZIE, *Poetry,* January 2004

Poet-critic: there is a temptation to read the hyphen as a subtraction sign, as if every brainwave of the latter robbed the world of the former's next villanelle or sestina.

DAVID WHEATLEY, *The Dublin Review,* Spring 2002

It's said that a trained musician can tell by looking at a musical score whether it's any good or not. A trained poet can do the same by looking at a poem, even before you start to read it.

DUNCAN BUSH, *English Studies,* no. 5, 1994

I don't mind if people read [my poems] or not, just so long as they don't make too many claims about them without having read them.

PAUL MULDOON, *Artvoice,* February 2006

Poetry, more than most writing forms, is an incestuous business, and competent reviewers are likely to be, if not inimical to the reviewee, or married to/living with/slavishly devoted

Poets have a responsibility to write serious reviews and essays about their contemporaries, even when the prospect seems daunting. Call it literary jury service.

JOEL BROUWER,
Harvard Review,
Spring 1997

༄

to/pupil of him or her, then in some way bound symbiotically to the author under scrutiny.

RICHARD PINE, *Irish Literary Supplement*, Spring 1992

I think most critics would agree that poets are "the irritable race." Given a mixed review, a poet usually fastens with a vengeance on a critic's one misgiving.

ALICE FULTON, *Parnassus* 16, no. 2

Literary theory is good clean fun but it's about as much use to me as a chocolate saucepan.

IAN DUHIG, *Thumbscrew*, Autumn–Winter 1995

The literal-minded should be kept from poems.

P.J. KAVANAGH, *Times Literary Supplement*, 6 August 1999

Many critics consider themselves superior to the work of literature, especially when the work expresses a personal or subjective experience. They know so much more than the poem, and they forget that the poem is what they know.

DENIS DONOGHUE, *Times Literary Supplement*, 15 July 1994

Criticism is misdirected creativity.

NUALA NÍ DHOMHNAILL, RTÉ Radio 1, September 1995

When an editor insists on a textual change, he or she is posing that imperative question: "Surely you're not leaving the house looking like that!?"

BILLY COLLINS, *Dear Editor*, 2002

LOST IN TRANSLATIONS

Translation is like describing one animal in terms of another. What you read outside its original language is a convincing rhinoceros, but the actual poem is an elephant.

FERGUS CHADWICK, *Acumen,* May 1997

Reading a poem in translation is something like watching a film with the sound turned down.

WAYNE MILLER, *Boulevard,* Spring 2005

"To read a work in translation is like kissing a beautiful woman with a handkerchief over her face," observed Vissarion Belinsky. He must be talking about poetry.

MURRAY BAIL, *The Guardian,* 10 September 2005

It should surely, by now, be axiomatic that poetry cannot be translated in a way that will preserve anything of the flavour of the original. Poems are custom-built churches in which the poem's own voice... can sing freely; but one so specifically calibrated to maximise the resonant *potential* of that voice, that another voice, upon entering the same space, is almost guaranteed to fall flat.

DON PATERSON, *The Eyes,* 1999

It is one of the bitter truths of life that all poetry, whether great or less great, is untranslatable. Whereas music is universal, each good poem is ultimately shut off inside its particular language, and there is no way of appreciating its unique effect apart from knowing that language, and knowing it well.

JOHN WEIGHTMAN, *The Independent on Sunday*

"Prosaic" might describe the pleasure of translated poems, like lovemaking overheard from behind a closed door, where the listener hears the sound evoked by each caress but does not feel it on her skin.

SUZANNE GARDINIER, *Parnassus* 20, no. 1

⌣⁖

Poetry, rooted in the quiddity of words, remains untranslatable. Something of a worldview or an insight can be conveyed in translation, but the texture of poetic utterance cannot: a dilemma which has no solution.

GREVEL LINDOP, *Stand* 5, no. 3, 2004

One statistically proven reason for the feebler hold on life of most translations is that, in syntax, tone, vocabulary and range, they are less various than the original... Often they appear in a sort of nowhere language—inoffensive, unexceptionable, doomed.

DAVID CONSTANTINE, *The Independent*, 10 December 2004

If translation was possible then it would not be necessary to keep on doing it.

WILLIAM OXLEY, *Stride*, 2005

Translations of prose can even be accurate; translations of poetry only brilliant.

JOHN SIMON, *Dreamers of Dreams*, 2001

The poets who seem to develop a poetry's capabilities most tellingly, who seem to their linguistic communities to be the most "poetic" of all, are often precisely those whom it is most difficult to bring over into another language.

DICK DAVIS, *New England Review* 25, nos. 1 & 2, 2004

The more a poem depends on language to make its effect, the harder it is to translate.

CHARLES SIMIC, *The Paris Review*, Spring 2005

Inevitably, translation dissolves the original unity of form and content, which characterizes any poetry of substance and quality.

Daniel Weissbort, *Far from Sodom,* 2005

To translate poems conceived in specific meters and rhymes into free verse is like separating the soul from the body, like killing a living creature.

Nina Cassian, *Parnassus* 18, no. 2

Nothing—not words, not phrases, not even metres—mean precisely the same in one language as they do in another.

George Szirtes, *New Life,* 1994

Much rubbish is talked about translating poems into "identical metres." There is no such thing, for prosody is language-specific.

Clive Wilmer, *Times Literary Supplement,* 6 September 1996

[T]he poetic translator's greatest and most enviable gift: to be faithful to the language and world of the source text, but in a voice that is unmistakably the translator's own.

Bernard O'Donoghue, *Times Literary Supplement,* 18 February 2005

Translation always involves the translator taking a position, an aesthetic position and an ethical position. Does the translator wish to negotiate with, or to dominate, the poet she's translating? Is her main aim to enhance her own reputation, or does she want to introduce a new voice into English poetry...?

Sarah Maguire, *Poetry Review,* Winter 2004-05

If baseball is a game of inches, poetry is a game of words. Single words can weigh tons, but they float away to nothingness in approximate translation.

Clarence Brown, *The Hudson Review*

In translation, the integrity of the means justifies the end; in the version, the integrity of the end justifies the means.

DON PATERSON, *Orpheus*, 2006

⌣⋅

Where most translations fail is by choosing what is possible in English, rather than what is right in English.

CRAIG RAINE, *Thumbscrew*, Winter 1994-95

The translator's knowledge of *language* is more important than their knowledge of *languages*.

JAMIE MCKENDRICK, *Poetry News*, Winter 2002-03

Translation of poetry is, if it is any good, first and foremost poetry.

CHARLES TOMLINSON, *Poetry Review*, Winter 2002-03

Textures are harder (maybe impossible) to translate than structures, linear order more difficult than syntax, lines more difficult than larger patterns. Poetry is made at all these levels—and so is translation. That is why nothing less than a poem can translate another.

A.K. RAMANUJAN, *The Art of Translation*, 1989

Freedom from the words of the original combined with a deep love of its words lies at the heart of translation. In the act of true translation... there is a moment when all prior knowledge of a poem dissolves, when the words that *were* are shed as a snake sheds its skin and the words that *are* take on their own life.

JANE HIRSHFIELD, *Nine Gates*, 1998

Translation might work zonally rather than lexicographically. When a complicated concept appears without a direct equivalent, we distribute the various shades of its meaning through the text.

GEORGE SZIRTES online, 15 April 2007

To translate is not only to experience what makes each language distinct, but to draw close to the mystery of the relationship between word and thing, letter and spirit, self and world.

CHARLES SIMIC, *The New York Review of Books*, 3 November 2005

The worst thing in translation, it seems to me, is the appearance of being remote-controlled.

MICHAEL HOFMANN, cited in *The Guardian*, 29 January 2005

Translation is like dancing as a couple when you are not the leading partner.

GEORGE SZIRTES, *Poetry Ireland Review*, October 2005

When I'm translating and I have a text in front of me, it's like somebody is drowning, and you're trying to pull them out of the water. You know that you're only going to get the arms and maybe the foot, but you've got to go for it.

CLAYTON ESHLEMAN, *Poets & Writers*,
March–April 1995

Of the tight-rope acts of language, that of the translation of poetry is the most defiant. There is no safety net.

GEORGE STEINER, *The Sunday Times*

Translating a poem takes up to twenty times longer than writing a poem of one's own.

RICHARD MCKANE, *Agenda*,
Autumn–Winter 2004

There is nothing worse than translations, for example, that attempt to recreate a foreign meter or rhyme scheme. They're sort of like the way hamburgers look and taste in Bolivia.

ELIOT WEINBERGER,
Fascicle, no. 1, 2005

⤙∴

Certain poets—
Virgil, in particular
—seem untrans-
latable. The bag-
gage arrives, but
not the owner
who is on
another flight.

FERGUS CHADWICK,
Acumen, May 1997

⌣⋰

The experience of translating is as heady as
being in love—the excitement, the anticipa-
tion, the joy of meeting and joining with the
unknown.

JANE HIRSHFIELD, *Fooling with Words,* 1999

Living with poetry in translation is like living
with strangers: what often begins in beautifully
romantic exoticism concludes in misunder-
standing, impatience and, sometimes, hostility.

SAM HAMILL, *The American Poetry Review*

Most poems in translation are affairs. With
novels, I suspect, it's more like a marriage.

SEAMUS HEANEY, *The Paris Review,* Summer 2000

The translator's relation to his to-be-translated writer, or victim, is essentially erotic and an exchange of mental fluids that cannot be entirely
justified or explained.

RICHARD HOWARD, *The Paris Review,* Spring 2004

I'm tempted to say that translation is like tracing. Going over an original on onionskin paper.

MICHAEL HOFMANN, *Ashes for Breakfast,* 2005

In a way, translation dresses a poem in different clothes. The bone
remains, the appearance changes.

IFIGENIJA SIMONOVIC, *Striking Root,* 1996

To be a good translator is somewhat like being a good double-agent.

JULIA OLDER, *Poets & Writers,* July–August 1994

A poorly translated poem is like a badly told joke.

TERENCE DOOLEY, *Modern Poetry in Translation,* 3rd ser., no. 3, 2005

Translation can be seen as the activity of reading carried to its logical extreme.

RUTH FAINLIGHT, *Poetry Review,* Autumn 2005

I believe in bad translations, because... they awaken the reader's intuition. Whereas a good translation confines the material to its own achievement.

JOSEPH BRODSKY, *Verse,* Spring 1994

The point isn't to produce a version so culturally smooth that nobody would ever guess it was imported. There has to be something strange, novel and fascinating either about the style or cast of mind of the new piece.

GWYNETH LEWIS, *Strong Words,* 2000

The last 300 years of translation activity in Europe... have left us with a legacy of easy readability, where the cultural and social conditions of translation have been concealed; where texts have been made to assume local cultural values, accredited according to the benchmark of fluency and transparency.

SIONED PUW ROWLANDS, *Poetry Ireland Review,* Autumn 1999

The language most people in the twentieth century speak is particularly unpoetic and that's why there are many things that you can't translate into it. The more esoteric and hermetic the poetry, the easier it is to translate.

MICHAEL HAMBURGER, *Testimonies,* 1989

I see translation as a kind of midwifery... I did not create the child, yet I must ensure its safe passage into the world.

LEZA LOWITZ, *The Poem Behind the Poem,* 2004

❦

I don't feel good about two or more translations of a single poem. It's like the man who always knew the exact time when he had just one watch, but from the moment he had two watches he never knew what time it was.

MIROSLAV HOLUB, *Poets & Writers,* November–December 1992

Translation is a necessity, for the obvious reason that one's own language has only created, and is creating, a small fraction of the world's most vital books.

ELIOT WEINBERGER, *Fascicle,* no. 1, 2005

Whatever the approach, whatever the pitfalls, we have to translate: other traditions and their authors permit us a bravery and risk with our own language that we are simply unable to grant ourselves.

DON PATERSON, *The Times,* 3 February 2007

Poetry only ever changes and develops through translation.

SARAH MAGUIRE, RTÉ Radio 1, November 2005

The act of translation is an absolutely central part of a culture affirming inclusiveness.

TOM PAULIN, RTÉ Radio 1, March 2004

ANTHOLOGIES

Jealousy, rage, *amour propre*, factional in-fighting of Bosnian complexity—
yes, another anthology of contemporary poetry has been published.

HARVEY PORLOCK, *The Sunday Times*, 20 June 1993

Anyone who makes an anthology is almost certifiably mad.

PAUL MULDOON, BBC Radio Ulster

An anthology or selection of poems is... like a spread of cards, the poet
dealing out a string of queens, kings and aces, slapping one down after
the other in a mood of bravura and triumph.

ROSEMARY GORING, *The Herald*, 25 October 2004

While anthologies survive, the idea of poetic tradition survives. They
house intricate conversations between poets and between poems,
between the living and the dead, between the present and the future.

EDNA LONGLEY, *Poetry & Posterity*, 2000

The institution of the anthology... is at best a convenience for teachers
but otherwise a pernicious modern nuisance which keeps readers away
from *books* of poetry.

THOM GUNN, *Numbers*

Mixed anthologies, like mixed social gatherings, have their advantages
and their drawbacks. There's something to be said for excluding men,
now and again, in order to give women a chance to come into their own.

WENDY COPE, *Is That the New Moon?*, 1989

Making anthologies is like composing music with other men's tunes. The important thing may seem to be how many varied tunes the anthologist knows, but the craft lies in turning them into a shapely whole—a poem made out of poems.

BRIAN ALDERSON,
The Times

～

Women's anthologies are read primarily by women. They could even be viewed as the up-market version of the woman's magazine.

CAROL RUMENS, *Poetry Review,* Winter 1996–97

Normally there is no class of book more slipshod, more boring, more prejudiced, more snobbish, more exclusive, more incestuous, more narrow-minded, more arid, more ignorant, more canonical, more soulless, more soul destroying, more anti-poetic than a poetry anthology. The shelves of bookshops are stacked with the spines of these prodigies of spinelessness.

PAUL DURCAN, *Lifelines 2,* 1994

It may well be that our contemporary taste for anthologies is a sign of increasing superfluity, reflecting our desire for easily accessible, browsable, context-free literature—LiteratureLite.

IAN SANSOM, *The Guardian,* 3 April 1997

Every anthology published in my lifetime has been worthless as an account of contemporary literature... because of the form's spurious claim to completeness.

EILÉAN NÍ CHUILLEANÁIN, *Cyphers,* Spring 1992

It is a truth universally acknowledged—at least it should be—that an anthology is a book that omits your favorite poem.

DANA GIOIA, *Poetry,* April 2004

Anthologies are usually masquerades in which partiality is presented as comprehensiveness, individual taste or prejudice as historical objectivity and close personal friends as the future hopes of poetry.

DAVID KENNEDY, *PN Review,* September-October 2001

I love anthologies—the absolute emphasis on the individual poem, the way you can jump from century to century, the sense they give of poetry being both continuous and contained. And yet I hate them too—the false impression they give of many poets, the emphasis on "teachable" poems, the train wreck of taste that most of them become when dealing with contemporaries.

CHRISTIAN WIMAN, Poetry Foundation online, 2006

Most anthologies are full of poems between three and six inches long.

JOHN KERRIGAN, *The Irish Review,* Winter-Spring 1997

Making an anthology is a bit like packing a suitcase; you have to discard things to achieve the temporary closure of a unitary concept.

ALASTAIR FOWLER, *Times Literary Supplement,* 29 December 2000

Reading anthologies is a bit like getting drunk on a series of miniatures.

ROBERT NYE, *The Times,* 25 January 1996

Anthologies age as badly as fashion, and the pillbox hats and pearls of one generation must give way to the tattoos and tongue studs of another.

WILLIAM LOGAN, *The New York Times,* 16 April 2006

Good anthologies are reckoners. They remind you that nothing is certain, that all canons are conditional, the dust of their last reconstruction still floating in the air.

CARMINE STARNINO, *The New Canon,* 2005

POETRY AT WAR

Poetry and war go together like guns and ammunition.

RORY BRENNAN, *The Irish Independent,* 22 April 1995

War and poetry have come to seem to belong together, like love and songs, or landscape and painting.

JEREMY TREGLOWN, *The Independent on Sunday,* 23 April 1995

Like warfare, poetry can result from the collision between romance and reality.

LT. GEN. WILLIAM JAMES LENNOX JR., *Poetry,* April 2005

War poetry is the one literary genre that one hopes will never be extended.

BERNARD BERGONZI, *PN Review,* May–June 1992

Poets who die in battle tend to get praised for the wrong reasons, especially by elderly non-combatants.

MICHAEL MEYER, cited in *Financial Times,* 8 May 1993

Few poets write like war reporters, in the middle of an event.

CAROL ANN DUFFY, *The Observer,* 20 June 1993

Here is a simple matter: if you want to oppose war (or anything else for that matter), get your ass out on the street and risk something, but do not abuse poetry any more than it is already abused by writing (and then, dear God, reading aloud!) some piece of worthless crap.

ANNE BURKE, *Context,* no. 13, 2003

With [the Iraq] war on the horizon, American poets will man their invisible barricades and sound their warcries. That they will go unheard does not mean they would be better left unsaid.

Campbell McGrath, *Smartish Pace*

In a time of violence, the task of poetry is in some way to reconcile us to our world and to allow us a measure of tenderness and grace with which to exist.

Meena Alexander, *The Kenyon Review,* Winter 2005

Among poets themselves are some of the most aggressive people on the planet.

Blake Morrison, *The Guardian,* 11 June 2005

I didn't have time to write poetry before, but now I have had the time to become a poet.

Saddam Hussein, cited in *The Sunday Times,* 14 May 2006

War poetry can no longer be defined as in the 20th century as the poetry of soldiers. The "war on terror" has created a limitless war zone... In such a context we are all confronted by the potential identity of "war poet."

W.N. Herbert, *Poetry London,* Spring 2006

No individual poem can stop a war—that's what diplomacy is supposed to do. But poetry is an independent ambassador for conscience: it answers to no one, it crosses borders without a passport, and it speaks the truth. That's why, despite talk about its marginalization, it is one of the most powerful of the arts.

Ellen Hinsey, *Poetry Magazine,* February 2003

و.

We should write poems that take on the way that 9/11 has been grotesquely fetishized by this culture—including its poets.

LYNN EMANUEL, *Poetry Flash*, Winter–Spring 2006

The kind of poetry written to make us *feel better*, for example, after 9/11, is pro-establishment falsification, for it lets us pull the comforter back over our heads and go on sleeping.

DAISY FRIED, *Poetry*, January 2007

When I write poems protesting the [Iraq] war, I don't ever really feel they're going to change anything. Maybe the vague hope is they might sensitize one person who isn't sensitized to what is happening, or, probably more likely, you might find ways for people who already feel the way you do to articulate what they feel a little better.

C.K. WILLIAMS, Poetry Foundation online, 2006

Incantation is all we have against empire.

REBECCA BLACK, *Good Times*, 9 March 2006

Celebration, Consolation, Lamentation

Right from the beginning, poetry has pitched itself in dialectical opposition to its negative—everything that is non-poetry: vulgarity, banality, ignorance...

MARIO LUZI, *Poetry Ireland Review,* July 2005

Poetry is an antidote to the poison-level at which we often consent to live.

PENELOPE SHUTTLE, Poetry Book Society *Bulletin,* Summer 1998

Poetry has to a large degree resumed its 19th-century role as a comfort and consolation, a retreat from the rigors of the world.

ADAM KIRSCH, *The New York Times,* 26 April 1998

Poetry provides comfort precisely by going straight to the most painful spot.

CHERYL GATLING, *Rattle,* Summer 2006

The real horrors are so horrible that only minority pastimes like poetry will take them on.

WILLIAM SCAMMELL, *The Independent on Sunday,* 24 May 1998

The ultimate function of the poet is to praise. It may have taken somebody like Dante the long pilgrimage through the *Inferno* and the *Purgatorio* to get up to the praising point but nevertheless that is the end vision.

JOHN MONTAGUE, *Irish University Review,* Spring 1989

Poetry, in its seeking and questing, in its notice and naming, is one means of giving praise.

PATTIANN ROGERS, *The Dream of the Marsh Wren,* 1999

Nothing can maim a poet's practice like joy… We can all drum up a few happy poems here and there, but from Symbolism and the High Moderns forward, poetry has often spread the virus of morbidity.

MARY KARR, *Poetry*, November 2005

Wilfully rhapsodic poetry in recent years usually turns out to be dire. Melancholy might be poetry's more stable mood.

DOUGLAS DUNN, *Acumen*, April 1991

We prefer our poets to be wracked with anguish or, at least, chronically depressed and raving on Paxil. We want dark nights of the soul from our bards, not breezy afternoons. Happiness looks suspect; it appears obtuse, oblivious, smug.

ERIC ORMSBY, *The New Criterion*, April 2007

Writing is an extreme form of happiness.

TOM PAULIN, *The Sunday Telegraph*, 7 June 1998

The poet is like a mouse in an enormous cheese excited by how much cheese there is to eat.

CZESLAW MILOSZ, *The Paris Review*, Winter 1994–95

In a way, all poetry is love poetry because it's about praising the world. Even if it appears to be negative, it is praising what's absent. It's lamenting that something isn't the case, it has praise in its sights.

ROBERT GRAY, *The Sydney Morning Herald*, 14 February 2007

If you go too far towards affirmation then you risk losing the brutal, historic reality. But then, if you limit yourself to describing the ugliness of history and societal life, there's no poetry at all.

ADAM ZAGAJEWSKI, *Five Points* 10, nos. 1 & 2, 2006

Poetry that says *yes* has to swallow great goblets of darkness; and poetry that says *no* has to say no in the face of the fact that there must be reasons why the poet has chosen to continue to live in order to say it.

ROBERT HASS, *The American Poetry Review,* March-April 1997

Since poetry deals with the singular, not the general, it cannot—if it is good poetry—look at things of this earth other than as colorful, variegated, and exciting, and so, it cannot reduce life, with all its pain, horror, suffering, and ecstasy, to a unified tonality of boredom or complaint.

CZESLAW MILOSZ, *A Book of Luminous Things,* 1996

A good poem (with the exception of light verse, parodies, etcetera) has some sort of pain or moral urgency behind it that has compelled its writer into expression.

HELEN VENDLER, *The Paris Review,* Spring 2000

Can poetry ever come from a comfortable place? Doesn't there need to be a knife edge under the toes?

IMTIAZ DHARKER, BBC Radio 4, April 2006

Good literature... doesn't evade any of the terrible things in life. It faces them and faces them squarely, but puts them in a context in which they have a richer meaning than they would as simply raw, descriptive facts.

ANTHONY HECHT, *Humanities,* March-April 2004

An atmosphere of depression will arouse artists' attention over an atmosphere of prosperity nearly every time. Also true, ruins are beautiful to us; blues make us feel good; it is through the wound that we perceive the body alive alive-o.

C.D. WRIGHT, *Cooling Time,* 2005

❧

We should write out of grief, but not grievance. Grief is rich, ecstatic. But grievance is not—it's a complaint, it's whining.

LI-YOUNG LEE, *Breaking the Alabaster Jar,* 2006

Lyric poetry rescues pain from the jaws of pleasure.

PAUL HOOVER, *The American Poetry Review,* March-April 2005

People like it when I write about dead queers; they just don't like it when I write about live ones.

THOM GUNN, cited in *Poetry Flash,* May 1992

Holy Writ

Poetry is earned spiritually. It's earned with silences. It's earned, it isn't arrogated.

SEAMUS HEANEY, *The Christian Science Monitor,* 9 January 1989

Poetry is a kind of communion, the chore of ordinary talk made sacramental by the attention to what is memorable, transcendent, permanent in the language.

THOMAS LYNCH, *Boston Sunday Globe,* 25 January 1998

A poem is very like a prayer: it's shareable; you're talking to something that you don't know is there or not; you don't know if you've got a listener or not; it's a blank page just as heaven is a blank page; and you have this act of faith in poetry, just as you have in a prayer.

BRENDAN KENNELLY, BBC Radio 4, March 2004

I write quite a lot of sonnets and I think of them almost as prayers: short and memorable, something you can recite.

CAROL ANN DUFFY, *The Observer,* 4 December 2005

Religion is poetry in a lived sense.

THOMAS MOORE, RTÉ Radio 1, April 1999

Poetry has only three legs and religion sometimes has four. It's sometimes revelation—the fourth leg comes from heaven.

LES MURRAY, BBC Radio 3, July 1998

At its best, the lyric opens a door in the everyday and allows me to pass into the otherworld behind the taken-for-granted.

JOHN BURNSIDE, *Poetry Review,* Summer 2005

A poem is not, in the end, a prayer. Poetry is unaffiliated. Put another way, prayer unites faith with ceremony, while poetry unites language with experience. Prayer seeks communion. Poetry, community.

DAVID BIESPIEL,
The Oregonian,
24 December 2006

[P]oetry's awareness of itself as a partially opaque medium that seems to involve a force beyond itself has much about it of what is thought of as the holy.

C.K. WILLIAMS, Literary Imagination, Winter 2005

Forget about schools, styles, movements and the rest: poets fall into two temperamental categories, those who see angels, and those who don't.

ELIZABETH LOWRY, Times Literary Supplement,
6 March 1998

These days, "spiritual literature" tends to denote a genre with no practical application beyond the invocation of a sort of diffuse and torpid sense of well-being, amounting to—more sinisterly—little more than a sort of generalised call to political inaction.

DON PATERSON, Orpheus, 2006

If poetry can't cope with what God means in the late 20th century, then it doesn't deserve to remain a major art form.

R.S. THOMAS, The Independent, 27 February 1993

Strange that in our time there's so little interesting poetry of religious belief, especially since world events more and more are driven by belief (or the fanaticism of Eastern or Western Fundamentalisms).

W.S. DI PIERO, Poetry, October 2006

Poetry has to do with the non-rational parts of man. For a poet, a human being is a mystery... this is a religious feeling.

OCTAVIO PAZ, The Independent, 21 May 1989

Poetry is religious in its contemplation of experience under the eye of eternity. It helps us to live our lives in the face of destruction.

SEAMUS HEANEY, *The Sunday Times*, 30 January 2000

Most people don't believe in heaven, but everybody wants to go there, right? Now *there's* a topic for a poet.

DAVID KIRBY, *storySouth*, 2003

It's the only way I can figure heaven to myself, that eventually one day you get into the poem and live there.

LES MURRAY, BBC Radio 3

The kinds of truth that art gives us many, many times are small truths. They don't have the resonance of an encyclical from the Pope stating an eternal truth, but they partake of the quality of eternity. There is a sort of timeless delight in them.

SEAMUS HEANEY, *The Economist*, 22 June 1991

A poem is a kind of rhythm between the world and the spirit or soul.

DANIEL BERRIGAN, *AGNI*, no. 43

Poetry is the delineation of the human soul, and the human soul is a fuming abyss.

NUALA NÍ DHOMHNAILL, *Poetry Ireland Review*, Autumn 1992

Poetry is essentially the soul's search for its release in language.

JOSEPH BRODSKY, *Apollo in the Snow*, 1991

Poems show us that we are both more and less than human, that we're part of the cosmos and part of the chaos, and that everything is a part of everything else.

JULIA CASTERTON, *Poetry News*, Winter 2002–03

᠁

All religion is fossilized poetry. Poets are the real practitioners of the sacred.

LI-YOUNG LEE,
Range of the Possible,
2002

Poetry is the voice of spirit and imagination and all that is potential, as well as of the healing benevolence that used to be the privilege of the gods.

TED HUGHES, cited in *Times Literary Supplement,*
5 July 1996

Poetry speaks to something in us that so wants to be filled. It speaks to the great hunger of the soul.

LUCILLE CLIFTON, *The Baltimore Sun,*
29 September 2002

It sometimes seems that we have been caught up in a kind of delusive Reaganomics of poetry: paper reputations built on paper reputations, while the real spiritual debt goes unacknowledged and continues to mount up.

COLIN FALCK, *Agenda,* Summer 1993

Poetry is an art concerned with how we encounter the category of the Metaphysical, in daily practice.

CHRIS WALLACE-CRABBE, *Landbridge,* 1999

If you want meaning, read history, read philosophy, but poetry's not about meaning at all, at least not in the sense that they are. It's about connecting you back up to a primal feeling of unity.

DON PATERSON, *Verse* 20, nos. 2 & 3, 2004

The poet discovers the wholeness of the world. If he can't—it's not the world that is wrong or fragmented.

LUCIEN STRYK, *Poetry Ireland Review,* Winter 1996

Precisely because the word, in poetry, is not only a meaning but also a sound, a nascent rhythm, a physical presence, the poem interrupts a conceptual reading of the world, becomes an awareness of the unity that lies beyond the conceptual grasp, and thus gathers together all existing things through a single act of naming.

YVES BONNEFOY, *Modern Poetry in Translation,* Summer 1992

By its formal integrity a poem reminds us of the formal integrity of other works, creatures, and structures of the world... Thus the poet affirms and collaborates in the formality of the Creation.

WENDELL BERRY, *What Are People For?,* 1990

I still have a belief that poetry is in some sense (and I know it is an archaic sense) a sacred art: that it is doing things like the Adamic naming of creatures, paying tribute to spots of time or moments of inherent excellence—things that are not fully accessible to secular discourse.

CHRIS WALLACE-CRABBE, *Oxford Poetry,* Summer 1989

If poetry is to perform its real function it... must become, for both poet and reader, a path that somehow leads from time to the timeless; a process that constructs from the materials of the contingent—a particular life, a particular place, a particular day, a particular hand and brain and language—a way into the transcendent.

GREVEL LINDOP, *The Path and the Palace,* 1996

We deal with poets and poetry, which transcends all communication, except divine intervention.

MICHAEL KEOHANE, president of the Yeats Society, *The Irish Times,* 6 August 2005

CLOSED SHOP

Poetry is read only by poets and that's its sickness.

> CAROL RUMENS, *Poetry Review*

The thing that is wrong with the poetry world is that in it the poets and the critics are the same people.

> ANNA ADAMS, *Acumen*, April 1993

Poetry has removed itself by its own choice into something that is private, that comes out in little magazines, that only other poets read.

> DEREK WALCOTT, *Outposts*, Winter 1991

One of the obstacles to poetry's wider acceptance is its own carefully guarded prestige, which seals it off from the rest of the culture into a self-satisfied, self-perpetuating, and not especially welcoming museum world.

> A.O. SCOTT, *Slate*, 7 November 2000

The most generous interpretation of the putdown "Only poets read poetry" is that poems *make* us into poets.

> JAMES RICHARDSON, *Poetry*, August 1993

It is not necessarily bad news that more people write poems than read them: it suggests that the urge to create is itchier than the urge to consume.

> ROBERT WINDER, *The Independent on Sunday*, 21 March 1999

Who, really, is interested in the work of new poets—apart, of course, from other new poets, who notoriously pore over the work of the competition and bitch about other poets' incomes with an assiduity not exceeded by the vainest actresses?

PHILIP HENSHER, *The Spectator,* 5 June 1999

You are writing in the dark if you read no one but yourself. And in the dark you can't even read yourself properly.

PETER SANSOM, *Writing Poems,* 1994

Like philosophy, independent thought, and believing one's own nose, poetry perhaps has to be the province of the few.

HERBERT LOMAS, *The London Magazine,* April–May 1993

Poetry is not a fiefdom or a private domain. It is a city whose gates stand wide; which has never exactly welcomed its newcomers but has always found room for them.

EAVAN BOLAND, Ronald Duncan Lecture, 1994

It is tempting to say that anybody who thinks poetry is the most serious thing will not be capable of writing serious poetry because they cannot see what things are *really* serious.

BERNARD O'DONOGHUE, *Thumbscrew,* Summer 2000

We could say that great poetry is about something more important than poetry; we could even say that that's what makes it poetry.

BRUCE F. MURPHY, *Poetry,* August 2003

Poets write for each other, dedicate poems to each other, review each other, and read each other. Validation comes totally from within.

BERNARDINE EVARISTO, *Free Verse,* 2006

∵

One of the ridiculous aspects of being a poet is the huge gulf between how seriously we take ourselves and how generally we are ignored by everybody else.

BILLY COLLINS, *The New York Times,* 23 February 2003

Most poetry editors don't publish poetry for readers but for poets.

NEIL ASTLEY, *Free Verse,* 2006

Sometimes the poetry world appears to be a huddle of back-slapping, back-biting, self-aggrandising, self-mythologising, navel-gazing cliques which are far too self-important and self-protective to want to open out to poetry which draws on, for example, Black and Asian cultures.

BERNARDINE EVARISTO, *Free Verse,* 2006

PRESENT, PAST, AND FUTURE

If every generation wrote with the voice it knew from the past, contemporary poetry would still be in the style of Chaucer or Shakespeare.

ALISON CHISHOLM, *Writers' News*

Shakespeare's gift to our time is an extraordinary one: the power to view the past that shaped the present as if we were already citizens of centuries to come.

KIERNAN RYAN, *The Guardian*, 23 April 2005

It is the struggle to express the contemporary that makes poetry seem alive, and contemporary life can hardly be expressed in the forms used by poets four hundred years ago.

LOUIS SIMPSON, *Harvard Review*, Spring 1997

Ireland is one of the very few countries where you can be reactionary stylistically and still be considered absolutely relevant.

PETER PORTER, *Metre*, Spring 1997

I think of poetry as the cutting edge of language, the point of keenest change. Very few other art forms change to reflect their time and place as poetry does.

TOBIAS HILL, *The Guardian*, 5 June 2004

Only through poetry can human solitude be heard in the history of humanity. In that respect, all the poets who ever wrote are contemporaries.

CHARLES SIMIC, *The Unemployed Fortune-Teller*, 1994

Aesthetic shifts over time can be seen as a kind of crop rotation; the topsoil of one field is allowed to rest, while another field is plowed and cultivated.

TONY HOAGLAND,
Poetry, March 2006

If poetry depended on intellectuals for its survival it would be about as current as hiero-glyphics. They exhibit common scholarly errors of reading from the outside, of treating the "canon" as a corpse to be wheeled out for dissection practice by generations of medical students.

MICHAEL DONAGHY, *Wallflowers,* 1999

Poetry is a dialogue, with our contemporaries and with the past; it's no good toadying to ourselves, because the past won't toady to us and neither will the future.

WILLIAM LOGAN, *All the Rage,* 1998

What poetry might be is up for grabs. There is nothing inevitable about what poems written in twenty years' time will look like. There is no ultimate venue where poetry is booked to appear.

JOHN REDMOND, *How to Write a Poem,* 2006

Without tradition a poet is ignorant, without innovation a poet is irrelevant.

GLYN MAXWELL, *Fulcrum,* no. 4, 2005

All tradition was once innovation, or imitative of the innovative urge.

JOHN KINSELLA, *Fulcrum,* no. 4, 2005

There's a certain life-saving, safeguarding element in art that permits you to take language, which is after all a very ephemeral, evanescent thing, and draw a line around it and keep it fixed in place, so that it can last through centuries.

HARVEY SHAPIRO, *The Missouri Review* 21, no. 2, 1998

What the lyric poets want is to convert their fragment of time into eternity. It's like going to the bank and expecting to get a million dollars for your nickel.

CHARLES SIMIC, *The Unemployed Fortune-Teller,* 1994

[H]ow maddening in an economy that depends on throwaways, that a poem can last forever.

JEANETTE WINTERSON, *The Times,* 19 November 2005

A week is a long time in poetry.

PETER ROBINSON, *Untitled Deeds,* 2004

As computers and networks improve, poets share poems with a click of the SEND button. Perhaps this will not be a golden or silver or even aluminum age of poetry, but a silicon age.

PAUL ZIMMER, *The Southern Review,* Spring 2000

On the Internet, a poem gets reconfigured as information.

JAN CLAUSEN, *The Nation,* 24 July 2000

The problem with [the] use of Greek myth, as many contemporary poets have unwittingly shown, is that today those myths themselves have no cultic power; they exist for us only as literature. (This is true even of biblical figures, which had a genuine mythical force in our culture far more recently than the Greek gods.)

ADAM KIRSCH, *The New Republic,* 7 August 2006

People who cite their influences from their own generation are quite suspect. Just go to a library, just put your feet in the past. It will

Lyric poetry pushes us out of the restrictions and particulars of our time and circumstance; it lets us drift free from, but near to, the hard lines of contemporary reality.

DAVID GEWANTER,
Fulcrum, no. 4, 2005

Of the future's taste only one thing is certain: it will be ruthless. The few who happen upon periodicals like this one will look at all these poems into which we've poured the wounded truths of our hearts, all the fraught splendor and terror of these lives we suffered and sang—and they will giggle.

CHRISTIAN WIMAN, *Poetry*, November 2003

❧

just give you more range, it will just give you more reach.

GLYN MAXWELL, *Contemporary Poetry Review*, May 2006

Too much reading of those whose language and history and vision is by definition close to one's own can seem to overload the world with poems, dilute it, pollute it with poems: poems, poems, poems.

C.K. WILLIAMS, *The American Poetry Review*, July–August 2007

Poets must write in the language of their time, and since our time is one of linguistic chaos and disintegration, that's no small task.

CHASE TWICHELL, Poetry Book Society *Bulletin*, Summer 2006

In no time at all, cultural and historical differences are abolished and a poem written almost three thousand years ago comes to life on a page. Nowhere else in literature does one find the experience of living in the moment so vividly rendered as in lyric poetry.

CHARLES SIMIC, *The New York Review of Books*, 22 June 2006

Every poem has its own relationship to time that is different than your own; it's like its own time signature. Part of the work of reading a poem is to calibrate one's rhythm to that of the poem, much in the same way a Shakespearean actor has to adjust from 21st century colloquial language and speech to medieval diction, if the dialogue on stage is to be convincing.

MAJOR JACKSON, Poetry Foundation online, 16 November 2006

"Wake up," is what a poem says. It just says "Wake up." It's a different morning in each new poetry and you have to wake up into the morning that you are given, into the conditions of that day. You can't wake up into a theory; and you can't wake up into a prior moment in history. You have to wake up into the terms that you have.

JORIE GRAHAM, KCRW Radio, 30 March 2006

Like men and women who reach a certain biological age, lyric poets must lament a vanished and better time. The impulse seems hard-wired into our species.

SYDNEY LEA, *The Writer's Chronicle*, December 2006

Most of us live in a sort of linear and horizontal way, but what lyric poems and poetry are trying to do is probably to live in a vertical way down the shaft of one of those single horizontal moments.

EAMON GRENNAN, *The Kenyon Review*, Summer 2006

If poetry can't come to terms with the vocabulary of science and technology, it is leaving out a large part of human life and is so much the poorer.

R.S. THOMAS, BBC Radio 3, November 1991

Like two chemical reagents missing the necessary catalyst, science and poetry remain largely unreacted, despite well-meaning efforts on both sides.

PETER FORBES, *The Independent*, 16 November 2006

Alcohol and Pub Talk

Poetry is relaxation from the labours of inebriation.

UNATTRIBUTED, *Acumen,* January 1995

A poem is language distilled into premium whiskey, no mix, no ice, no little paper umbrella.

PENNY DYER, *The Chattanooga Pulse,* 24 May 2006

I like reading poetry at night—a doctor I know claims that this is because "poetry is the only thing you can read when you're drunk."

JOHN LANCHESTER, *The Sunday Times,* 1 June 2003

I've heard my own work being denigrated as being mere pub-talk. If that's the case, I'm very happy with the comparison. Any poetry that confines itself to the merely literary is half dead. And I enjoy pubs a lot more than poetry readings.

CIARAN CARSON, *The Irish Review,* Spring 1990

In a poet, too much sobriety is a dangerous thing.

TONY HOAGLAND, *Harvard Review,* Fall 1994

Write drunk, but polish sober.

DAVID BURNETT, *Quoins for the Chase,* 2003

He was once told by doctors that if he took another drink he would be dead. His response was to call in at the nearest bar on the way home.

PETER WAYMARK, on Charles Bukowski, *The Times,* 18 March 1995

The poets I know smoke less and drink less every year... The drink of the 1890s was absinthe; that of midcentury was gin; that of the 1990s appears to be Cranapple Juice.

ROBERT B. SHAW, *Poetry*, January 2000

Alcohol doesn't help you write; if it did, half the drunks in the world would be great poets.

GWYNETH LEWIS, *The Guardian*, 5 June 2004

> Poetry is... the alcohol content of any given piece of literature.
>
> GREY GOWRIE,
> *The Daily Telegraph*,
> 29 January 1994

Things that happen to poets are transmuted into something else: if a bee falls into a poet's gin, the ripples extend beyond the glass.

ALAN COREN, *The Times*, 24 August 1995

I should like people to read my work and think it was like drinking lemonade, only to find a little later that it was strongly laced. I'd want it to go down like lemonade but to hit them like vodka.

ALAN BROWNJOHN, cited in *The Guardian*, 7 October 2006

PHYSICAL POETRY

Poetry is a way of putting us back in touch with the deep rhythms of the body, rerooting words in the bodily life from which they spring.

TERRY EAGLETON, *The Times*, 3 February 2007

Poetry originated in song and dance. I don't separate the language of the poem from the language of the body.

STANLEY KUNITZ, *Interviews and Encounters with Stanley Kunitz*, 1993

When we talk about the body of a poem—its anatomy—the line is like a skeletal system, the sentence is like a circulatory system, and the image is like a central nervous system.

MOLLY PEACOCK, *How to Read a Poem*, 1999

Poetry is an utterance of the body... It is the language in thrall to the corporeal, to the pump and procession of the blood, the briefly rising spirit of the lung, the nerves' fretwork, strictures of the bone.

GLYN MAXWELL, *Strong Words*, 2000

Poetry is a bodily activity with a high voltage of muse energy.

SEAMUS HEANEY, *The Times*, 27 March 1999

Poetry is one of the ways to make a reconciliation between the body and the mind.

OCTAVIO PAZ, Lannan Literary Videos, 1991

Poetry is about as good as we can get at communicating without the aid of gestures, without the aid of our bodies.

PHILIP LEVINE, *So Ask*, 2002

I am a poet who happens to be black and a black who happens to be a poet. My poetic sensibility may not be predicated on the colour of my skin, but the colour of my skin certainly generates my poetry.

FRED D'AGUIAR, *Strong Words*, 2000

Poetry is thought clouded by feeling, made flesh, registered along the sinews, in breath and bowels.

GERMAINE GREER, *The Independent on Sunday*, 7 May 2000

Poems made of blood and muscle, music and memory, are the ones that will endure.

MAXINE KUMIN, *Planet on the Table*, 2003

Poetry is the most intimate of the arts, and at its strongest can produce an almost physical reaction in the reader, a shying-away, as from the too close proximity of another's flesh.

JOHN BANVILLE, *The New York Review of Books*, 13 July 2006

Reading good poems requires fierce brief sensual attention akin to lovemaking itself.

GREY GOWRIE, *The Spectator*, 26 August 2006

Poetry subtly takes command of our breathing and dances with it; a sob built into a line will reverberate in the diaphragm and cause it to signal the brain for tears, and laughter can similarly be produced without any joke needing to appear in the text.

LES MURRAY, *Meanjin*, April 1988

Like philosophy, poetry is a contemplative form, but unlike philosophy, poetry subliminally manipulates the body and triggers its nerve impulses, the muscle tremors of sensation and speech.

CAMILLE PAGLIA, *The Daily Telegraph*, 5 March 2005

⌣∴

As well as between tongue and teeth, poetry happens between the ears and behind the left nipple.

DOUGLAS DUNN,
The Observer,
23 March 1997

Poetry is chiseled breath.

JEFFREY MCDANIEL, Here Comes Everybody blog, 17 May 2005

Verse is the voice that sails on breath.

GLYN MAXWELL, *Poetry Review*, Winter 2006-07

There is a primal covenant between voice and text. I feel the line when I look at it, there's a musculature there. It is a kinetic action, not just an eye movement.

SEAMUS HEANEY, *The Times*, 27 March 1999

Poetry is—even if you don't speak it out loud—something that you get in your ears, your mouth, lips... So knowledge in poetry is always coming through at the level of experience rather than at the level of concept.

JEROME J. MCGANN, *The Cambridge Quarterly* 22, no. 4

The medium of poetry is a human body: the column of air inside the chest, shaped into signifying sounds in the larynx and the mouth. In this sense, poetry is just as physical or bodily an art as dancing.

ROBERT PINSKY, *The Sounds of Poetry*, 1998

I sometimes think of a good line as a mouth dance, requiring the mouth to undertake a variety of movements that might well imitate expressions of human emotions.

GEORGE SZIRTES online, 25 February 2005

When you read good poetry aloud, your lips pout and stretch, your tongue jives, your whole mouth is vigorously exercised.

MICHAEL LONGLEY, *Poetry Ireland Review*, Summer 1999

Poets are regressive creatures who have never got over the sensual thrills of babbling. While mature men and women use language to buy shares and wage wars, poets love to relish the shape and flavour of words on the tongue.

TERRY EAGLETON, *The Times,* 20 January 2007

Poems scan naturally on alternate beats, not every which way, because such is our flesh: We walk, march, or dance on exactly two feet, two alternating feet, not every which way on amoeba pseudopods.

PETER VIERECK, cited in *Contemporary Poetry Review,* November 2005

Walking can animate the body and senses in a way conducive to poetry's wandering alertness, moving through things, looking around—purpose without system.

ROBERT PINSKY, *The American Poetry Review,* May-June 2005

A Hopkins line brings you to your senses: like hearing a woodpecker at dawn, or walking across a beach of small crunching shells.

SEAMUS HEANEY, *The Independent on Sunday,* 31 March 1991

Hopkins had me. I called in sick to my construction job and spent a day wandering through a park trying to memorize the lines that tremoloed from the back of my head to my ravenous tongue which whipped them to pieces.

PETER E. MURPHY, *Poetry Daily*'s Poet's Pick, 29 April 2005

There is nothing escapist about the poetic enterprise, if you're prepared to have your heart cracked open and your brain cells rearranged.

GARY GEDDES, Poetry Book Society *Bulletin,* Summer 1996

From a very early age, when I read a poem, it was as if the poet's burning taper touched some charred filament in my rib cage to set me alight.

MARY KARR, *Poetry,* November 2005

LABELS AND CATEGORIES

The consumerist systems of our age love labels: poets ought to hate them.

PETER JAY, *Times Literary Supplement*

Categories and labels appeal to inattentive minds... And the better a writer or a particular work, the less useful any label that may be applied to him.

ROBERT PINSKY, *The Washington Post*, 10 July 2005

Almost none of the poetries I admire stick to their labels, native or adopted ones. Rather, they are vagrant in their identifications. *Tramp poets*, there you go, a new label for those with unstable allegiances.

C.D. WRIGHT, *Cooling Time*, 2005

There's a natural tendency to categorise artists; but we are die-hard individualists, so we insist on wriggling out of these categories.

PHILIP CASEY, *The Irish Times*, 10 November 1994

Writers are more concerned with trying to name and bear witness to the particularities of the world and our experience in it than we are with assembling work that provides neat categories for analysis.

SHARA MCCALLUM, *Smartish Pace*

All adjectives are diminishments. I want to be a poet, not a right-handed Protestant male New Hampshire poet with large feet.

DONALD HALL, *Poets & Writers*, September–October 1994

The adjective *neglected* may be applied to practically *any* poet from the past, even from the recent past.

RICHARD TILLINGHAST, *The Gettysburg Review*, Summer 1995

Obviously, I am a gay writer because I write about gay themes, but I also write about other things and I don't want to be restricted in the way that somebody would be called a landscape painter or a writer of boys' stories.

THOM GUNN, *San Francisco Examiner,* 11 January 1998

Critical short-hand can become an alternative to reading, with a poem or poet, once labelled, being forever consigned to one corner of the territory or another.

DAVID HERD AND ROBERT POTTS, *Poetry Review,* Winter 2004-05

Every narrowing of what contemporary poetry is supposed to do bears with it an equivalent narrowing in the definition of a human being.

DOUGLAS OLIVER, *PN Review,* September–October 1995

Real poems have themes, but they don't have subjects. That's why any division of poems into "love poems," "nature poems," "protest poems" or what have you has nothing to do with what actually goes on in a real poem.

MICHAEL HAMBURGER, *Testimonies,* 1989

Writing nature poems does not make one a nature poet, just as a poet who experiments is not necessarily experimental. It makes sense that a poet would resist these labels, if only because they imply one's approach to poetry is fixed.

TERRANCE HAYES, Poetry Foundation online, 8 June 2006

Don't categorise yourself as a Black or ethnic poet. There's no need to, the media will do that for you. If you see yourself simply as a poet, it will free you up to write about whatever you want.

VALERIE MASON-JOHN, *Free Verse,* 2006

The word "poet" is a noun that sheds off adjectives.

SEAMUS HEANEY,
BBC 1, December 1995

Moving On

The greatest difficulty for the poet is how to go on being one.

MICHAEL HOFMANN, *London Review of Books*

It can be rather devastating for a writer to finish a book and have nothing in the pot on the back of the stove.

RITA DOVE, *The Writer's Chronicle*, October–November 2005

The ability to write poetry can be withdrawn as easily as it is given. To be suddenly empty of poetry is a frightening thought, like an abandonment.

HELEN DUNMORE, Poetry Book Society *Bulletin*, Spring 1994

Any anxiety about the quality of what one has written cannot compare to the anxiety over the possibility that one's last poem is going to turn out to be one's Last Poem.

BILLY COLLINS, *The Recorder*, Fall 2003

A poet's talents exist in productive tension for only a decade or so. Before, the language is all main force, the subjects mistaken, the voice immature; after, the poet often hardens into manner, his subjects written to extinction.

WILLIAM LOGAN, *The New Criterion*, June 2001

We forget how rarely a poet of substantial early achievement "develops," as well as how common it is to have simply a decade or so of real originality over the course of one's life. That we can't know this about ourselves is... a kind of grace.

CHRISTIAN WIMAN, *Poetry*, November 2001

The poet's first social responsibility, to continue the art, can be filled only through the second, opposed responsibility to change the terms of the art as given.

ROBERT PINSKY, *Poetry and the World*, 1988

When a poet runs out of childhood, what do you do?

EILÉAN NÍ CHUILLEANÁIN, RTÉ Radio 1, March 1999

Poets grow in different ways, some in skill, others in range.

ROBERT B. SHAW, *Poetry*, May 1995

As soon as you are not moving in poetry, you are dead. Mere repetition is like the onset of freezing.

DAVID CONSTANTINE, Poetry Book Society *Bulletin*, Winter 1991

It may be unavoidable that the virtues of every poet's work are in the end responsible for its defects.

CHARLES SIMIC, *The New York Review of Books*, 7 April 2005

It is really too bad that once a poet has *become* a style, he might do well to break it up and start over.

CALVIN BEDIENT, *The Southern Review*

Each poet who is seriously exploratory keeps rebelling against his or her own framework of ideas. Many such rebellions are necessary to keep one's art alive.

MARK HALLIDAY, *The Writer's Chronicle*, February 2002

> If I knew where poems came from, I'd go there.
>
> MICHAEL LONGLEY, *The Observer*, 24 March 1991
>
> ∿

As you get older, you get the hang of things. And just when you're getting the hang of everything, it's time to die!

MICHAEL LONGLEY, *Five Points* 8, no. 3

It is not so dif-
ficult to kindle
the poetic fire in
the first place as
to keep it going,
hot and bright,
through a whole
lifetime.

THOM GUNN,
AGNI, no. 44, 1996

⌣

Some things are constantly changing. Some things never do. Poets and their poetry keep track of each.

THOMAS LYNCH, *Boston Sunday Globe,*
25 January 1998

If you're falling through space, poetry is a kind of parachute that rights you, and allows you to land on your psychic or spiritual feet.

STANLEY MOSS, *Jewish Quarterly,* Winter 2004

When the energies implicit in the activity are exhausted, when there's really nothing more to say, nothing that won't be just trying to pad out a little more, you know a poem's done.

ROBERT CREELEY, *Rattle,* Summer 2003

You keep working on it until you're tired of it, or lose interest—and that's how I know that a poem is finished.

RITA ANN HIGGINS, *The Irish Times,* 11 June 2005

There is a point when the poem has lost its magical intimacy with you and become an external object. That's when you usually know whether it has failed or succeeded.

LES MURRAY, *The Paris Review,* Spring 2005

Every poem is a sort of fit of desperation how to end it.

HUGO WILLIAMS, Poetry Book Society *Bulletin,* Summer 1994

To the reader, a poem may seem to be about love or separation or cele-bration or whatever. But to the poet who is in the process of writing the poem, the poem is about only one thing: its completion... to make a thing that can stand on its own after you leave the room.

BILLY COLLINS, *Fugue*, Summer 2001

It's so easy to be caught up in the premature urge to tidy, to polish and prettify and generally smooth over, something that could only have benefited from the chance to grow.

SUSAN WICKS, *Contemporary Women's Poetry*, 2000

A bad closure is not a closure but someone waving goodbye when they haven't in fact gone anywhere.

GEORGE SZIRTES, *Poetry*, February 2006

The drawback of overtly modest poetry... is that it must be of definite use, providing a payoff, a certain illumination of localized experience. There is something cynical in insisting on resolution; it's like demanding a receipt of a poem.

BENJAMIN LYTAL, *Los Angeles Times*, 1 January 2006

The kind of poetic closure that interests me bleeds out of its ending into the whole universe of feeling and thought. I like an ending that's both a door and a window.

STANLEY KUNITZ, *Interviews and Encounters with Stanley Kunitz*, 1993

There comes a point where I'll write a poem which I realise is the first of the next book, and then the new collection is complete.

MICHAEL LONGLEY, *Books Ireland*, Summer 1995

By finishing one work, one has actually learned something that allows one to go on to make the next.

MEENA ALEXANDER,
The Kenyon Review,
Winter 2005

❦

In every book there is a poem that belongs to the last one.

EILÉAN NÍ CHUILLEANÁIN, *The Canadian Journal of Irish Studies* 20, no. 2

A finished poem is also the draft of a later poem.

MARVIN BELL, *Poet's Market,* 2004

A poem is a lamp, and it's got just enough oil to last for you to write the poem down... The next one you start from scratch.

LI-YOUNG LEE, *Breaking the Alabaster Jar,* 2006

BEYOND WORDS

Words are the enemy of poetry.

RUSSELL EDSON, *Metre,* Spring–Summer 2000

However remarkable the text may be, its poetic quality depends on its author having known how to keep alive in it the light of what is beyond language.

YVES BONNEFOY, *Times Literary Supplement,* 12 August 2005

Poetry can exist without paper and ink... It has its roots in ceremony, ritual, song, dance and rhythm. Peoples who have no written literature, or are pre-literate or illiterate, still produce poems, those rhythmic arrangements of words.

MICHAEL LONGLEY, *The Belfast Telegraph,* 2 November 2006

The poem is an act beyond paraphrase because what is being said is always inseparable from the way it is being said.

EDWARD HIRSCH, *How to Read a Poem,* 1989

Language is not commensurate to the world. Something slips in the telling.

CAROLYN FORCHÉ, Dublin Writers Festival, 16 June 2005

Poetry springs from a level below meaning; it is a molecular thing, a pattern of sound and image.

NUALA NÍ DHOMHNAILL, RTÉ 1 television, July 1995

I find language is well after the fact; and the fact is a way of seeing, feeling, thinking that is pre-linguistic, that is in blocks of imagery, in blocks of feeling.

GARY SNYDER, Lannan Literary Videos, 1991

Although poetry comes to us in words, it indicates an unspoken understanding, a language of sign and gesture. Poetry's stories and descriptions fuse into images and metaphor. Haiku is an extreme example. Being so short on words, it is almost an art of mime.

RUSSELL EDSON,
Parnassus 16, no. 1

◡:

There is no such thing as a silent poem.

GILLIAN CLARKE, BBC Radio 4, July 2000

Poetry is the closest literary form we have to silence.

MARIANNE BORUCH, *The Southern Review,*
Spring 1994

Poetry is only there to frame the silence.

ALICE OSWALD, *The Observer,* 19 June 2005

A poetic form is essentially a codified pattern of silence. We have a little silence at the end of the line, a bigger one at the end of a stanza, and a huge one at the end of the poem.

DON PATERSON, *Poetry Review,* Summer 2007

It's not just language that we use to write poems. We use silence, too. In fact, we use language to inflect silence so we can hear it better.

LI-YOUNG LEE, *Breaking the Alabaster Jar,* 2006

A poem for me displaces silence the way your body displaces water.

BILLY COLLINS, *The Cortland Review,* Spring 2005

What you leave out of a poem is as important as what's in. Maybe more.

RUTH PADEL, *Contemporary Women's Poetry,* 2000

The astonishments of poetry, for me, reside most vividly in its capacity to make a reader receive utterable and unutterable realities at once.

JORIE GRAHAM, *American Women Poets in the Twenty-first Century,* 2002

Poetry is an experience of limits: it travels around the borderlines of what can be named and what must be left unnamed.

KEVIN HART, *Landbridge*, 1999

A poem permits us to live in ourselves as if we were just out of reach of ourselves.

MARK STRAND, *The Making of a Poem*, 2000

Poetry for me is always reaching for something that's slightly beyond what I know, slightly out of reach.

DAISY FRIED, *The Philadelphia Inquirer*, 17 December 2000

One has to maintain a distance, an air pocket, between the poet and the poem—a pocket of objectivity. The poem isn't an expression of what you could say better in ordinary language, or in theoretical language.

ANNE STEVENSON, *The Cortland Review*, November 2000

Through imagery in particular, but also through the evocative and bodily force of sound and rhythm, a poem enables us to realise that greater part of our being and experience which does not think and for which ideas are, as for other creatures, inaccessible.

DAVID BURNETT, *Quoins for the Chase*, 2003

There is a shortfall between what language can express and what an individual can feel; metaphor can go some way towards bridging that gap.

SIMON ARMITAGE, BBC Radio 4, June 1992

Poetry needs metaphor, which is the rhyming of concepts, more than it needs rhyme, which is the analogy of sound.

BRIAN PHILLIPS, *Poetry*, June-July 2004

What they say "there are no words for"—that's what poetry is for.

MARVIN BELL,
Poet's Market, 2004

⌣

Poetry discloses something that lies not so much in its words themselves as in what we see above and through them, in an experience that is more than purely verbal.

DAVID GERVAIS,
PN Review,
May–June 2002

⌇

Metaphor is a way of showing sameness by difference.

GREG DELANTY, *PN Review,* March–April 2007

Given that poems themselves are metaphors, I find overt metaphors more and more embarrassing in poems.

HUGO WILLIAMS, *Strong Words,* 2000

We didn't have metaphors in our day. We didn't beat about the bush.

FRED TRUEMAN, BBC Radio 3, August 1996

All good similes depend upon a certain essential heterogeneity between the elements being compared. The simile asserts a likeness between unlike things, but it also draws attention to their differences, thus affirming a state of division.

EDWARD HIRSCH, *The Washington Post,* 9 November 2003

I find myself increasingly impatient of any kind of writing, prose or poetry, which does not bring with it the coiled energy, the dark tincture of the unconscious.

NUALA NÍ DHOMHNAILL, *The Irish Times,* 16 May 1992

Poetry springs from the dream mind, the unconscious. Poetry is never comfortable in language because the unconscious doesn't know how to speak.

RUSSELL EDSON, *Double Room,* Spring–Summer 2004

When a poem arises from the psychic deep, it can possess soothsaying force. The emotional mark it makes can be so unexpected that it feels more like impersonal revelation than personal utterance. And when a poet gets in this close and this deep, you stop admiring and start being commanded.

SEAMUS HEANEY, *Poetry Ireland Review*, Autumn 2003

With music, with cadence, with form, poetry speaks for what cannot be spoken as well as what can. It does not baffle or confound the due process of thought, but opens a corridor between head and heart.

ANDREW MOTION, *Strong Words*, 2000

Post-Poetry Tristesse

Having cold water thrown over your dreams is part of being a writer.

DAVID WHEATLEY, *The Irish Times*, 17 October 1995

Humiliation is the invariable lot of poets, but each poet, and each new generation of poets, learns to be humiliated in different ways.

BLAKE MORRISON, *The Guardian*, 3 November 1995

If you have doubts about the poem you have written, the kind of doubts that make you want to ask a friend what he or she thinks, don't bother. Trust the doubts.

WESLEY McNAIR, *Mapping the Heart*, 2003

Sooner or later even the poem I'm most proud of lies lifeless on the page before me, completely inert and without merit; and I have no idea where another will come from, or when.

ANTHONY HECHT, *The Paris Review*, Fall 1988

Words come, well ordered, the fluent vowels, the strong consonants binding the poem together. All seems to be well... And then, just when the end seems to be in sight, just when it is time to deliver the final hammer-stroke, something goes wrong, the poem falls to pieces in your hands. Or you know, beyond a doubt, the shape of it is wrong. Reluctantly, you throw it on the scrap heap.

GEORGE MACKAY BROWN, *The Masked Fisherman*, 1989

If the poet is not finally willing to be relentlessly honest, if the poet is not willing to fail in his or her expression, to be and appear to be silly, sentimental, wrong, then the poet is probably not going to accomplish anything other than the learning of competency or skill.

DAVE SMITH, *Range of the Possible*, 2002

Fear of failure narrows a poet's potential.

JOSEPH BRODSKY, *Conversations with Joseph Brodsky*, 1998

The real forcing house of good poems is the poems that fail, the ones that never appear. Those are your real teachers.

EAVAN BOLAND, *New Hibernia Review*, Summer 2006

It takes just as much work to write something that is a failure as it takes to write something that is good. You just might not know until the end of it that your idea wasn't a good one and that it's a failure, but you have to see it through.

ERICA FUNKHOUSER, *The Boston Globe*, 24 May 2007

The penalty of being a lyric poet is the law of diminishing returns, the temptation to repeat oneself unconsciously or even consciously.

R.S. THOMAS, Poetry Book Society *Bulletin*, Autumn 1995

The most difficult thing is the generation of excitement. That is why poets are so panic-stricken. They are afraid that the unexpected, accidental kickstart that sends poems into action will desert them.

SEAMUS HEANEY, *The Sunday Times*, 8 October 1995

Poetry is a tremendous school of insecurity and uncertainty. You never know whether what you've done is any good, still less whether you'll be able to do anything good tomorrow.

JOSEPH BRODSKY, *The New Yorker*, 8 January 1996

ᶜ∶

The demise of poetry remains poetry's favourite subject. Like someone in a state of manic hypochondria, [poetry] continues to search for signs of its own ill-health.

SIMON ARMITAGE, Poetry Book Society *Bulletin,* Autumn 1993

DEATH BY POETRY

No-one in a literate culture is able to kill their enemy with a poem, though no doubt a good many would like to try.

> MARTIN DUWELL, *Scripsi*, March 1992

He very nearly killed me on his bicycle one night... What a way to die—under a bike cycled by a poet in the dark!

> JOHN RYAN, on Monk Gibbon, RTÉ Radio 1

There's no posterity to write for. I'm writing now for mutated arthropods.

> PETER READING, *Oxford Poetry*, Winter 1990-91

Perhaps poetry is always elegy, for us and for itself. An anagram allows me to conclude: Posterity—it's poetry.

> EDNA LONGLEY, *Poetry & Posterity*, 2000

To say death is regrettable is only saying something about death, but to communicate that feeling is saying something about life.

> BERNARD O'DONOGHUE, *Oxford Poetry*, Summer 1999

There's one subject in lyric poetry, and that is that you have this existence and at the end of it you're going to experience non-existence.

> BILLY COLLINS, *The Independent*, 31 May 2003

Writing is like dying: it's lonely and nobody else can do it for you.

> FRANCIS HARVEY, *The Irish Times*, 16 April 2007

A funeral is very much an exercise in language, symbol and ritual. All of these things that we do when someone dies are the stuff of writing.

> THOMAS LYNCH, *The Clare Champion*, 2 September 2005

Even grief needs to be playful in poetry.

PETER PORTER,
BBC Radio 3,
January 1996

⌣:

There is always an element of the erotic in a poem about death. In fact I would venture that all one's feelings about death are a kind of elegy for the erotic, just as all poems about age have that element.

STANLEY KUNITZ, *The Wild Braid,* 2005

Every line of verse is doing its best to wriggle free of death. The whole achieved poem is a deed of life, in the face, in the teeth of death.

DAVID CONSTANTINE, *Strong Words,* 2000

I write because I would like to live forever. The fact of my future death offends me. That the people and things I love will die wounds me as well. I seek to immortalize the world I have found and made for myself.

REGINALD SHEPHERD, Reginald Shepherd's Blog, 10 February 2007

This is one sense of poetry. A little concoction of words against death. It's almost the instinct against death crystallized.

MIROSLAV HOLUB, *Times Literary Supplement*

The dead know nothing and we cannot speak with them. / Still, in that silence, let me write: *dear friend.*

ELAINE FEINSTEIN, *Poetry Review,* Winter 2005-06

Poetry is a way of talking to your loved ones when it's too late.

TED HUGHES, cited in *The Daily Telegraph,* 2 November 1998

What are the uses of elegy? To confirm that loss is real, that individual disappearance matters; that the rupture in the known world is pointed to, held up for attention, shared.

MARK DOTY, Poetry Foundation online, 2006

Poetry gives the griever not release from grief but companionship in grief.

    DONALD HALL, *Poetry,* November 2004

Writing is remembrance; but it is also forgetting, because an elegy suggests that the deceased is somehow put away in their proper place so that the elegist can move on.

    DAVID KENNEDY, *Poetry Review,* Winter 2005-06

Poets are like pigs, only worth money when they're dead.

    TED HUGHES, cited in *The Independent,* 16 November 1993

Nobody these days knows a poet is alive until he or she is dead.

    PHILIP HOWARD, *The Times,* 19 November 1993

Writing poetry is my way of celebrating with the world that I have not committed suicide the evening before.

    ALICE WALKER, cited in *The Guardian,* 15 January 2005

Death is what gets poets up in the morning.

    BILLY COLLINS, cited in *San Francisco Chronicle,* 9 January 2005

INDEX

ABOUT THE EDITOR

Dennis O'Driscoll was born in Thurles, County Tipperary, Ireland, in 1954. His eight books of poetry include *Weather Permitting* (Anvil Press, U.K., 1999), which was a Poetry Book Society Recommendation and was short-listed for the Irish Times Poetry Prize; *Exemplary Damages* (Anvil, 2002); and *New and Selected Poems* (Anvil, 2004), a Poetry Book Society Special Commendation. His work is included in *The Wake Forest Series of Irish Poetry, Volume One* (Wake Forest University Press, 2005). His latest collection of poems is *Reality Check* (Anvil, 2007; Copper Canyon Press, 2008).

A selection of his essays and reviews, *Troubled Thoughts, Majestic Dreams* (The Gallery Press, Ireland), was published in 2001. He is editor of the *Bloodaxe Book of Poetry Quotations* (Bloodaxe Books, U.K., 2006) and its American counterpart, *Quote Poet Unquote* (Copper Canyon, 2008).

O'Driscoll received a Lannan Literary Award in 1999, the E.M. Forster Award from the American Academy of Arts and Letters in 2005, and the O'Shaughnessy Award for Poetry from the Center for Irish Studies (St. Paul, Minnesota) in 2006.

A member of Aosdána, the Irish academy of artists, Dennis O'Driscoll has worked as a civil servant since the age of sixteen.

The Chinese character for poetry is made up of two parts: "word" and "temple." It also serves as pressmark for Copper Canyon Press.

Since 1972, Copper Canyon Press has fostered the work of emerging, established, and world-renowned poets for an expanding audience. The Press thrives with the generous patronage of readers, writers, booksellers, librarians, teachers, students, and funders—everyone who shares the belief that poetry is vital to language and living.

Major funding has been provided by:

Anonymous (2)

Sarah and Tim Cavanaugh

Beroz Ferrell & The Point, LLC

Lannan Foundation

National Endowment for the Arts

Cynthia Lovelace Sears and Frank Buxton

Washington State Arts Commission

For information and catalogs:

COPPER CANYON PRESS
Post Office Box 271
Port Townsend, Washington 98368
360-385-4925
www.coppercanyonpress.org

This book is set in Legacy Serif, a font designed by
American type designer Ronald Arnholm after close
study of Nicolas Jenson's 1470 Eusebius. Display
quotes set in Reminga Titling, designed by Xavier
Dupré. Titles set in Pontif, designed by Garrett Boge.
Book design and composition by Valerie Brewster,
Scribe Typography. Printed on archival-quality paper
at McNaughton & Gunn, Inc.